S0-AYA-090

Balance +

Food, Health + Happiness

Beatnik

Beatnik

P O Box 8276, Symonds Street, Auckland 1150, New Zealand
www.beatnikpublishing.com

First published in 2019 by Beatnik Publishing

Text and recipes © Rachel Grunwell 2019
Photography and styling © Aimee Finlay-Magne 2019
Endspaper Photography © Garth Badger and Alice van Schaik 2019
Design, Typesetting and Cover © Beatnik Design Ltd 2019

All of the recipes in the Bowled Over section, and the recipe for Mango Tango
Chia Pudding on Page 238 were developed for, and published in, **Good magazine**.
They are reprinted here with their kind permission.

www.Good.net.nz

This book is copyright. Apart from any fair dealing for the purposes of private
study, research or review, as permitted under the Copyright Act, no part may be
reproduced by any process without permission of the publishers.

Printed and bound in China.

ISBN 978-0-9941383-8-5

Balance +

Food, Health + Happiness

RACHEL GRUNWELL

Contents₊

Overview +

This book is for anyone who wants to be healthier and happier.

Keen to shed some stress? You're reading the right book. But if you're looking to shed kilos on a restricted diet, go and find a bikini-body trainer. You won't find anything here on how to get buff or formulas for building rock-hard abs. It's not what this book is about.

This book is a guide to inspire you to move well, eat well, think well, feel well and live well. There are tips and inspiring stories to uplift you, your mind, body and soul, as well as ideas to help you live your best life.

Be warned: not every page will resonate with you. Choose a chapter you're curious about and start from there. That's right, you don't have to read the book from start to finish or do everything I recommend. You choose where you want to read, learn and grow. If you hate yoga, then for goodness' sake, skip that chapter. I include yoga in this book because it's a zen-inducing practice, and both yoga and mindfulness are recommended by medical experts for de-stressing. I teach these important skills to high-flying corporates.

I'm not an expert at everything, nor is anyone. That's why, in these pages, I'm introducing you to some wise and inspirational minds by bringing together a global community of thought leaders, change-makers and trailblazers. Many are authors too. They are from places like the US, Europe, Australia and New Zealand, and they specialise in many areas. Think emotional intelligence, psychology, neuroscience, nutrition, yoga, medicine, sports science, fitness and business. They are all, in my view, rock stars.

As you're reading, highlight some stuff
you love and be brave enough to try ideas.
Don't be afraid to mess up and draw on the
pages and leave them less than perfect.

I share some tips of my own in here too. I'm more of a wellness geek than a rock star, though. Actually, I'm a co-ordinator who has helped to gather this powerful tribe of wellness gurus together.

The wellness experts in this book can help you to transform – if you choose. I use the word 'choose' on purpose. You have the power to choose to transform your life at any moment. The only barrier stopping you is you. And that barrier is often linked with fear. So take note of the advice you read in here. Focus on progression to live a better life. Avoid being perfect.

As you're reading, highlight some stuff you love and be brave enough to try ideas. Don't be afraid to mess up and draw on the pages and leave them less than perfect.

There are some nutrient-dense recipes in this book. I've included healthy smoothies and gluten-free snacks, and you'll also find sweet treats and cakes. This book is all about balance. Apply this philosophy to everything. Have your cake and eat it too, I reckon. Savour treats sometimes. Just be smart enough not to have cake for breakfast, lunch and dinner. You get the idea – life is for living. So silence that mean-girl voice in your head that makes you feel crippled by guilt every time sugar passes your lips. Break the rules and enjoy some sweet stuff sometimes. It's okay. Self-loathing is more toxic than any kind of sugar.

Please remember, the idea of perfection is just an illusion. We all have our struggles at one time or another. And every struggle is different. We often stumble in this slow and often unsteady waltz through life. So instead of finger-pointing, gossiping and judging, use your energy to focus on living a happier life that uplifts you as well as others.

One of the most powerful messages I share in this book is about ditching perfectionism. Instead, focus on balance. Improving your health and happiness is about adopting small, healthy habits often. Over time, these habits become part of your lifestyle. The all-or-nothing approach will never work. Trying to do everything at once is daunting and overwhelming. Small steps work best. Successful people are people who keep showing up – that's my philosophy. These people are all in. You know, they show up to fitness workouts and try to eat healthily as a way of life. Successful women are not superwomen. They are brave enough to keep taking steps and striving to be the best they can be. They are not afraid of tripping up. Nor should you be afraid.

Please quit feeling guilty when you screw up and fail at trying a new health idea along the way. Come on, we all stuff up sometimes. Look at stuffing up as useful instead – be proud that you tried. Learn something from the situation and grow. Trying means everything. The secret to doing anything is to work hard, and, little by little and over time, you can improve. You can always start fresh any time you choose.

Choose 'you' today by choosing to make your health and happiness a priority. This is in no way selfish. You deserve this. I promise if you adopt a healthier approach, then you will feel better and look better. Your health is your true wealth. You are worth working on. You'll also likely end up inspiring others to follow in your footsteps.

Now, flick through and choose a chapter to help you to live well. Be brave and try something.

If I can do this, anyone can.

About the author
Unfit mum to multi-marathoner and wellness expert

I've gone from writing geek to wellness geek. I'm an award-winning journalist, and I used to cover high-court murder trials and question police and write front-page stories. I even challenged lots of leaders in government over policy over the years. My favourite writing topics were education and social issues. I loved sticking up for the 'little guys' who genuinely needed help.

It was through luck that an editor assigned me a weekly fitness column in the **Herald on Sunday** newspaper seven years ago. I was on maternity leave after having my son, Finn, and was keen to do some freelance writing that didn't take up a lot of time.

Back then, I was an unfit, stressed-out investigative journalist who loooooved sugar. I had no idea how to get fit. But I was curious to learn. For the fitness column, I tried (and survived) hundreds of fitness challenges. I did flying trapeze from the height of a three-storey building – despite a fear of heights. I tried BMX riding with Olympian Sarah Walker. I surfed in Hawaii. I even danced with professional dancer, Aaron Gilmore, from the **Dancing with the Stars** show. I was terrible!

Along the way, I fell in love with running. At first, I struggled to run/walk for 20 minutes around the block. It was hard and I hated it. But, now, I've learned to love this sport, and I've conquered 21 marathons within five years. I'm now a yoga teacher too, who specialises in restorative yoga.

Choose 'you' today by choosing to make your health and happiness a priority. This is in no way selfish. You deserve this.

And I'm a qualified personal trainer. I coach people to be fitter, healthier and happier through individually tailored plans and coaching. I love helping others to transform.

I'm grateful to be fit and healthy. For me, fitness is more about the mind work than the body work. Yeah, this mum of three boys is happy to actually have abs, but the real game-changer for me was finding flow through exercise (For more about 'flow', see Chapter 5). Exercise fuels my health and happiness levels. Thank goodness my husband, Damien, a network architect (IT expert), loves the healthy way of life too.

Going from being a stressed-out journalist to a wellness geek is a pretty unlikely leap — for anyone. So I talk about my own journey when trying to convince others that change is possible. If I can go from eating, or almost inhaling, a block of chocolate each night while slumped on the couch watching telly to being addicted to CrossFit and drinking kale smoothies, then anyone can change!

By the way, just because I'm a wellness geek doesn't mean I'm happy all the time. Only dogs are happy all the time. Life is a rollercoaster for everyone. I just know more tools to help me de-stress and feel happier — that's the difference. An editor remarked to me once, 'It must be hard living up to being a wellness expert, Rach.' I told him, no, it's simply about striving to live life in balance. That's all. I'm still not perfect!

Back to that idea of transforming. Here are some of the leaps I've made since I started to believe in myself and invest in being healthier seven years ago. I used to struggle to push my toddler in a pram around the block and never imagined I'd be capable of running a long way. Now I'm a multi-marathoner and also help guide disabled athletes through events. I used to be terribly uncoordinated. Now I'm a qualified yoga teacher. I used to fidget in meditations. Now I teach this practice. I used to be scared going down hills on a bike. I've since conquered a hairy, scary, hilly 100km cycle race. I did this alongside TV star Mike McRoberts. We stopped for coffee halfway through the race and enjoyed the journey of that adventure.

What I've learned through all these health and fitness challenges is that it doesn't matter if you have little talent at cycling, running or even dancing. The health benefits of moving your body and conquering a challenge mean everything. Movement and good food fuel your mind and every cell in your

At first, I struggled to run/walk for 20 minutes around the block. It was hard and I hated it. But, now, I've learned to love this sport, and I've conquered 21 marathons within five years.

body to be well and to fight disease. So don't think of fitness or good food as merely ways to shed kilos, and don't focus on the number on the scales. These things fuel your entire wellbeing. They can even rewire your brain. You do not have to be a product of your environment, either. So quit the excuses.

I grew up in Rotorua, a magical and mystical place. It is renowned as a place for adventure. It boasts lots of stunning lakes and forests. It is a place with many beautiful and unique Māori legends and stories. The Māori traditions and myths give this place a soul. The history here is truly a treasure (called taonga in the Māori language).

Rotorua has natural geysers that attract a lot of tourists. There are natural geothermal mineral waters that people travel from all over the world to experience. At the Polynesian Spa, there are acidic pools for relieving aches and pains and alkaline pools to nourish your skin. I co-lead health retreats here and help people to reset and rejuvenate.

My English-born parents moved to New Zealand when I was born – for a better, more nature-filled life. I have an older brother, Jamie, and younger sister, Bex. My parents, Nick and Christine, used to take us kids on walks at the weekend through the majestic forests in Rotorua. I resented this like a true teenager back then. I thought it was such a drag. I now see they were trying to teach me healthy habits, but, of course, I viewed it as parent-inflicted torture. All I wanted to do was lock myself in my room and talk all day on the telephone to my boyfriend. You see, you can lead someone to healthy habits, but you can't make them adopt these habits. They've got to want to do these things for themselves – and in their own time.

Dad was always a runner, and Mum exercised too. But we weren't health freaks by any measure. Just an average family. We had homemade fish and chips every Friday. Dad cooked because Mum was out working. We'd drool

The health benefits of moving your body and conquering a challenge mean everything. Movement and good food fuel your mind and every cell in your body to be well and to fight disease.

over those golden fries in anticipation. Even before Dad planted the giant plate of golden, chunky wedges on the table, we kids would have our forks at the ready. We'd stab as many chips off the plate as we could. You'd learn to never put your pinky finger in the way. You'd never want to risk your digit ending up on someone's plate. Within point-five seconds, all the chips and oozing fat would be piled up on our plates. We'd then count our chips, and if someone got more, there would be squabbling and even violent-sounding screams. 'They got MOOOOOOOOORE. It's not faaaaaaaair!' one of us kids would wail.

Dad would divvy the chips up amongst us – and then put the lion's share on his own plate and cackle. When Dad laughs, all you see is his Adam's apple moving. His chin tilts to the ceiling, and he enjoys laughing loudly and outrageously.

I couldn't wait to grow up so I could have the biggest share of the chips in my own house. Fast-forward to today and my kids know the words 'superfood smoothies' better than 'fries'.

Yes, I do sometimes wonder whether my efforts to raise my kids on healthy foods will backfire. My kids have grown up knowing what kale is. They know what goji berries are. So they may rebel and end up with stringy, oily French fries overflowing in their households when they leave home. It happens. When they're bigger, they can make their own choices.

Actually, my youngest son, Finn, who often wears a superhero cape around the house, declared the other day, 'When I grow up, I'm going to buy a fire engine and an ice-cream truck.' I smiled. He loves the superpowers of firemen, which is just so cute. And I hope he always finds joy in eating ice cream. I believe in living life in balance. Eat your ice cream. Eat cake. Eat sugar. Have that celebratory wine if you want. Just follow the general rule that these things shouldn't be scoffed all the time. Have them sometimes,

> I couldn't wait to grow up so I could have the biggest share of the chips in my own house. Fast-forward to today and my kids know the words 'superfood smoothies' better than 'fries'.

savour them and then pile the good stuff up on your plate the majority of the time. I live by that 80/20 rule. Most of what I eat is good for me, but I live life in balance and eat treats sometimes. It's okay.

I've not just lived but thrived since I became a wellness writer. I simply couldn't ignore all the experts I was interviewing through my wellness-writing work. It really was lucky that I was offered the wellbeing column all those years ago. I would have likely said yes if I had been asked to pen the weekly wine page, and I'd be a different person today.

Through the wellbeing learning curve of my work, I've transformed. I've gone from being an unfit mum to a multi-marathoner. I've gone from being an uncoordinated goofball with zero self-awareness to being a qualified yoga teacher (with slightly more grace and, thankfully, a tad more self-awareness). I used to be so serious and staunch; now, I'm more understanding and empathetic and a bit softer around the edges. I used to suffer badly from foot-in-mouth disease (i.e. saying the wrong thing at the wrong time – all the time). I'm still nowhere near perfect at that. But at least I'm more aware of this failing and I'm more mindful to press pause before speaking.

Most importantly, my fitness and health work and the way I choose to live my life now are ultimately about inspiring my kids. I care about being a good role model. My greatest wish is that if I am healthy and fit and taking on challenges, my kids will be inspired to follow in my footsteps.

If you aren't inspired to make a healthy change for yourself, then do it for the people you love.

Resisting the culture of busy+

Almost every day, I hear a conversation that goes something like this:

How are you?
I'm good – just busy.
Oh, that's awesome.
Okay, see you around sometime.

I hate it. Nothing shuts down connecting with others more than saying you are busy. It signals that you are too busy for them. When did being busy become some badge of honour? Being too busy is a broken idea in our society. Everything on this planet could do with slowing down. Otherwise, we spin out of control. I want you to cull the word 'busy' from your vocabulary. I want you to view 'busy' like a swear word and never say it. None of us should ever be too busy for loved ones and friends. Sometimes you have to stop, give time to others and put everything else on pause. It's important to be a good friend. This is about being a decent human being.

Life tends to be on a speed setting. We multitask and never catch our breath. We focus our attention on digital devices rather than the people we love. We remember to recharge our phones but not ourselves. We are disconnected and believe that being busy is okay. How did this become normal?

Consider for a moment how much time you give to those people you love and who matter. I'm talking about your partner, family and those friends who love you for being you. I'm talking about those friends who

Life tends to be on a speed setting. We multitask and never catch our breath. We focus our attention on digital devices rather than the people we love.

care about you on your darkest days. The ones who make you feel happy. They deserve your full attention. Life is about connection, community and collaboration. It's about people, not stuff. Authentic and real relationships are what life is about.

Now, consider who you are choosing to spend a lot of your time with. Spend time with loved ones; unglue your fingertips from your phone, laptop, TV and iPad. Be aware of giving the valued people in your life the most valuable gift you can give: yourself. Your presence. Your undivided, not digitally driven, attention. Let them know that you hear them, see them and 'get' where they are at. Tell them you love them often. Reach out to them and hold them tight. Hug other humans often. When you wrap your arms around another, your heart soars. It's magic. You can feel their heartbeat, their warmth, their energy. There's this chemistry of connection. It goes deeper than skin; it makes your body chemistry change.

Don't reserve hugging for special or celebratory times. Hugging is a soul kind of thing but also a brain thing – so my oldest son, Zach, told me after a lesson at school. His class studied the topic of love. Zach chatted to me about dopamine, serotonin, adrenalin and oxytocin. He told me about what these chemicals do, including, in his words, 'help us to feel safe and feel the pleasure of love'. His understanding of 'chemical love' blew me away.

I then told him my definition of aroha. Aroha is the word for love in the Māori language. I told him my definition of love was him. In those magic moments when he was born, I felt the electricity of love ripple through

> 'A powerful way to give presence is to be a good listener – so you can tune into when others need help.'

my veins. I couldn't stop tears from flowing. My heart shifted to another gear I never knew I had. My love for him never fades. Okay, I don't like him sometimes when I have to repeat the words 'clean up your room'! This is normal life with a teenager.

Anyway, my message here is to give presence and make time for those we are lucky enough to have in our lives. A powerful way to give presence is to be a good listener – so you can tune into when others need help.

This brings me to **Neha Sangwan**, MD. She is the author of the book **TalkRx: Five Steps to Honest Conversations that Create Connection, Health and Happiness**. I met this stunning doctor at the worldwomen17 conference in Auckland. Her words and outlook on life showed beautiful insight.

She spoke about our society's need to have more honest conversations that create connection. We need this for the sake of our health and happiness. She said we needed to listen on a heart level. I had no idea what that was, back then.

Dr Sangwan says listening from the heart allows you to understand how someone is truly feeling, but it requires listening to more than the words they are saying for the underlying emotion. Resist being distracted or interrupting the talker, and give this person your full attention. Next, get curious and ask questions. 'Curiosity solves so much,' Dr Sangwan says. Then, when you find out what is truly going on with your friend, the next step is to acknowledge their feelings. Then ask what they value (so they feel heard). Dr Sangwan says this can be an 'invisible bridge between hearts'.

Dr Sangwan tells me that medication is the answer to many problems presented to doctors. But so much could be resolved through better communication, she insists.

'Whenever I say I have the most powerful tool to use, people kind of expect me to pull out a wand and do some kind of superpower experience for them. But, really, it's so much more simple. Could it be that the quality with which we listen to someone else is really pivotal? Listening determines how much information we take in – and it's one of the biggest gifts you can give someone else.'

Later, over a Skype call, I ask her to explain the five levels of listening.

'People tend to listen at different levels depending on their surroundings and state of mind. Most people only listen on a surface level because they are distracted, don't care or are self-focused. Even when someone listens more closely, they often only focus on the words being said. However, it's listening with an open mind and heart that allows you to hear what you may have been missing. It's the secret of people who have solid, consistent, understanding and loving connections that last for decades.'

Dr Sangwan says many people think communication is easy. 'The quality of your relationships reveals how well you've been able to listen.'

She likens it to learning to ride a bike. 'It takes your focus, awareness and presence. It's not really about your physical attention – it's about being truly present. When you are, you will see miraculous results.

'One of our biggest needs is to feel heard and valued. Everyone has a unique perspective to bring to the table.'

Dr Sangwan's perspective is unique in the medical world, and I want to know how she ended up in that field. I Skype her at her home in San Francisco. Her soft and warm-sounding voice pauses for a big dramatic moment. She speaks now in a deep, more serious tone. It's like that dramatic and meaningful pause you might get in music. It's more powerful than any noise.

Dr Sangwan describes her younger self as 'a good Indian child'.

'Life was about math and science all the way.'

'People were saying things like, "I've disowned my son," or, "I haven't talked about anything since the war."' Dr Sangwan knew that on a heart level these patients needed to address those issues if they were to ever get well.'

She trained as a doctor, and in the beginning, she got a lot of joy from this career. She felt a bit like a 'rock star'. She was helping to save lives in a hospital.

'But then I started seeing the same patients a few years later. They would come back in with another heart attack or health issue. It was a revolving door.'

Dr Sangwan says modern medicine is very good at getting people through a crisis, such as a car crash, broken bones, heart attack, stroke or surgery.

But she started to struggle with being a traditional doctor who only took care of acute crises rather than solving the underlying problems. She felt if she could get to the root cause of ill health, then patients would be empowered to care for themselves and stay out of the hospital.

'Everyone is so scared [in the hospital]. Doctors talk in scientific language, and people can't really take in what's happening. I saw several areas where we could improve our care.'

Dr Sangwan noticed that stress was at the root of many patients' concerns, and often the stress was coming from communication issues. 'People were saying things like, "I've disowned my son," or, "I haven't talked about anything since the war."' Dr Sangwan knew that on a heart level these patients needed to address those issues if they were to ever get well.

So she'd give them five questions to contemplate. She would ask them to journal about their answers, and then she would talk to them the next day. She calls this 'an awareness prescription':

1. Why this? Why your heart? What message is your body trying to give you?

2. Why now? Why did it need to get your attention in this moment?

3. What signals might you have missed along the way? 'My hope is not to blame others here but to help them pick up the clues early,' Dr Sangwan says.

4. What else in your life needs healing? 'I'd look at physical, mental, emotional and spiritual health here, because it's all connected.'

5. If you spoke from the heart, what would you say?

Dr Sangwan did this exercise with thousands of patients over the years. She vows everyone knew the answers to every question.

'Their answers consistently revealed the action that would lead to their own healing.'

There's nothing more powerful than the physical breakdown of someone's body to take them directly to looking at their health on multiple levels,' she says.

Dr Sangwan says we need to be connected to our purpose and meaning in the world. We need to realise what we do matters. And feeling heard and valued 'is a deep part of that'.

I'll never forget listening to Dr Sangwan talk to hundreds of women at that conference in Auckland. Everyone was still, nodding their heads and listening. I will never, ever forget this line: 'We can have it all in life if we know what we value.' It was the first time someone had said I could have it all in life. I had always thought that was a myth. What she meant was that if we knew what we valued, then we knew what we should focus our attention on. This could help us to feel fulfilled.

On our Skype call later, I probe her further: 'Can we really have it all?' Her reply: 'I do think we can have it all. We have grown as a world outside of ourselves. We care about image, body, what we look like, how much we make, what position we are in the workplace, how many people report to us. We care very deeply how other people view us, and I think we have lost awareness.'

She says that saying 'no' should never be seen as a negative thing. Saying no to others is sometimes about 'saying yes to me'.

She says rather than caring about the status you have, ask yourself, what is it that you value? What rejuvenates you? 'Tragedy or things that surprise us, like unexpected things, can be a wake-up call,' she adds. 'So get clear on your values. Prioritise those values. Do something meaningful and purposeful.'

She says changing her work focus from traditional medicine to 'internal medicine' has become her 'superpower'. It lights her up. It helps to create a world she wants to live in.

Dr Sangwan tells me that sometimes you can't have everything you want all at the same time. And with age, we can become more open to powerful ideas that we may not have been open to before. She uses herself as an example here.

'I didn't previously understand the power of meditation. But I now realise that breathing, meditating, having quiet and time alone and personal space is powerful.'

So she now makes time for these things and sets boundaries around when to say 'no' to stuff that doesn't resonate. She says that saying 'no' should never be seen as a negative thing. Saying no to others is sometimes about 'saying yes to me'.

'It's turning down the volume of me if I don't [say no],' she explains. She adds that if you don't say no when you need to, then you can end up resenting others.

I tell Dr Sangwan this is something I have been personally working on. I used to say yes to everyone and everything all the time. It saw me almost face burnout. I now prioritise the people I surround myself with better.

I'm not perfect at it, but I'm better. Motivational speaker **Jim Rohn** famously said that we are the average of the five people we spend the most time with. So, spend time with people who are uplifting.

Otherwise, people who bring you down can suck the joy from your life. This doesn't mean ditching anyone who annoys or disagrees with you. No way. Rejoice in meeting people with different perspectives. Live with different opinions with ease. That's tolerance. What I mean is keep clear of the people that only bring misery to your life. Sometimes we simply outgrow these friendships. People change and can go down different roads.

Elena Brower teaches people about cultivating the art of attention and parenting consciously. Based in New York, she is a yoga and meditation teacher, a speaker and the author of **Art of Attention, Practice You: A Journal and Better Apart**.

I heard her speak for the first time at a yoga festival called Wanderlust in Taupō. The Wanderlust festivals are in many places around the world. They showcase amazing speakers, yoga, meditation and music and promote healthy living. I've been to these festivals in Hawaii, Sydney and Melbourne, and they're always good for the soul.

I remember noting Elena's make-up-free, gorgeous, glowing skin. She later told me in a Skype chat that she credits taking vitamin C for her complexion.

That day at the festival, when I heard her speak, she shared some tips on how to be an 'awakened parent'. Elena's talk centred around telling the truth and always being kind. She said you did not always need constant eye contact with your kids. That was a myth.

'Sometimes they may feel more comfortable sharing things or asking questions without full eye contact.'

This advice was gold. I gave my kids more space whenever they appeared to want to share something sensitive. Now they can open up more, if they wish, without my laser-beam eyes upon them.

I've come to understand from Elena's talk that I'm meant to be less of a hovering parent. Now I aim for my kids to communicate with me without needing to look me in the eyes. They're more open and willing to share this way.

She advised too to 'give your kids a voice'. For example, it's helpful to let them be part of plans, when you can, to give them a voice and say. 'Create a space where everyone can have a say,' Elena advised. 'Consider their ideas and feelings and try to give them some choices.' A great example she gave was asking your child if they wished to do their homework when they got home from school or instead in 10 minutes. 'That is much nicer than being dictated to,' she said.

Elena said when your child is frustrated, 'These four magic words can change everything: "How can I help?"'

This is the magic formula for connecting with your kids. 'There's no extra sauce.' What she meant was there was nothing extra or more you needed to add to this. You just needed to say those four words to connect with your child.

These four words have since been a powerful connector with my kids. They don't always want my help. But when they need my help, this opens the door to their knowing I'm here. They know I'm trying to listen. I'd like to help.

Elena asked the audience to 'take care of yourself' too. She said we must give ourselves permission to do this. This is so our children see that we as parents value ourselves, and this is important. 'They need to value themselves too,' she said.

She then advised the audience, 'Choose the frequency of your being.' Choose wisely how you behave, talk and present yourself to the world. After all, she said, how we acted was how our kids learnt how to act too. Elena had the audience chuckling when she gave a great example around this. She said, for example, if we slam doors, then how can we expect our own children not to be a door-slammer too?

I gave my kids more space whenever they appeared to want to share something sensitive. Now they can open up more, if they wish, without my laser-beam eyes upon them.

If your child did something unkind, she said, ask them, 'What was the spirit behind it?' This is because they may not realise their actions were unkind. They may have had a different intention.

Elena often teaches about a concept she calls the Do-Over, to help smooth relations between parents and children. She asks her son one question at bedtime each night.

'Was there anything I could've done better today?'

In her talk, which she delivered with her son, she modelled how this created healthy communication, a safe space for more questions and deeper conversation. 'This is where the "gold" is. Ask this question so your child is empowered to have a voice and feel heard.'

I've since put this into play and I've found my youngest two sons are really receptive. It really works. They love the attention and time spent together. I can see they appreciate being heard and that this ritual of connection before sleep-time resonates. They gently tell me how I could have improved as a parent each day!

With my oldest teenage son, I've found a different approach works best. He usually comes to me later at night, when his brothers are in bed, to chat quietly about what is on his mind or to share some news about his day. This is when he is open to communication and I think he feels more relaxed. That's perhaps just the window for him when he wants to connect on his terms; children really are all unique and different. But pausing to give them more presence is what I'm always trying to do more of with my kids.

By the way, the parent should never expect the kid to ask in return what they could do better as a child. When they are older, they may choose to add that part, Elena said.

Lastly, she said to speak the truth to your kids – and to everyone, in fact. 'When you tell the truth, they tell the truth.'

I was so inspired by Elena's parenting advice that I asked her for five happiness tips. These were in my wellness column for **Good magazine**.

I love how she communicates these important tips in a beautiful and unique way:

1. Get plenty of rest and sleep. Seven hours. And remember that naps are never an indulgence. They are invitations to your immune system.

2. Meditate. Even five minutes a day will help you cultivate and sustain the attitudes of your choosing.

3. Surround yourself with people who inspire and uplift you. Stay close and attentive to the nourishment they provide, and return the favour.

4. Move your body. Even 15 minutes a few times a week will boost your mood, elevate your interactions and keep your circulation strong.

5. Empower others. Sharing encouragement, helping others as you rise up and giving others your time will bring you joy and clarity.

I ask Elena on another chat via Skype about how to live life in balance. She prefers the term 'reverence'. She explains:

'We're aiming to have spaciousness enough in mind and body to be able to deal with all the polarities and all the tensions on any given day. Life is really about, instead, having realistic reverence.'

'What's that?' I ask.

'It means I can't be perfect. I can be respectful. And when I'm respectful, I can slowly turn my mind towards being really reverent, which only helps everyone around me,' she says.

I ask her next how one can master the art of attention.

'Understand that your attention is your best and finest commodity,' she says.

'It's no easy feat to be attentive in day-to-day interactions. But when you do, you can feel a sacredness from someone – like a glance shared, a kindness shared. There's something special about that.'

Stress is a choice. 'There are other ways you can look at things without you compromising your immune system. That's all that stress does.'

'Make sure you have rituals in your life, whatever that means to you. If that means clearing a space and meditating or taking a bath or even cooking your own meals to relax.'

An art to feeling less stressed is 'taking more time for rituals'.

'Make sure you have rituals in your life, whatever that means to you. If that means clearing a space and meditating or taking a bath or even cooking your own meals to relax.

'If you have a practice, it's very rare that you'll lose focus and lose your cool. Your practices should help you to hold it together. And if you don't hold it together and for some reason you falter, then make sure you forgive yourself first and then forgive others.'

Elena says to practise rituals like yoga. 'It can help you accumulate time in that neutral state, so this becomes an easier space to be in.'

I ask how you can stay neutral when, say, dealing with a difficult person.

She explains that by accumulating practice through your rituals, you can become calmer and live in a better state. 'You can bring this calmness to these situations,' she explains.

Elena believes in forgiveness, too, for relinquishing stress. 'Keep forgiveness really close by and available to you so that it's never far from you and never foreign to you. It's very important in our families and in our relationships that we are very ready to forgive often. It keeps our space clear. It keeps our creativity flowing.'

She recommends that we put our own 'habits and tendencies' that don't serve us well under the microscope too. You know, what you do that doesn't help you to live happily. Assess whether you have any negative habits and resolve them or lose them. 'Negative ways of acting and living can drain your energy.'

When I speak with Elena, I feel like she chooses her words carefully. There is no rambling. No wasted time. The pauses almost feel uncomfortable, because I haven't mastered this awareness quite as much as her. I note 'awareness' as something I personally need to work on more. How about you?

Elena advises that everyone should keep learning to flourish. 'Keep learning to broaden your mind and be willing to be teachable. Putting yourself in the way of great teachers is very important. Ultimately, how you live is a choice. Keep up your practice [rituals], take care of yourself, take care of each other.'

Elena says we are not all raised equal. Assess the role models you had when you were growing. Then assess whether you will choose that or another way of doing things.

'You have to be willing to observe and be willing to change what you know and what's familiar with you. You can choose to take it in another direction. Be willing to look at what you know and address the most painful examples that you had in your life. Then choose consciously how you are going to carry yourself going forward.

'And, by the way, don't blame anyone. Ever. Whatever you remember of growing up, don't blame anyone. Just go forward and choose who you would like to be and find role models that represent who you would like to be.

'Make that your mission. You are going to see some stuff you don't like. Hardship. There were bad people and bad examples. So just know that they had a certain number of tools in their toolbox. Then consciously do things differently.'

'Keep learning to broaden your mind and be willing to be teachable. Putting yourself in the way of great teachers is very important. Ultimately, how you live is a choice.'

Belly laughs and petting cats.

We live in an age when mindfulness is trendy. We need an antidote to anxiety and stress. This helps us to harness stillness.

In today's world, being stressed has become the normal, everyday state for many of us. But we need to be mindful that long-term stress can harm our body and beauty. Living life being busy and constantly on adrenalin can affect the appearance of our skin and our happiness levels. It can give us rollercoaster emotions and interfere with our digestive system. Stress can promote excess cortisol. This can slow the metabolism (so losing weight becomes a battle).

Living life in constant top gear can also lead to burnout or feeling overwhelmed. This can potentially spiral into depression. It is a very real concern. Anxiety and depression are a burden on many lives.

It's important for us to find strategies to live more in the moment. We need to take time to relax and also exercise to de-stress.

From my own personal experience, I know how important this is. I've struggled with some extremely stressful times in my life. Everyone struggles on occasion. No one is bulletproof. I've found some strategies that help me to de-stress and bolster my happiness levels.

Here are some ideas:

1 Exercise fuels happiness – it's scientifically proven. So choose something that 'moves' you. I feel good when I run; for me, it's a form of moving meditation. I feel free and alive when I'm out in the fresh air, sunshine or rain. I delight in seeing beautiful places as I plod along. Running allows me the space to think. The 'runner's high' truly exists. Being fit and strong helps with my energy levels, and having running goals helps to motivate me. I'm no longer bothered about whether my bum looks big in a pair of jeans. I care more about how my body can be healthier and how running helps me feel mind-strong.

2   Yoga helps me to unwind and centre myself. It empowers me, grounds me and takes me to my 'bliss place'. I belly breathe while stretching out, and this helps to slow my heart rate and calm my nervous system. The yoga way of life is about striving to live a good life and to be kind to others. I'm not perfect at it, but it has taught me to be more mindful with everything I do. It's helped me so much that I've trained to become a yoga teacher, and I love helping others with this tool. One of my favourite relaxation techniques is to lie still on a mat for five minutes with my hands by my sides. I close my eyes. I focus on slow inhalation (for about four seconds), then slowly exhale (for around six seconds). I slow my breath and tune out from my to-do list. I am then mindful to relax my whole body, one part at a time, from the tips of my toes to the top of my head. I always feel calmer after this practice. The best thing is this can calm my nervous system in a matter of moments.

3   Getting at least seven-and-a-half hours of sleep each night helps me tap into my inner calm. Some people need more than this, and kids need even longer.

4   I eat 'real food' and make sure I don't indulge in too much caffeine, alcohol or sugar. For me personally, those things can be like rocket fuel and make me too wired and tired if I have too much.

5   There's a huge power in being playful. Belly laughs are gold. Being silly with my kids, swinging on a swing and just generally letting my hair down. When you have kids, there's nothing like hopping on a swing next to them and giggling your head off. I love doing this and seeing who can swing the highest. My youngest son, Finn, also loves nothing more than when I grab his hands and spin him around in circles outside. I'm not sure who squeals the loudest. This is when I shake stresses and truly reawaken. Play is necessary for mental, social and inner spiritual health.

6   Playing the saxophone is something I have done since I was 11. It transports me to another time and place and it's a stress-shaker.

7   Essential oils can be bliss. Lavender calms and soothes me. I like it on my pillow at night. I give it to my yoga students too. I give them a drop on their wrists near the end of yoga to help them relax. It's a beautiful smell.

8   Planting my toes in the sand at a beach and looking out to the endless blue, blue ocean. This is such a happy place for me. So too are climbing mountains and being in nature in general. Nature nurtures. If you are close to nature, you are closer to feeling 'well'.

'Talk more to friends and family about feelings. Another helpful skill is recognising problems that are causing anxiety and prioritising the issues, so everything is not overwhelming and can be targeted in steps.'

I interviewed Professor **Tony Dowell** once for a newspaper article about depression. He's a Professor of General Practice at Otago University in Wellington.

He said resisting stress and feeling happier was often about finding joyful things to do and then simply doing them often. Activities that could help some people achieve a zen-like state included stroking a cat, watching a comedy, fishing, baking and gardening. 'It's all about finding the things that brighten our days.'

I asked Tony to tell me more about anxiety and depression.

'These feelings can be very disabling and crippling,' he said, adding that anxiety could spiral into agitation, low mood, sadness and severe depression. 'Anxiety affects kids as young as eight here in New Zealand. [Fear about things like monsters and the dark are] a normal part of childhood. But children can become distressed if they're not listened to and supported with their feelings.

'Teenagers too can get anxious. Thankfully, teachers and adults are better at spotting symptoms and taking them seriously. Those aged between 20 and 50 often struggle with relationships and family pressures. While mature folk can get unsettled too.'

However, anxiety could be 'very treatable', said the professor. 'Talk more to friends and family about feelings. Another helpful skill is recognising problems that are causing anxiety and prioritising the issues, so everything is not overwhelming and can be targeted in steps.'

He said help for mild symptoms was accessible through lots of websites and doctors were now well trained in spotting symptoms. Doctors could give clients 'a good hearing' and could be a great 'gateway' for further help if required, usually suggesting 'talking therapy' but also medication if it was clinically indicated. Counsellors and clinical psychologists have expertise and experience with a range of psychological therapies.

Tony said there was a new trend towards shorter periods of therapy (about three sessions), which had successfully helped people. 'This is now regarded to be highly effective. So people shouldn't be frightened that they will be working in therapy for years.'

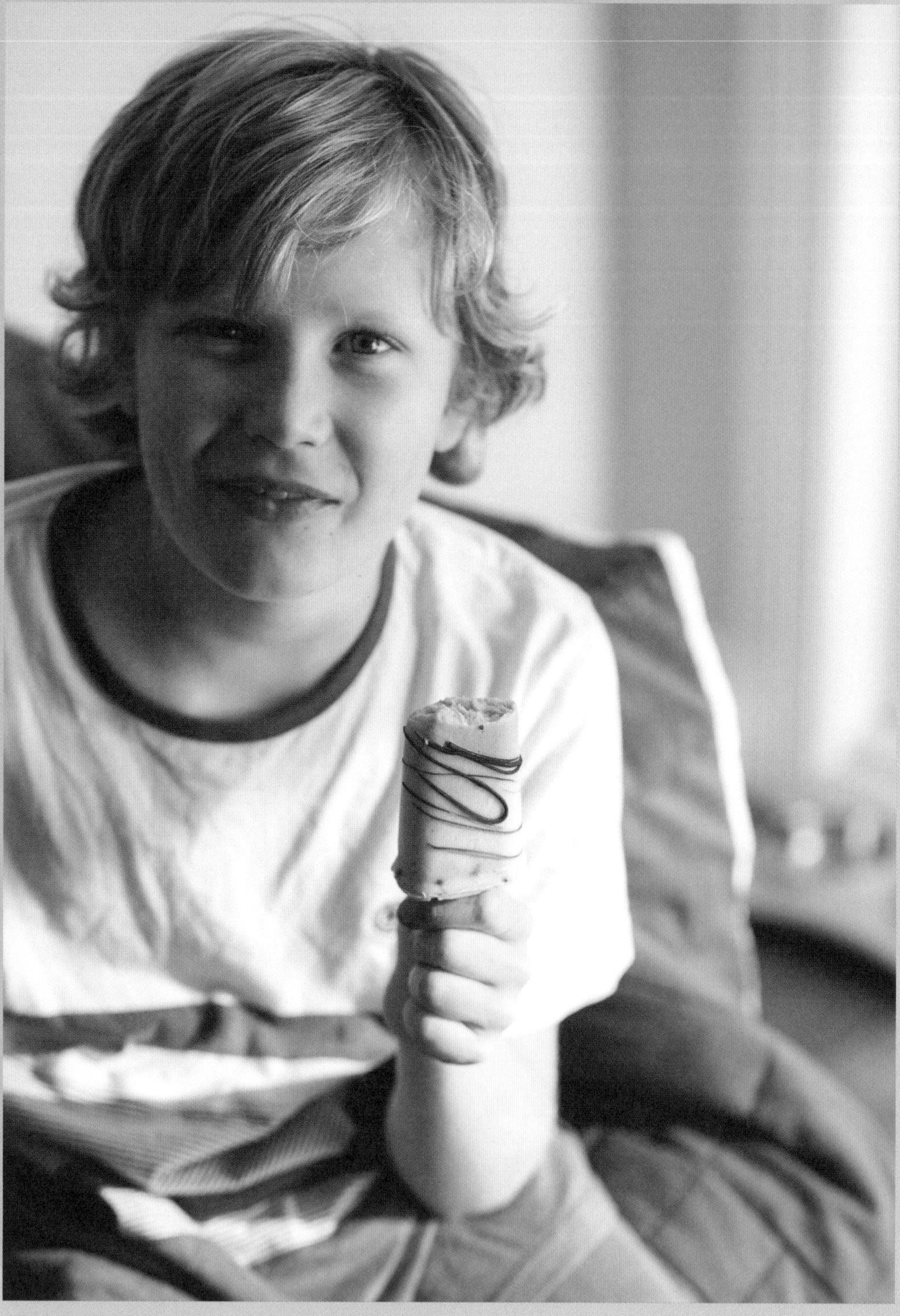

Bowled Over₊

Prepare for your mouth to water. Here are some nutrient-dense, delicious and whole-food recipes, originally developed for Good Magazine and now collected here for you to enjoy. Most of these recipes take only a few minutes to make — except the ice-blocks. These offerings come in either a bowl, glass, cup or on a stick... You know, smoothies, juices, milks, lattes, ice-blocks or frappés. Give them a whirl!

Summer Bliss Strawberry Smoothie

Smoothies are an easy way to inject nutrients into your diet. There are, however, a few common pitfalls when making smoothies to be aware of. The first is setting yourself up for 'smoothie fatigue'. In essence, some people learn just one or two smoothie recipes and thrash them day after day. This gets boring – fast. It also means you end up having the same nutrients repeatedly, which is not smart nutrition-wise. Change your smoothie recipes often to consume a wide variety of nutrients. This will keep your taste buds interested too.

Another mistake is packing in too many ingredients. This can turn your smoothie into an ugly brown swamp-like colour. It can also make them taste yucky. Worse still, if you add too many ingredients then you can end up swigging your entire day's calorie intake in one quick hit. Adding too much fruit can also transform your smoothie into a 'sugar bomb'. You don't actually need much fruit to make your smoothie taste sweet. A little fruit can go a long way.

So, keep smoothies simple, not too sweet, change them up often, and make sure they taste good so you enjoy them.

1 cup **strawberries**, washed and hulled

¾ cup **cashew milk** – recipe for this is below (or use almond milk, which works nicely too)

1 **frozen banana**, skin removed

1 handful **ice**

1 pinch **cinnamon**

1 tsp **flaxseed oil**

Throw everything into a blender and blend for roughly 30 seconds, or until smooth. If you feel like being super fancy, top with a sprinkle of granola and some edible flowers if you have them growing in the garden (I grow a wall of them in the backyard at my place).

For an extra antioxidant boost add 1 tsp of powdered berries (there are lots of these on the market – just find one that you like the taste of). Or just leave it out. The recipe is delicious on its own.

Cashew Milk. Place ⅓ cup of raw cashews in a cup and cover them with water. Leave these to soak for about three hours (or overnight if you wish). Then drain the water and wash the cashews with some more fresh water. Next place the soaked cashews in a blender with 1 cup of filtered water and blitz this until it is smooth. You can use a muslin cloth to filter the cashew milk and leave the pulp to the side. But I tend not to bother removing the pulp when I make cashew milk. I separate the pulp when I make almond milk though, for instance, as it results in a silkier texture.

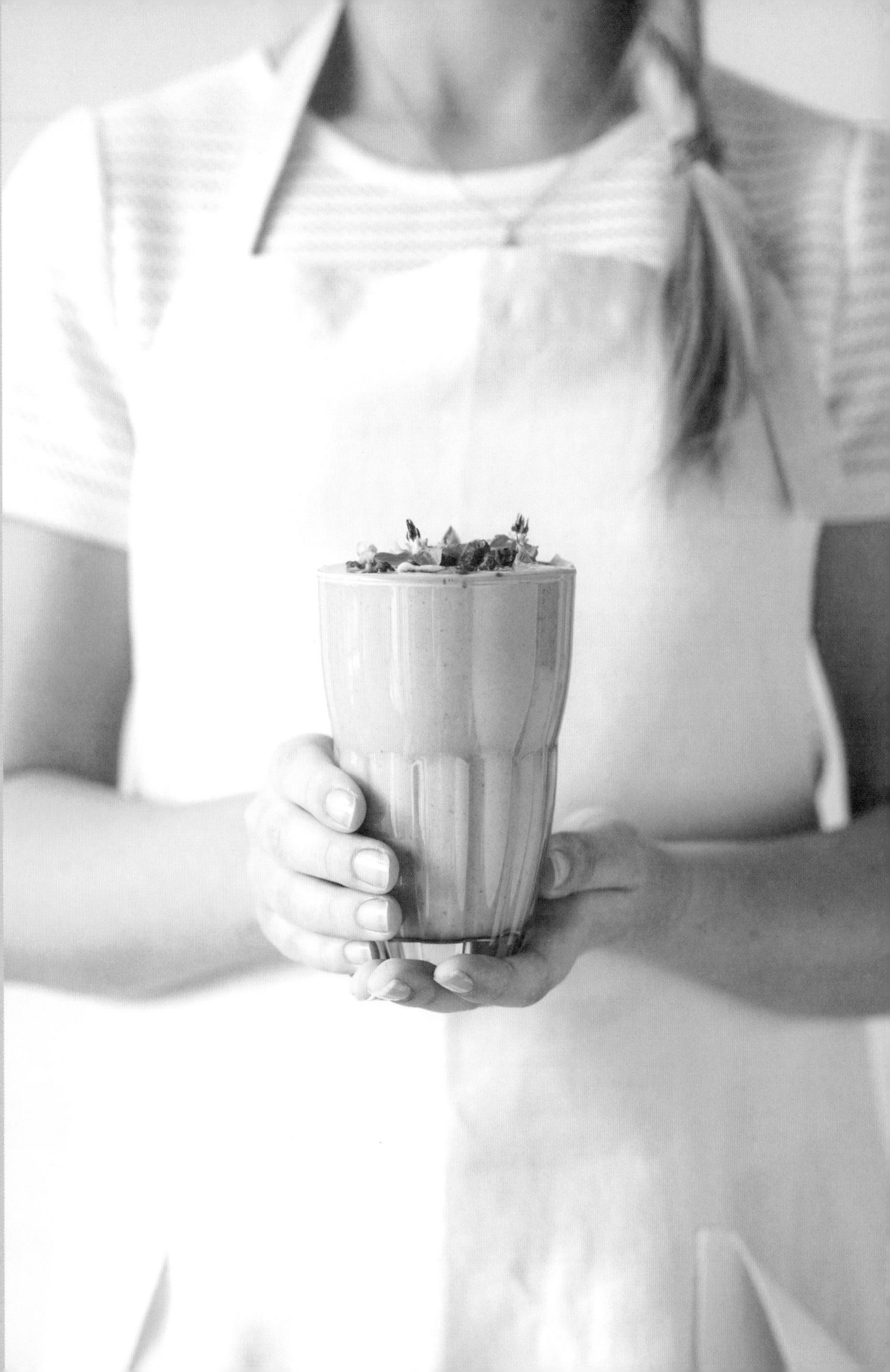

Beetroot Energiser Juice

There are so many benefits to beetroot juice. Beets have antioxidant and anti-inflammatory properties. They are awesome for the cardiovascular system, so have them for your heart health.

The colour always pops out at me when I make beetroot juice; I love it. But that vibrant colour comes at a price! I used to avoid using beets because they are so messy to prepare, but I got over that because I know they are packed full of goodness. To avoid red-stained fingers from preparing beets, wear kitchen gloves. Or just handle them quickly with bare hands and wash your hands with warm soapy water immediately afterwards.

3 medium **beetroot** (roughly 200g)

½ **green apple**, core removed

3cm chunk **fresh ginger**, skin removed with a sharp knife

1 cup **coconut water**

good squeeze **lime juice**

Peel and cut the beetroot into 3cm chunks and place into a powerful blender. Add the green apple to the beets. Then add the remaining ingredients: ginger, coconut water and lime juice. Next, blitz this all in the blender. You can use less ginger if you like, but I love the kick of flavour from this amount. Ginger is also known as an anti-inflammatory. I love using fresh organic veg and ginger for this recipe. Blitz everything to liquidise, then pour through a sieve for a silky-smooth consistency. Discard the pulp (or save it for making something like beetroot crackers) and pour the juice into a glass to drink. I sometimes double the recipe and keep it in a jar in the fridge. This will last for a few days.

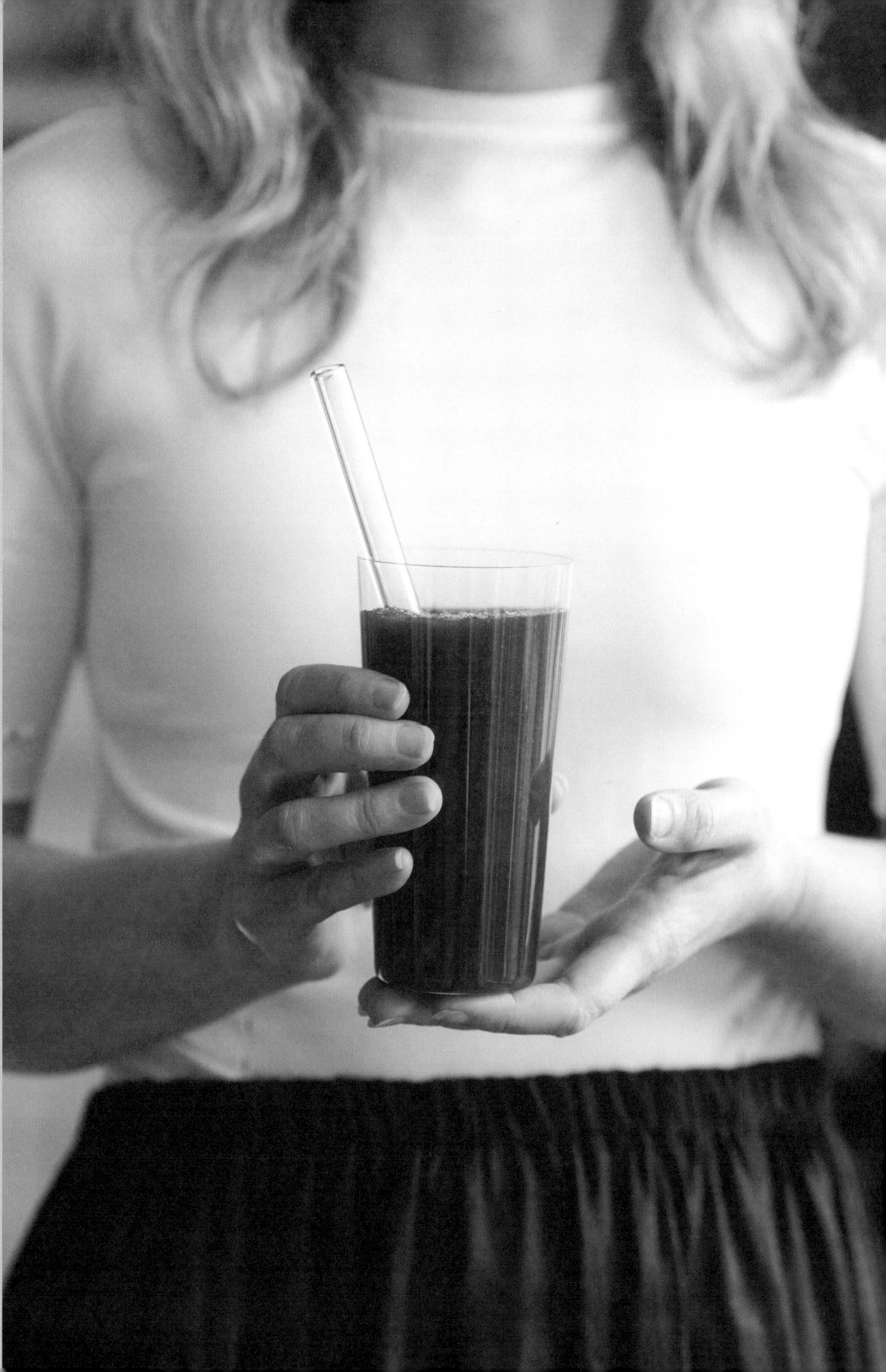

Beetroot
Crackers

I eat these crackers instead of traditional bread sometimes, paired with a veggie bowl, boiled eggs, salmon and avocado (and a grind each of salt and pepper and squeeze of lemon juice). Or pair them with a chickpea, avocado or white bean dip. I'll sometimes have these beetroot crackers with just sliced avocado on top (with a grind each of salt and pepper and a squeeze of lemon juice too, of course). Or how about cottage cheese and tomato on top?

Beetroot pulp (left over from making juice from three medium-sized fresh beetroot)

¾ cup **linseed** (half of it ground in a blender, the other half kept in its natural whole form)

1 cup **ground raw almonds**

small **clove garlic**, skin removed

1 **egg**

salt + pepper

Turn the oven on to 160°C and line a flat tray with baking paper. Or if you have a dehydrator then use that instead, if you prefer.

Mix all the ingredients in a bowl and then use a spoon to spread out the mixture evenly over the paper. Keep it about ¼ centimetre thick.

Bake in the oven for roughly 1 hour until firm and crispy (you may need to turn up the temperature or leave them to bake for longer depending on the oomph of your oven). Just test them to see that they are firm like crackers and then you will know they are done. While crackers are still warm, cut into desired squares. Leave them to cool on a wire rack. Then place them in an airtight container until you want to eat them. I usually eat these within a few days while they are fresh.

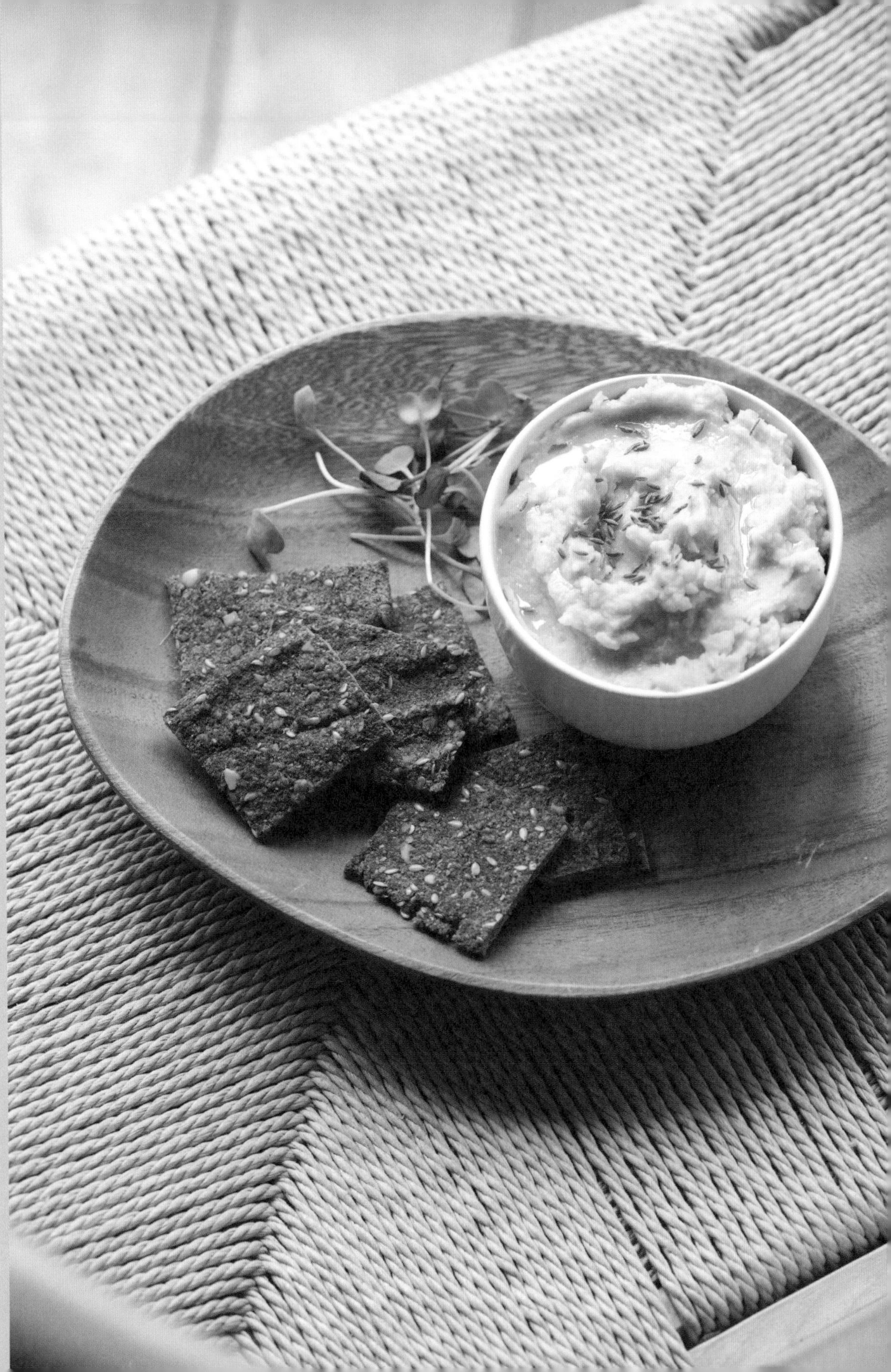

Popeye's Greens in a Cup

Spinach grows like a weed in my garden for most of the year. I hack it back regularly when I make salads or smoothies. I love nothing more than a green smoothie after teaching yoga; this fuels my body and soul. This smoothie is so full of goodness. It boasts lots of antioxidants and nutrients. Spinach is known for containing iron.

A great way to get my kids on board with loving greens is I tell them that Popeye ate greens to get superpower strength. Actually, my kids love this smoothie without any bribery because of the sweetness of the added pear. They guzzle this back like mini Popeye chaps. I hope you love it too and get a kick out of this smoothie's 'superpowers'.

4 medium **spinach leaves**

250ml **coconut water**

½ chopped **pear** (Bosc variety ideally), remove pips (if pears are not in season, just use tinned ones)

½ **avocado**, skin and pip removed

4 **ice cubes**

1 tbsp **coriander**

2 **mint leaves**

Wash the greens under water. Then place the leaves and the rest of the ingredients into a blender, mix, pour into a glass and savour.

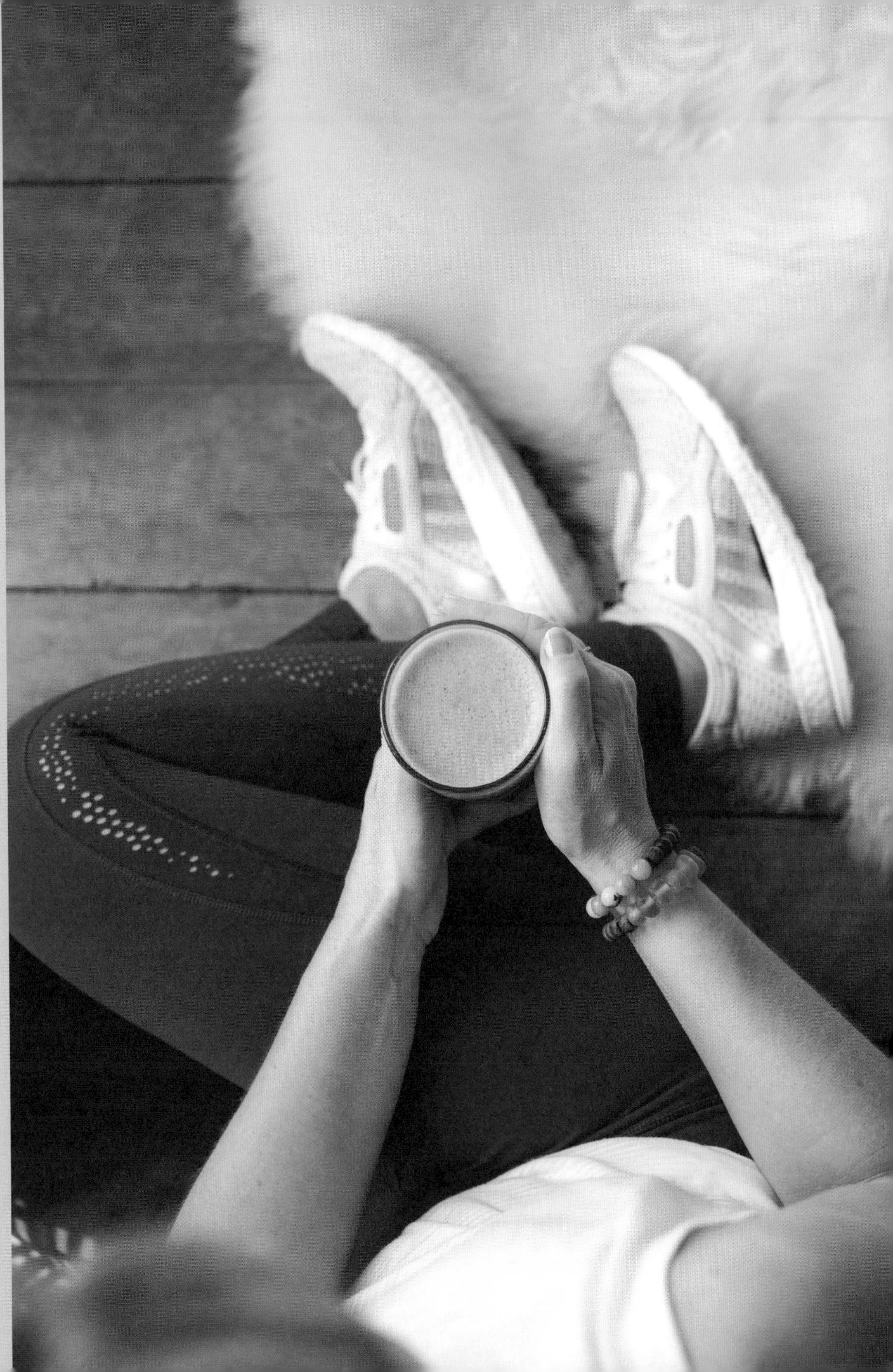

Green
Mean
Machine

Green smoothies are a great way to start the day, and you can use whatever is growing in your garden. Spinach is one of my favourite leafy green vegetables to use in smoothies because it thrives in the garden most of the year and is so easy to grow. It doesn't need a lot of care and attention! I love that it boasts lots of nutrients and antioxidants and also contains lutein (which is good for sparkling eyes). But you can use kale or silver beet instead if you wish. Any option will fuel your body beautifully. The parsley in here may look like a token gesture, but don't underestimate its superpowers. Parsley has anti-inflammatory properties, is alkaline, boasts iron and vitamin C and is also an antioxidant. So the little things do make a difference in this blend.

Meanwhile, feel free to use a squeeze of lemon instead of lime, or use water instead of coconut water if you prefer. My recipe is simply a guide, and you are welcome to mess with it a bit. I will simply be chuffed to have inspired you to up your greens.

For an extra wellbeing boost, add a scoop of green powder nutrients (if you happen to have this in your cupboard at home). However, it is nutrient-rich already and doesn't require the powder.

¼ **cucumber**, peeled and chopped roughly

5 **spinach leaves**, washed under water

½ cup **pear**, fresh with pips removed, or you can use them from a tin if they are not in season

½ cup **coconut water**

2 sprigs of **parsley**

ice (roughly a handful)

squeeze of **lime**

Place all the ingredients in a blender and blitz until smooth. Pour into a glass and devour.

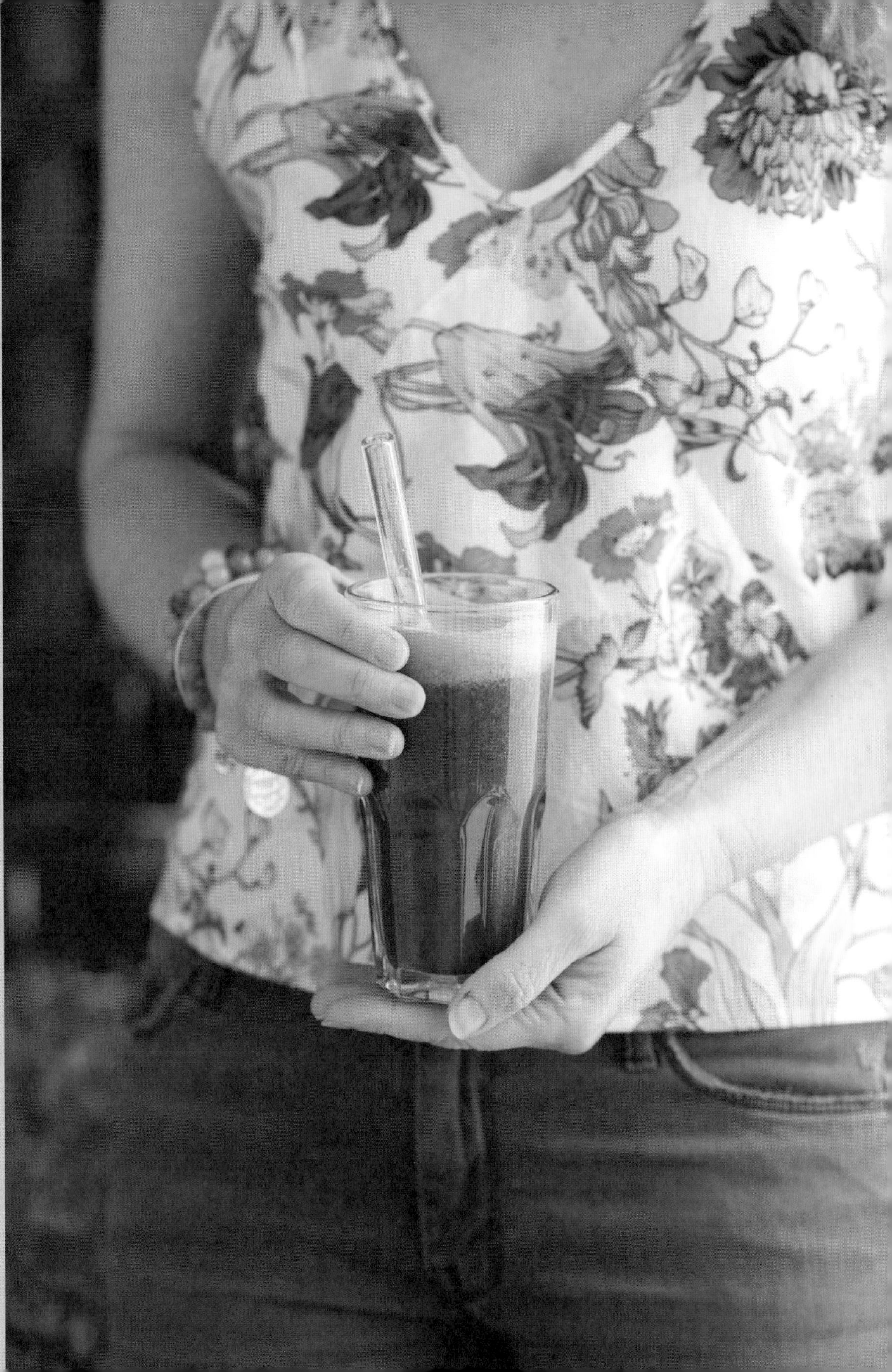

Oh Goodness Green Cleanse

Maybe they enjoy these healthy treats because they've grown up with them – long may this last!

Plant-powered smoothies are full of goodness. This one is thirst-quenching as well as a great way to inject more greens into your day, and you'll find its vibrant colour irresistible.

I liken this smoothie to summer in a glass; sweetened just enough with pineapple and banana, its hero ingredient is the fresh, young coconut, which is soft in texture. As well as having a lovely flavour, coconuts contain antibacterial properties. For an extra protein boost, add 1 scoop of protein powder (a vanilla flavour is a good option).

I always drink my smoothie slowly and mindfully, savouring the goodness, whereas my young son Finn slurps his up in seconds, leaving behind a cute green moustache. Sometimes Finn requests this smoothie after school, saying, 'I'll have that green one with the pineapple, okay, Mum?' So I raid our spinach patch and whip it up, the whole process taking only a few minutes. If pineapples aren't in season and affordable then I just use the tinned stuff.

I love that my kids often have nutrient-dense smoothies for snacks, rather than highly processed foods.

5 **spinach leaves**

¼ cup **coriander leaves**

½ **avocado** (skin off, pip out)

1 tsp **lime zest**

1 tbsp **lime juice**

¼ cup **pineapple pieces**

flesh of 1 **young coconut**, any brown bits removed

250ml of the **coconut's water**

Put all the ingredients into a blender and blitz. Pour into a glass and savour – with stillness, and appreciation of the moment, if you can.

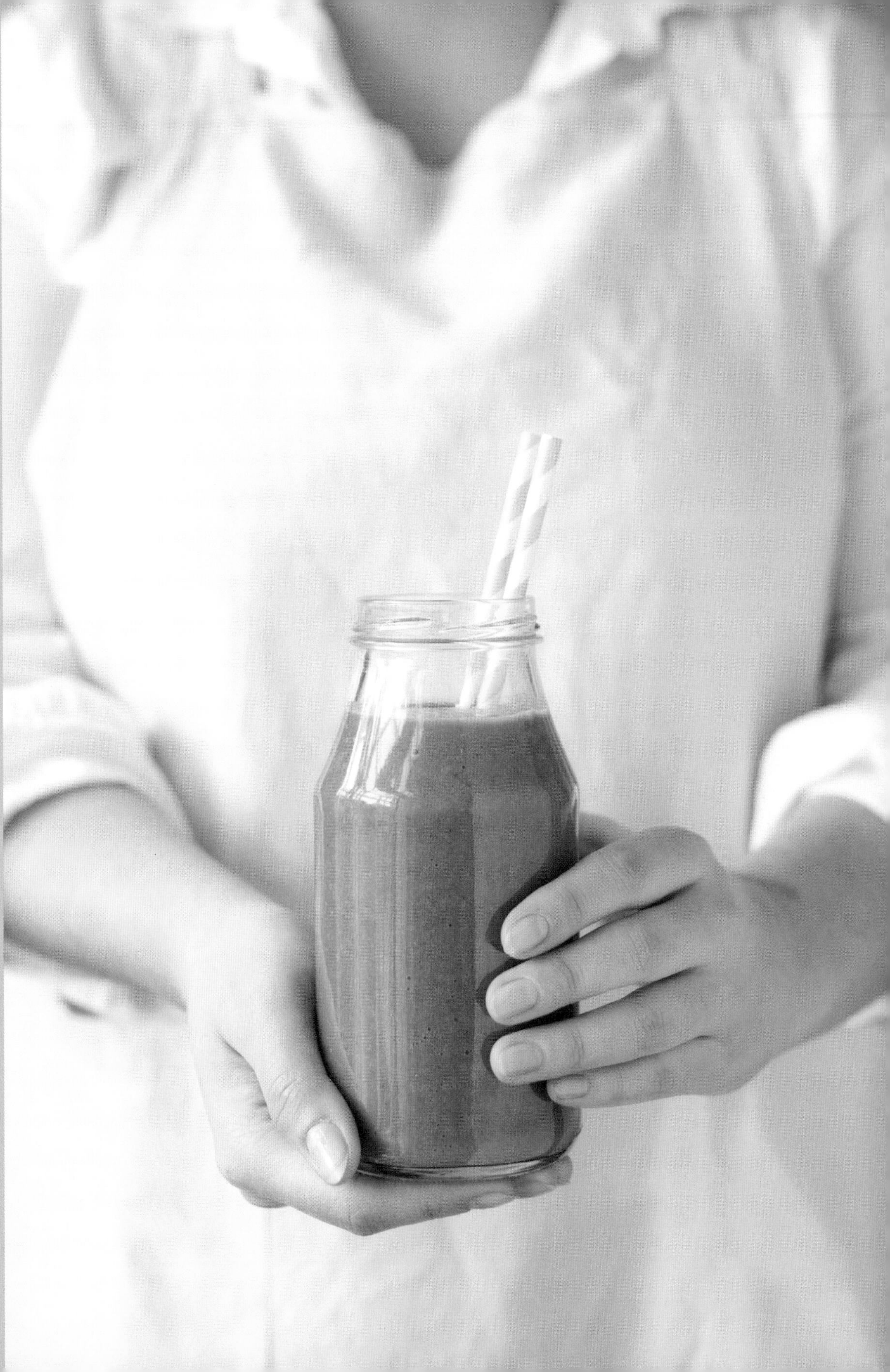

Spiced-Up Turmeric Latte

*If you haven't tried a turmeric latte yet, you are in for a truly lovely experience. A good turmeric latte tastes creamy, spicy and earthy and leaves you feeling full. My first turmeric latte left me disappointed, but I know now that it had been made with water and so wasn't creamy-tasting enough. Thankfully I tried another one at Matcha Mylkbar in Melbourne, and that's when the love affair began. The knowledge that this brew is soothing and has incredible anti-inflammatory properties makes it even more appealing. Fellow foodie **Kelly Gibney** has a beautiful version of the turmeric latte in her book **Wholehearted: Inspiring Real Food for Every Day**. Or if you are in Auckland, treat yourself to **Megan May**'s turmeric offerings at one of her Little Bird Unbakery cafés. Here is one version I make at home which I love; it's goodness in a cup.*

¼ cup **raw cashews**

1 cup **filtered water**

½ cup **coconut cream**

1 tsp **fresh turmeric** (scrape off the skin with a teaspoon then grate. Alternatively, use 1 tsp powdered form)

2cm piece of **fresh ginger** (or use ½ tsp powdered form)

1 tsp **mānuka honey**

½ tsp each of **ground cinnamon** and **nutmeg**

1 tsp **coconut oil**

1 grind of **black pepper**

Soak the cashews in the water for three hours first. Then put them in a sieve and wash them clean with more water. Place them and everything else in a blender (except the coconut oil and pepper) and blitz, then heat in a saucepan on the stove. Add the coconut oil while it's heating. When warm, pour into a cup, top with a grind of pepper and savour.

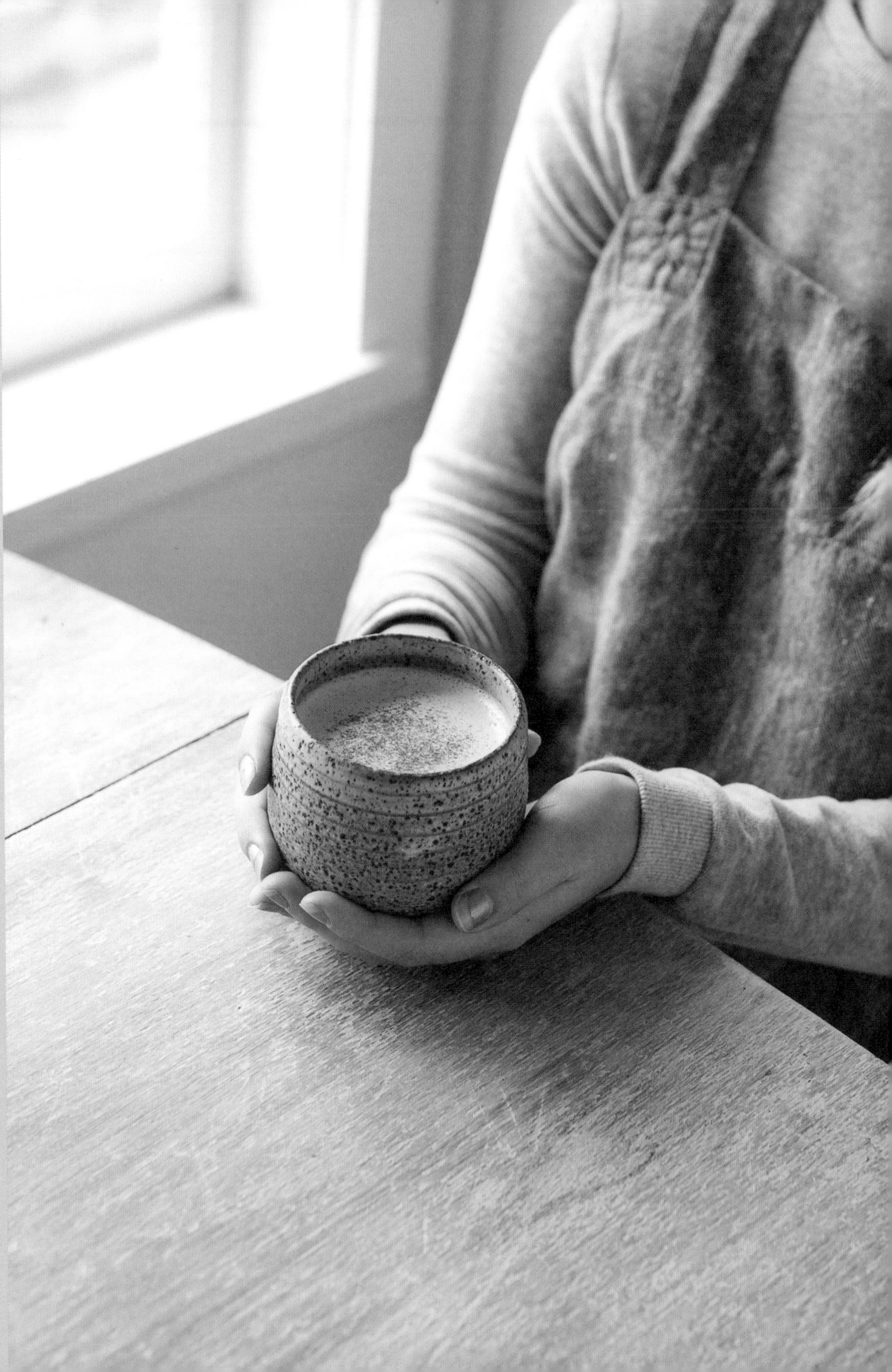

Ginger
Fire
Injection

The supermarket is full of juice products, but many contain added sugar on top of the natural fruit sugars already present. So I make my own. This way, I know they're full of goodness. It's easy – even my kids love to create their own drinks.

The trick is to resist using lots of ingredients, otherwise they can look and taste like a science experiment. Another tip is to use vegetables and fruits that are in season (i.e. what's cheapest or readily available from your garden or on sale at the local market). I often use vegetables, fruits and herbs from my garden. Or I buy them from a store in my village where a grandmother in her 80s serves me (her family runs this store and I love supporting local businesses when I can).

I'd also recommend investing in a decent juicing machine that can deal with harder produce like ginger and apples, and be sure to get one that's easy to clean.

I love this recipe because I'm a big fan of the warming taste of ginger, which is perfect for winter and can aid digestion too.

2cm chunk **fresh ginger**, peeled

1 **green apple**, core removed

2 **oranges**, peeled

squeeze of **lime juice**

Put the ginger, apple and orange through a juicer and pour the juice into a gorgeous glass. Add the lime and stir. Lastly, sip and savour!

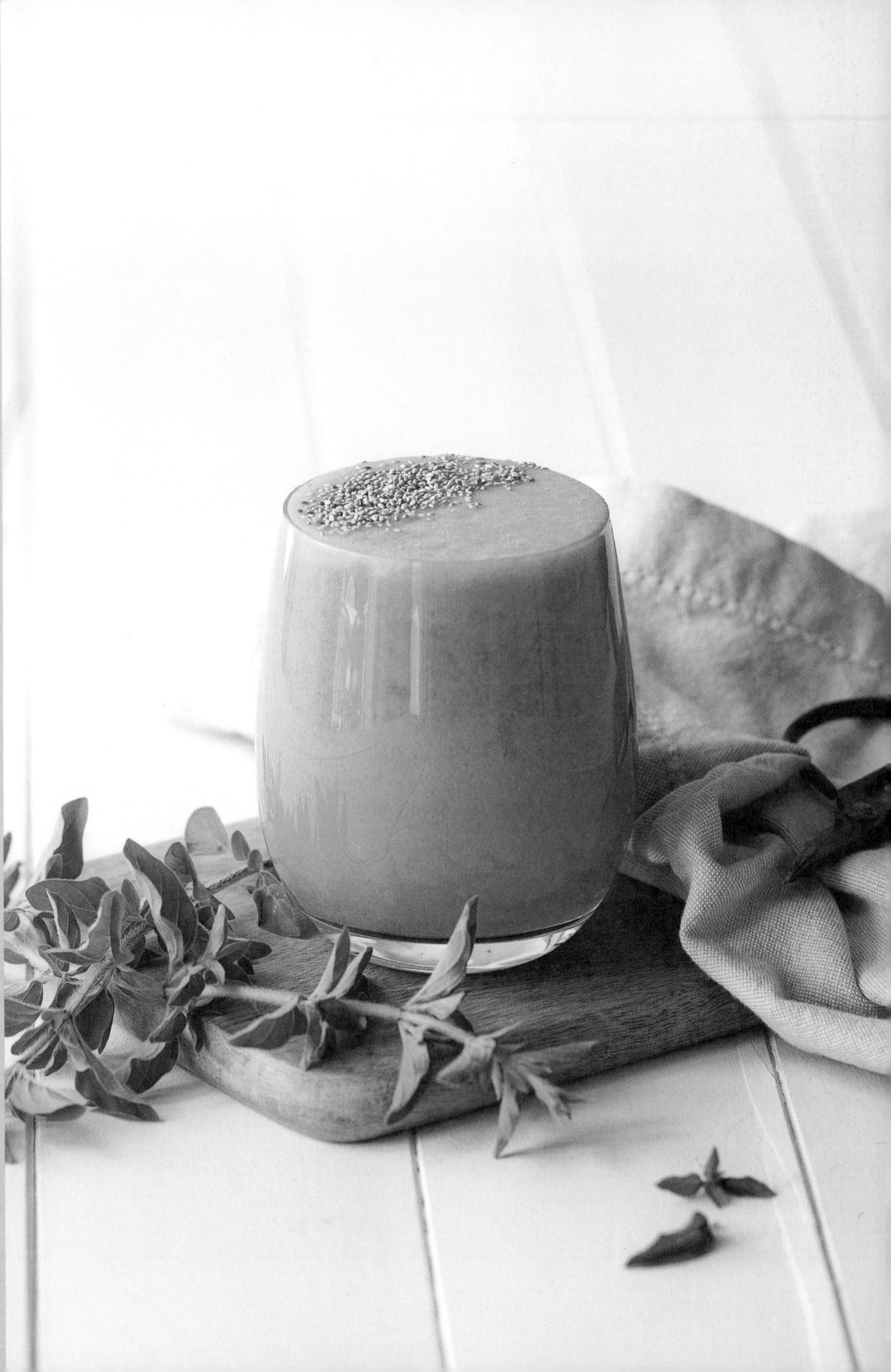

'Matcha' Made in Heaven Iceblocks

If you make your own iceblocks for the kids, then you know exactly what goes into them. These have some good ingredients, including matcha powder. Matcha is green tea leaves that have been ground into a fine powder. Makers of the tea reckon it can enhance energy, metabolism, detoxification and even immunity. I can tell you that my kids smile when they eat these.

1 cup **coconut cream**

1 cup **water**

1 ripe **avocado**, skin and pip removed

2 tbsp **maple syrup**

½ tsp **matcha powder**

1 cup **dark chocolate bits**

TOPPING:

½ cup **dark chocolate**

Place the iceblock ingredients (except the dark chocolate bits) into a blender until mixed. Pour into iceblock moulds, leaving 1cm space free at the top. In this space, place about 1 tsp of the dark chocolate bits. Repeat the process for each iceblock. Leave overnight to freeze. To make the topping the next day, melt the chocolate in a double boiler (also called a bain-marie). That is, put the chocolate in a glass bowl and then place this bowl into a pan that has a centimetre of water in the bottom of the pan and gently heat. The water will heat up in the pan and gently and evenly heat the chocolate in the glass bowl. Once the chocolate is melted, place the iceblocks on a board and then use a spoon to drizzle chocolate lines across the iceblocks. This makes them look super fancy.

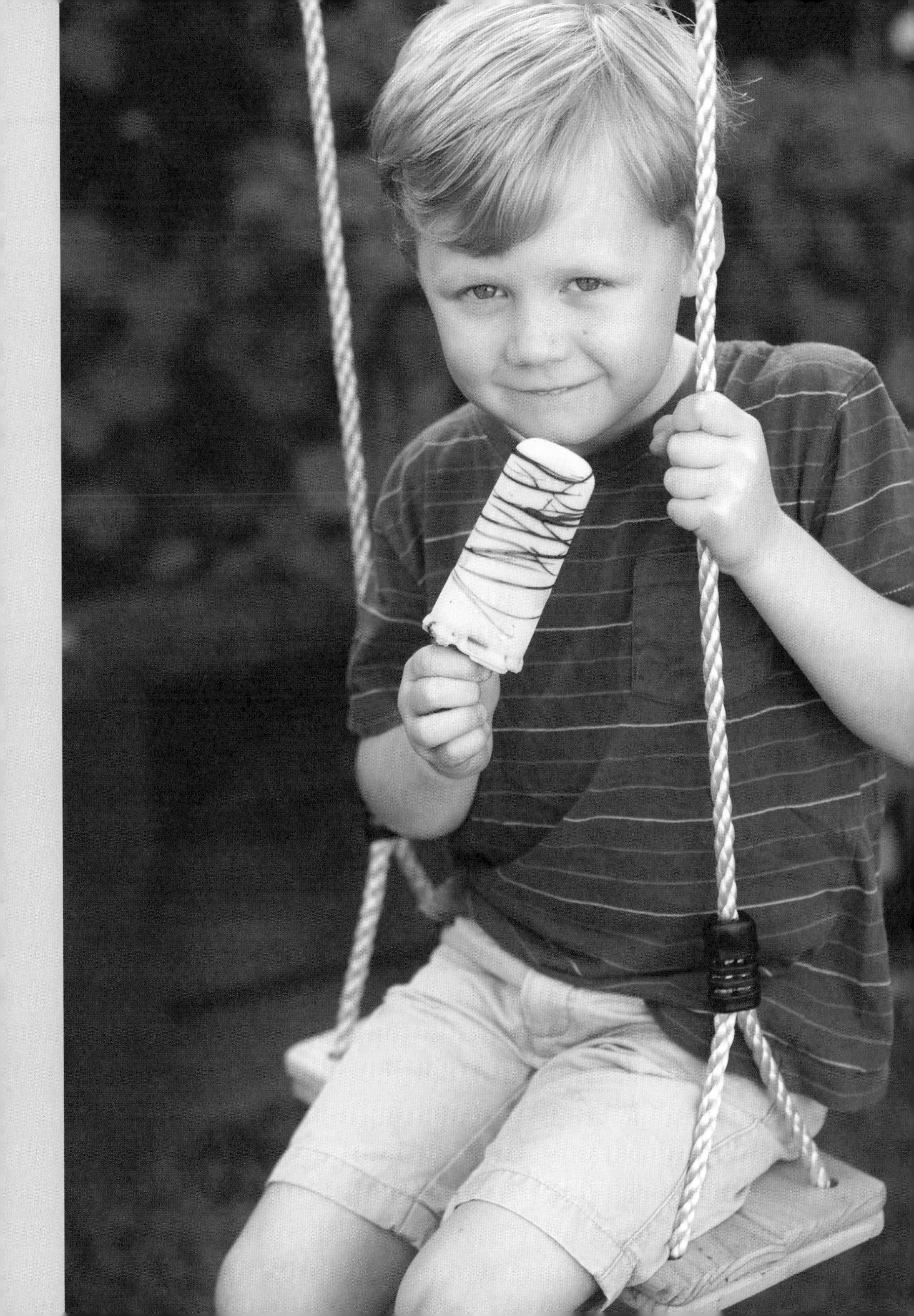

Pineapple Mint Froth – Juice or Iceblocks

Coconut water is so hydrating, and it's the base of this recipe. But the rock-star ingredient is pineapple. This yellow fruit contains vitamin C, manganese, fibre and bromelain. The latter is a protein digesting enzyme.

This juice is easy and delicious on a hot day. You get a two-for-one recipe with this idea, too. You can make the exact same recipe into iceblocks. The family will love drinking this frothy drink in a glass or eating it in its icy form. My kids have taste-tested this recipe and love it. The benefit of making your own iceblocks is that you know what they contain, of course.

1 cup **pineapple**

1 cup **coconut water**

small handful fresh **mint leaves**, washed under a tap

½ **lime**, squeezed

Roughly cut up the pineapple (removing the skin), put this into a blender with the rest of the ingredients and blitz until frothy. Pour the liquid into a glass, add a few ice cubes and a straw and enjoy quenching your thirst! This is a great non-alcoholic drink to offer guests, too, if they want an alcohol-free option.

To make the iceblocks, pour the same liquid into iceblock moulds and leave overnight to set.

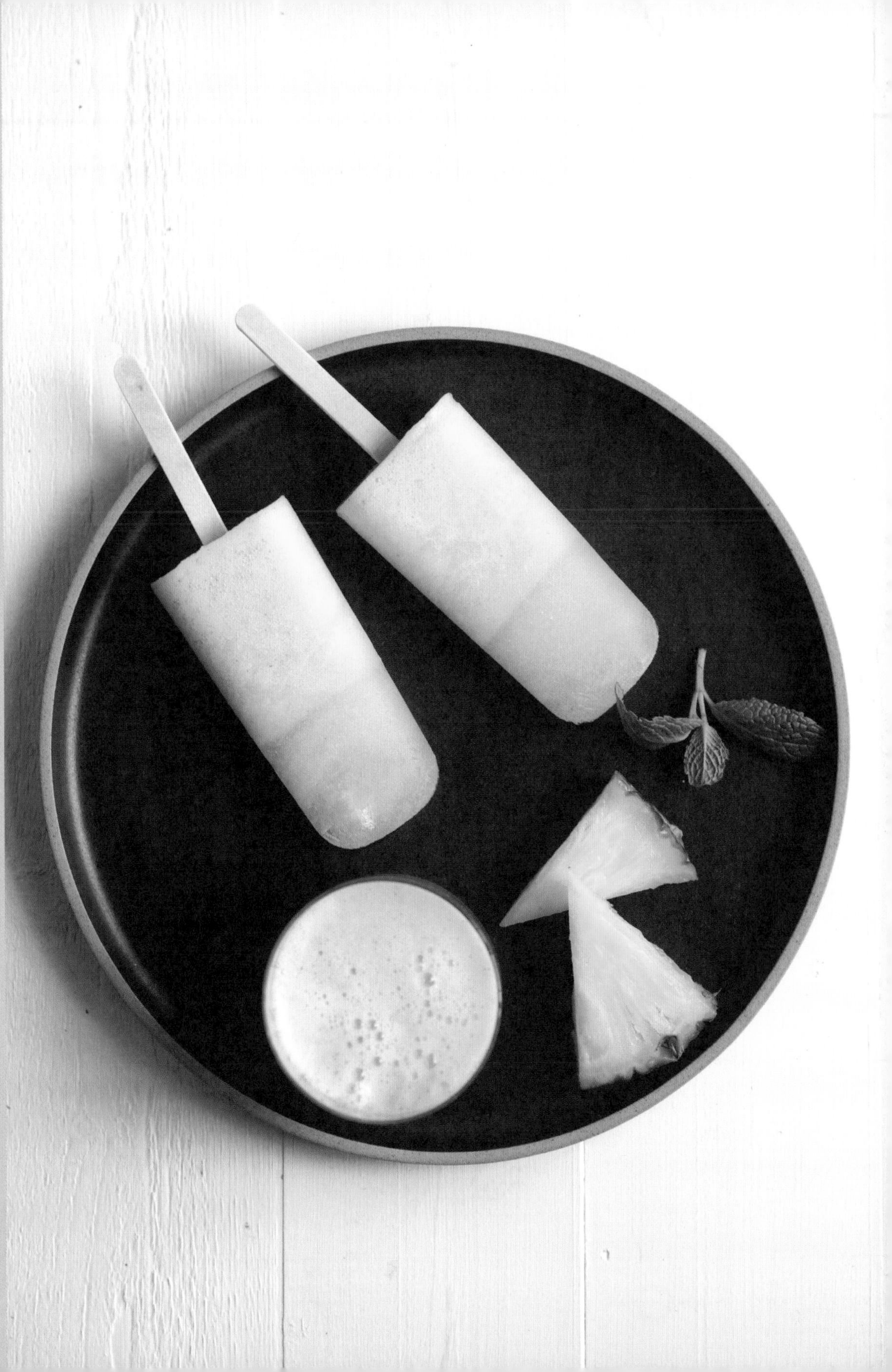

Choc Raspberry Smoothie Bowl

SERVES 2

This recipe can be used in two ways – in a bowl or frozen into iceblocks.

I also sometimes double or even triple the recipe and have a smoothie bowl and leftover mixture for making iceblocks.

My kids love these iceblocks. They are a healthy option for an after-school treat. They are preservative-free, gluten-free and dairy-free. And who doesn't like the combination of chocolate and raspberries, right?

1 cup **water**

¼ cup **cashews**, soaked previously for two hours in water and then water removed and rinsed with fresh water

2 **frozen bananas**, skin removed

1 tbsp **cacao powder**

¼ cup **coconut cream**

pinch of **salt**

½ tsp **vanilla essence**

1 tsp **honey**

RASPBERRY CHIA:

½ cup **raspberries**

1 cup **water**

2 tsp **honey**

¼ cup **chia seeds**

OPTIONAL TOPPINGS FOR THE SMOOTHIE BOWL:

handful **granola**

sprinkle of **raspberries**
(use freeze-dried raspberries or fresh ones if they are in season)

Put all the first list of ingredients for the smoothie bowl into a blender and blitz until smooth. Leave to the side.

Next, make the raspberry chia by blitzing the raspberries, water and honey in a blender and then gently stir in the chia seeds and leave for 30 minutes to plump up in the fridge. To make your smoothie bowl, pour the choc smoothie mixture into a bowl and then spoon as much raspberry chia on top as you like. We then sprinkled a handful of granola and raspberries for added crunch and flavour. You can add as much of this (or as little) as you desire.

ICEBLOCKS:

This same smoothie bowl recipe mixture (and the raspberry chia) can double as nutrient-dense iceblocks. Just put roughly a tbsp of the chia recipe into iceblock moulds first and then fill with the chocolate smoothie recipe mixture to get the two layers. Then pop these into the freezer overnight. For added chocolate sweetness and flavour (as well as wow factor), I then remove the iceblocks from their containers and drizzle melted dark chocolate on top of them. A photo of the ice block version of this recipe is on page 33.

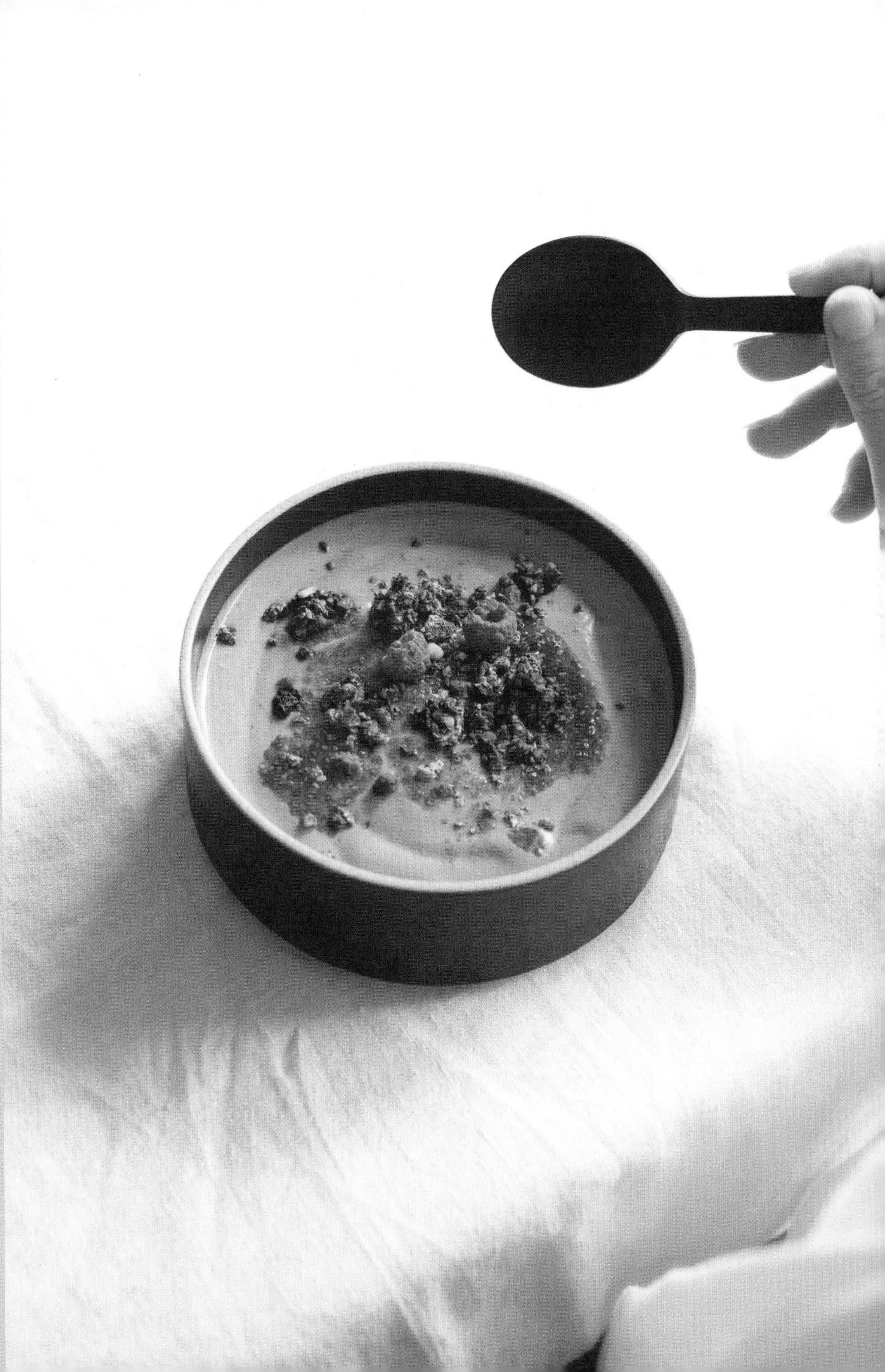

Strawberry Blonde Smoothie Bowl

Smoothie bowls are so much more than a quick snack that you'll devour in one hit. Savour your smoothie bowl as a full breakfast or lunch option. Be creative and layer nutrient-dense ingredients on top, like natural muesli or oats, granola, raw nuts, coconut chips or fresh fruits that are in season. Or just use whatever is handy in your fruit bowl. I love to add protein powder to mine if I eat them after running or teaching yoga. I'll even put shavings of dark chocolate on top of my kids' smoothie bowls. They like them so much that I can never make a sneaky smoothie bowl for myself. I always end up lining up the bowls and making them for my kids as well.

The hero ingredient in this recipe is strawberries. This fruit is a source of vitamin C, which is crucial for lots of processes in the body, including immune function and collagen creation (promoting healthy, youthful skin).

1 punnet **strawberries**, leaves removed

½ cup **almond milk**

2 **frozen bananas**, peeled

1 tsp **raw maca powder**

3 **Medjool dates** (pips removed)

4 **ice cubes**

1 tsp **mānuka honey**

pinch each of **vanilla bean powder** and **cinnamon**

1 tsp **lime juice**

Place all the smoothie ingredients in a blender and mix until smooth then place into two bowls. Top with a swirl of yoghurt and your favourite topping. This one has slices of orange and banana, strawberries, bee pollen and freeze-dried raspberries. But feel free to use whatever topping you desire and have at hand.

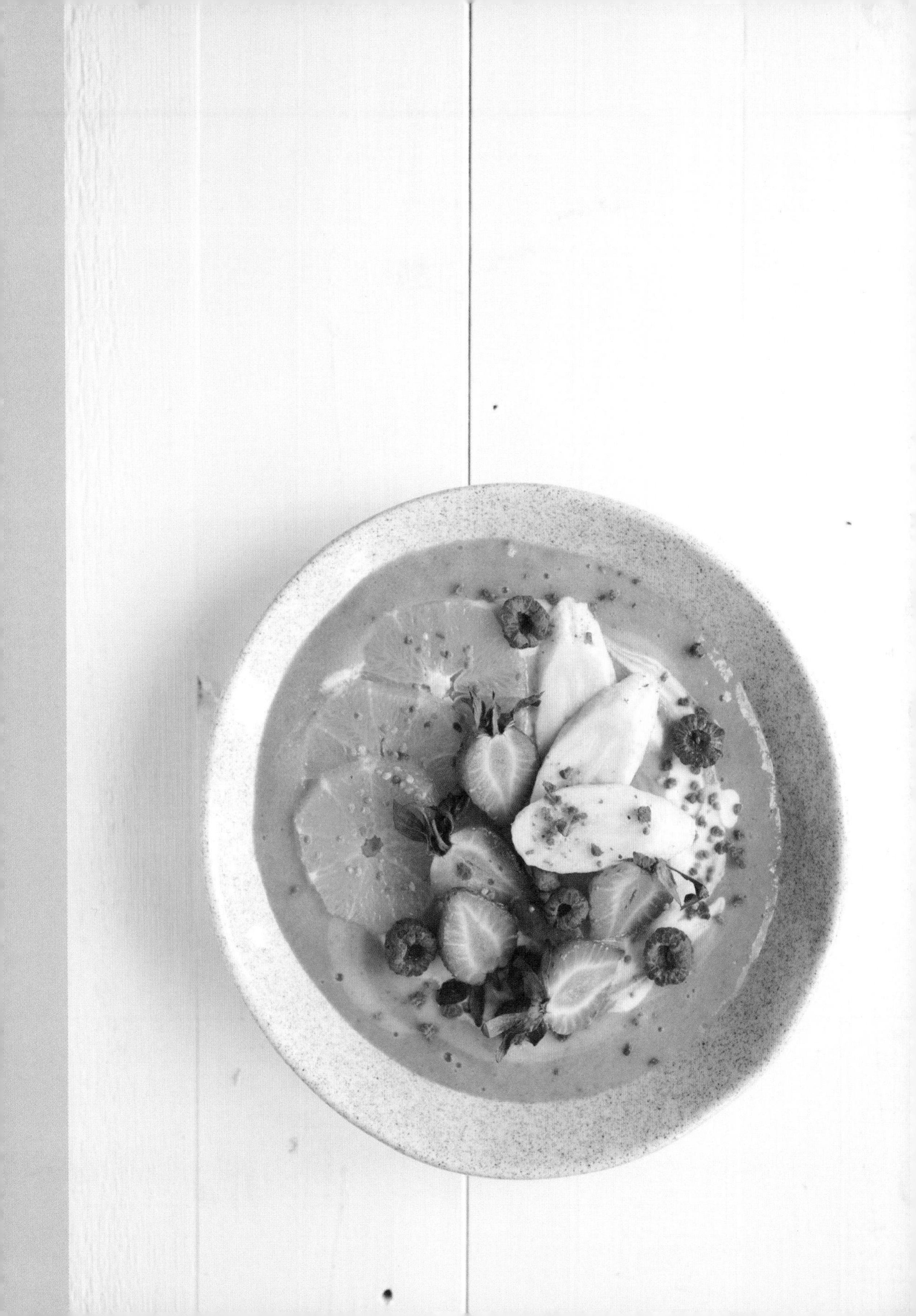

Blueberry + Coconut Escape

Blueberries are the hero ingredient in this richly dark, thick and creamy smoothie. Blueberries are wonderfully rich in antioxidants, which can help to counteract premature ageing. They're also deliciously sweet, so add them to things like porridge at breakfast time or have them on their own as a mid-afternoon, or night, snack. Another healthy snack I love is blueberries with natural yoghurt. My kids love to snack on them frozen from the freezer and I know when they have been into them – their blue lips are a giveaway!

1 cup of **coconut water**

1 cup of **blueberries** (frozen or fresh)

1 **banana** (frozen ideally), skin off

drizzle of **maple syrup**

handful of **ice**

2 **mint leaves**, washed and torn

Place all the ingredients into a blender and whiz them together. Now it's ready to pour into a smoothie bowl or glass – and enjoy. For an extra protein boost add one scoop of protein powder. However, there's no need for the protein powder. It's delicious on its own. I poured this smoothie into a bowl and ate it with a spoon. Garnish it with whatever nutrient-dense toppings you love to eat. There are no rules with toppings. I used some of my homemade muesli (the recipe is in this book). If passionfruit are in season, then squeeze one of these on top with some coconut yoghurt instead. This recipe will make enough for two people.

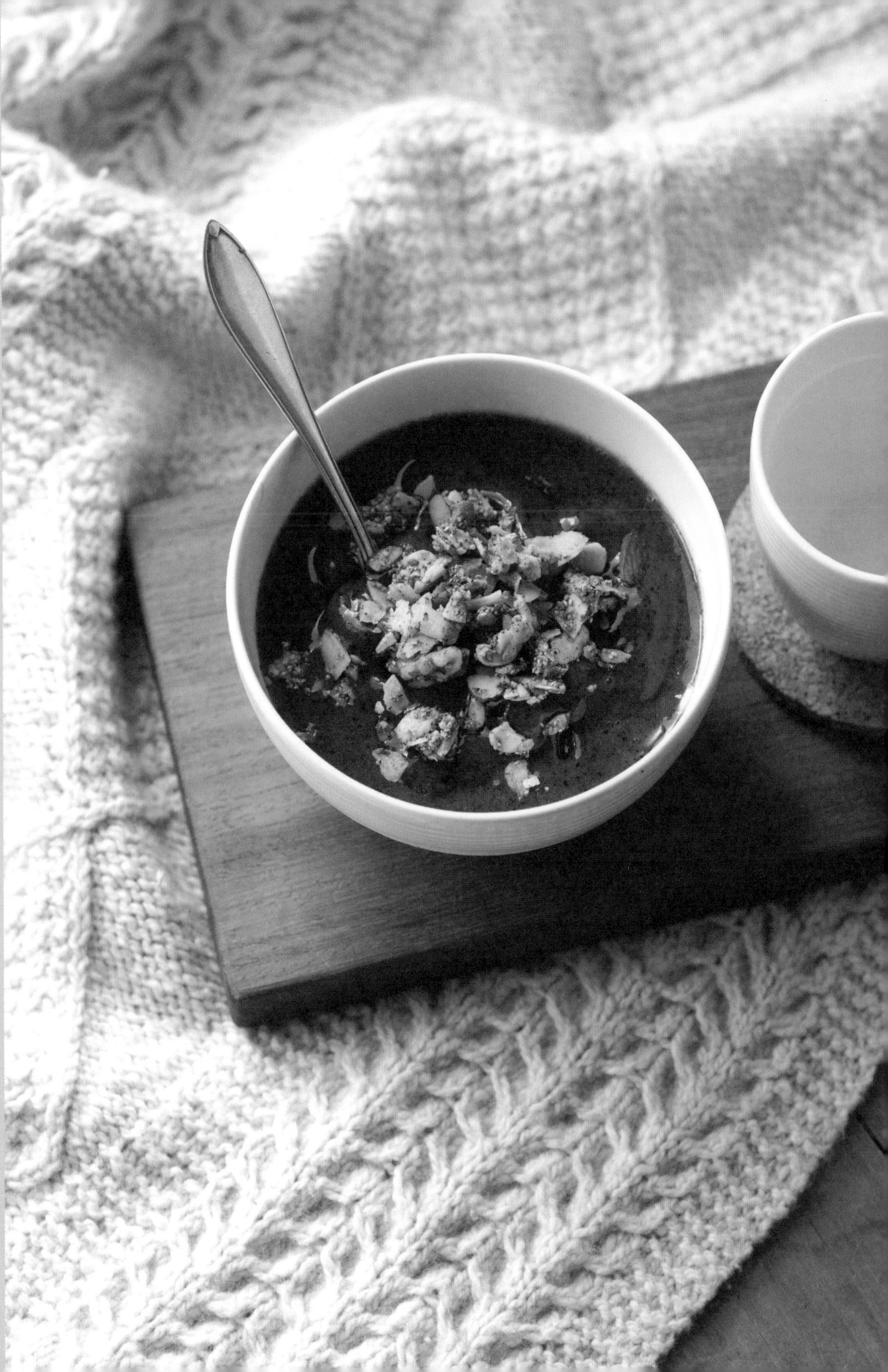

Chocolate Lovers' Dream Smoothie Bowl

Avocado is the star ingredient in this decadent chocolate smoothie, which could just as easily be whipped up for dessert. I'm so lucky to get avocados sometimes from two of my yoga students – they own an avocado farm, which is the ultimate, right? I love avocados as they are delicious but they are also a 'real food'. The healthy fats in avocados are good skin-food! This smoothie bowl was styled by topping it with coconut chips, pomegranate seeds, cacao nibs and bee pollen with a swirl of coconut yoghurt for added 'wow factor', but you don't need all these toppings as the recipe is deliciously decadent on its own.

My kids love it as much as I do. You can make it in just a few minutes then pop it in the fridge for a snack later. It's healthy and nutritious and I don't feel one bit guilty when I scoff it.

1 ripe **avocado**, skin off, pip removed

1 **frozen banana**, skin removed

3 **Medjool dates**, stones removed

½ cup **almond milk**

1 tbsp **cacao powder**

1 tbsp **almond oil**

Place all the ingredients in a blender and process to a smooth consistency with no flecks of avocado. Pour the mixture into two smoothie bowls and then 'dig' it out with a spoon. You can save one bowl for later or give it to someone else in the house when you whip it up. Add a topping if you feel like being a fancy-pants.

For a protein boost, add 1 scoop of protein powder.

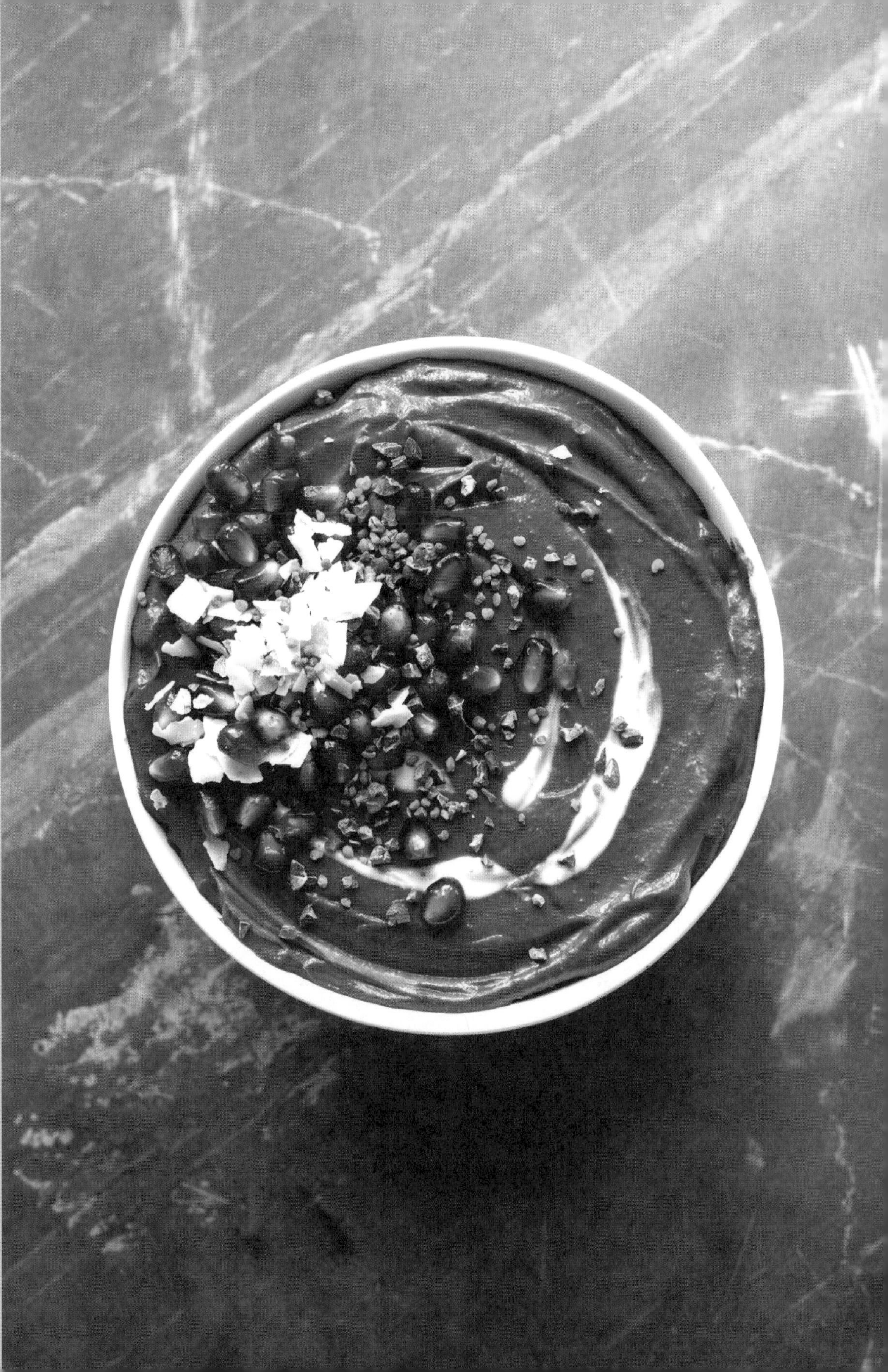

Choc Bomb Indulgence

This chocolate treat isn't only divinely decadent but also boasts a host of superfood ingredients such as mānuka honey, which has wonderful anti-inflammatory and antibacterial properties. Chia seeds, too, are a hero ingredient. As well as being on trend right now, these little powerhouses are a great source of protein, fibre and omega-3, just to name some benefits. However, the ultimate hero will be you, if you whip this recipe up for a loved one.

1 **banana**, peeled

¼ cup **cacao powder**

2 tbsp **cashew butter**

1 cup **cashew or almond milk**
(or any milk you have on hand)

¼ tsp **vanilla bean powder**

½ cup **filtered water**

1 tsp **rice malt syrup**

1 tsp **mānuka honey**

¼ cup **chia seeds**

pinch of **salt**
(I like to use natural mineral salt)

TO GARNISH:

2 tbsp **coconut yoghurt**

chocolate, shaved (use a high-quality dark chocolate)

½ tsp **cacao powder**

Place all the ingredients except the chia seeds in a blender. Mix until smooth then place the mixture in a bowl. Stir the chia seeds through the mixture.

Leave mixture in the fridge for 30 minutes so the chia seeds can plump up. Swirl yoghurt around the inside of a clean jar, then pour in the chia mixture to give a marbled look. Top with shaved chocolate and a dusting of cacao powder. I added edible flowers for that fancy look, but these are not essential, of course. I just add them because they grow abundantly in my garden.

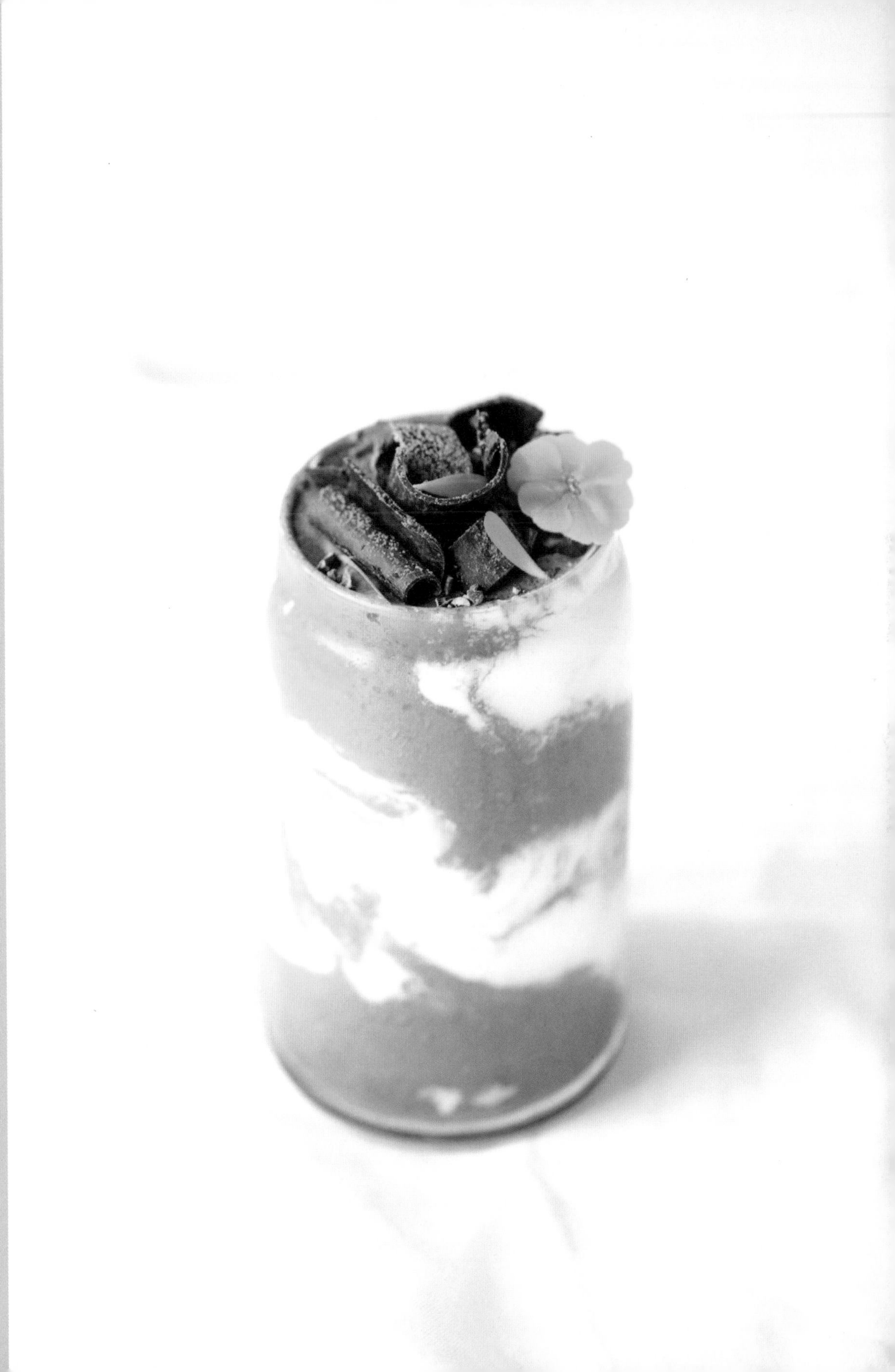

Peanut Butter Frappé

SERVES 2

Peanut butter is so popular in kitchen cupboards. Who else remembers racing home from school to raid the pantry and make peanut butter and honey sandwiches? It's a great energy food, full of good fats, to fill our tummies and fuel our bodies when we are active. I think I love peanut butter even more as an adult. I sometimes put it in celery and eat it as a snack. For a sweet pick-me-up, I spoon peanut butter into plump Medjool dates. If you want to take this to the next level, dip these in melted dark chocolate. They're heavenly. I never want to share these with anyone if I make them!

The key ingredient in this frappé is the humble peanut butter. This recipe is a definite favourite with my kids. It's delicious, thick and creamy and has the consistency of ice cream. It's also dairy-free and gluten-free.

1 **frozen banana**, peeled

4 **Medjool dates**

4 tbsp **peanut butter**

1 tsp **almond oil**

pinch **vanilla bean powder**

2½ cups **ice**

¼ cup **filtered water**

Put all the ingredients into a blender and blitz until smooth. If it's too thick, add a bit more water so it can blend more easily. Be careful not to over-blend, though, as you don't want it reduced to a liquid. Pour into two cups or jars, and sprinkle peanuts on top if you feel like being a bit flashy. Share this frappé with a friend or your kids, and drink it slowly and mindfully so that you can savour the delicious, creamy flavour. I dig mine out with a spoon. Smile, too, as you eat – because we could all do with some more positivity, as well as good, nourishing food.

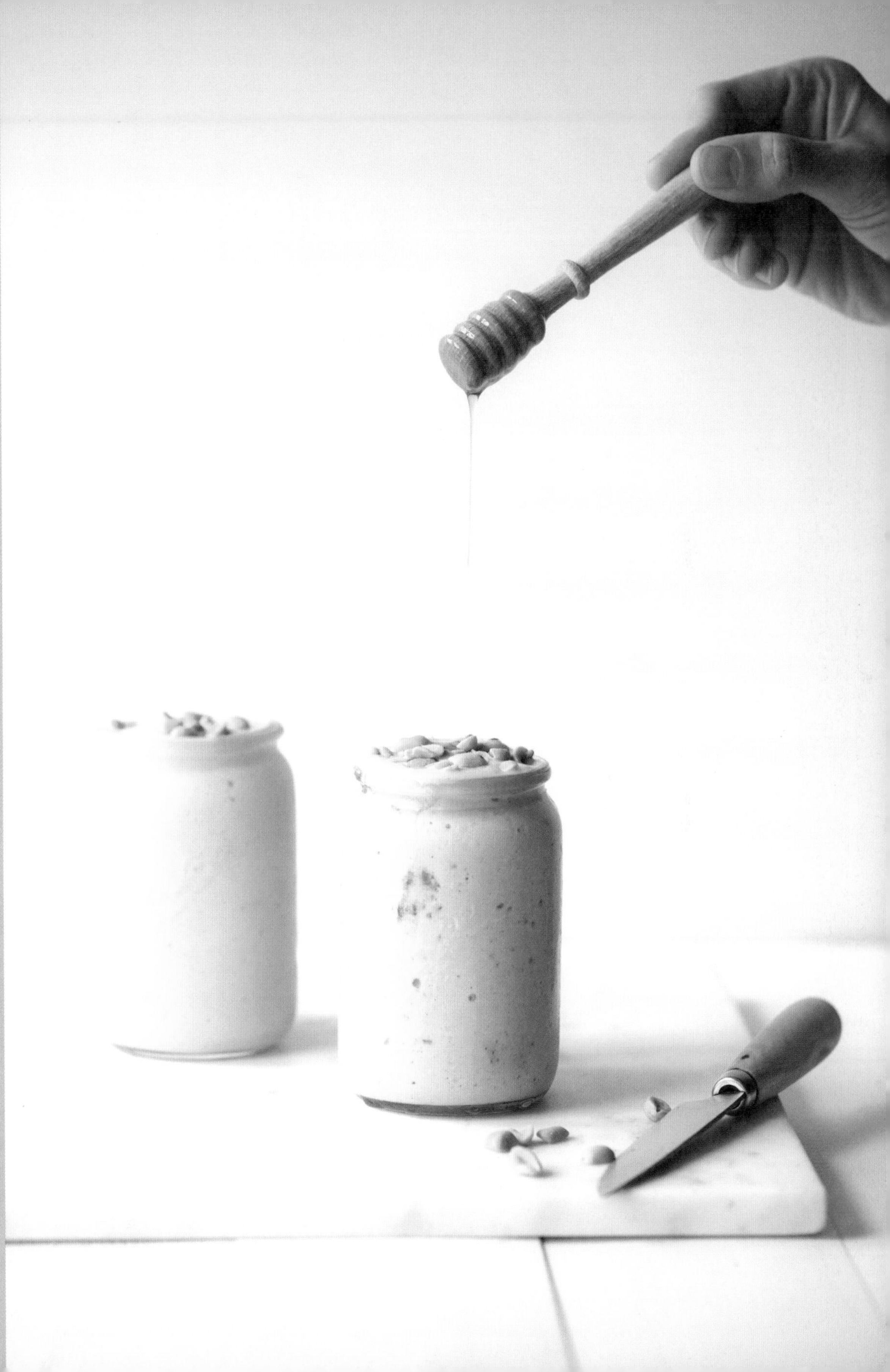

Choc Honey Frappé

On a summery day, there's nothing like an ice-cold slushy-style chocolate drink. And did I mention chocolate? This is sooooo good. To make it extra chocolatey I sometimes add half a cup of high-quality cacao powder (instead of the quarter cup recommended). Just use the amount of cacao to suit your taste buds. If you don't have flax-seed oil at hand, then this is still delicious without it. I love adding this ingredient, though, because it has omega-3 fatty acids. There are no preservatives in this cup. Just good stuff.

1 tsp **mānuka honey**

1 frozen large **banana**, skin removed

pinch **vanilla bean powder**

½ cup **almond milk**

¼ cup **dark cacao powder**

1½ cups **ice**

1 tsp **flax-seed oil**

pinch **salt**

Put all the ingredients into a blender and blitz until smooth. Then pour the thick mixture into a glass. I topped this one with bee pollen because I had it in my cupboard. But it's absolutely fine without any topping (and cheaper, of course!). Or try adding strawberries on top if they are in season. You can use a straw to slurp up the drink or eat it using a spoon.

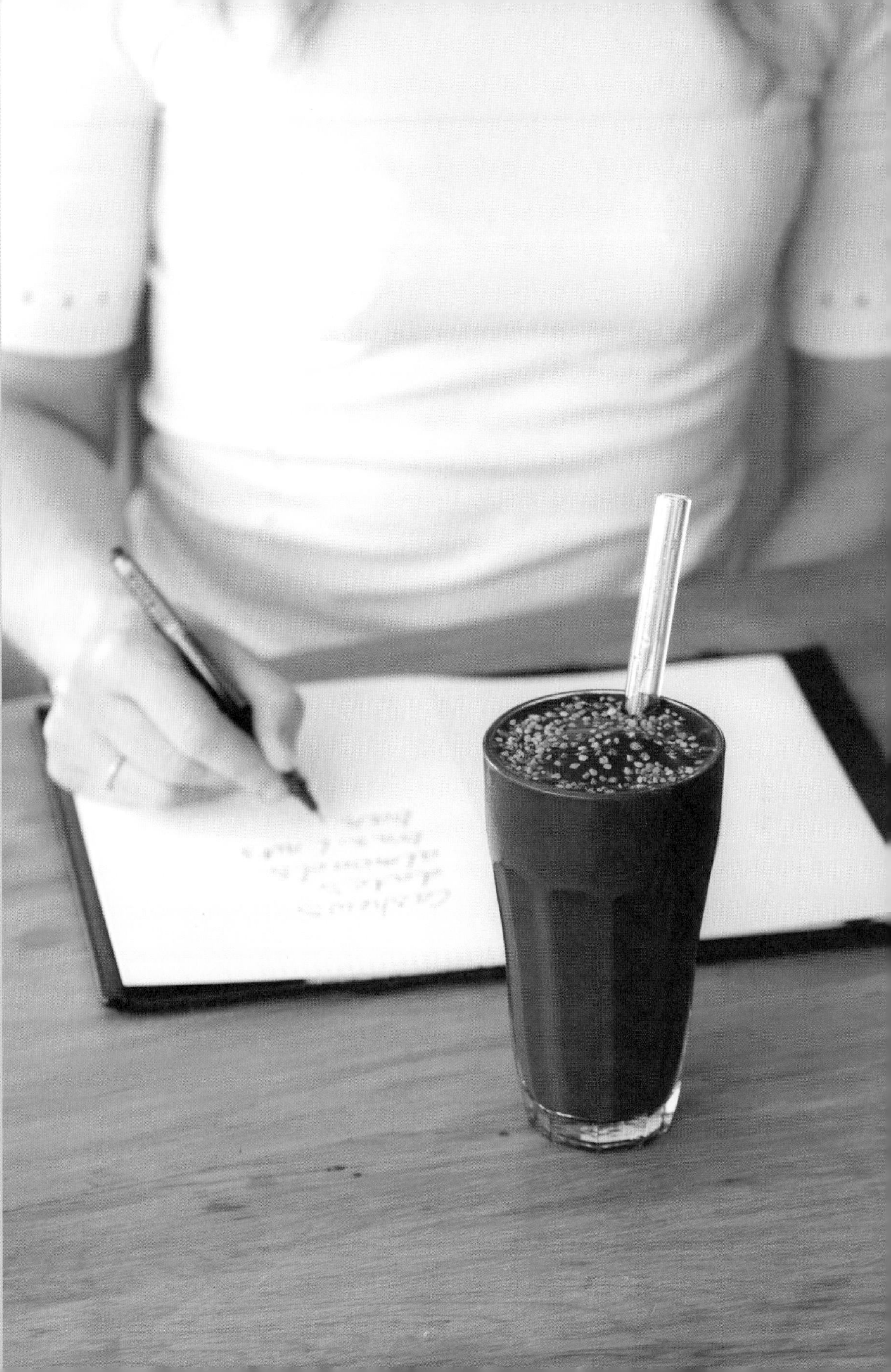

Home-Made Chocolate Coffee Hazelnut Mocha

SERVES 2

I first started making nut milks after meeting my husband, who is dairy-intolerant. He grew up on a dairy farm and had to help with milking the cows every morning while growing up. But his intolerance meant he could never drink the fruits of his hard labour. In fact, as a baby he had to have goat's milk because he reacted so badly to the cow's milk. So sometimes some things do not agree with our bodies. Tune in and eradicate anything from your diet that doesn't help you to feel well, and talk to an expert if you're unsure about any allergies.

I've come to love making nut milks for drinking because they are so delicious as well as being full of goodness. This chocolate version is divine. I have to stop myself from drinking the lot in one sitting.

1 cup **hazelnuts**
(soaked overnight in water)

2 cups **filtered water**

¼ cup **cacao powder**

6 **Medjool dates**

2 pinches of **vanilla bean powder**

shot of **coffee** (optional)

Place the soaked nuts in a blender with the rest of the ingredients (except the coffee). Blend until smooth and then put it through a muslin cloth (or sieve) to separate the milk from the pulp. Place the silky-smooth milk in the fridge to drink when you wish and leave the nut pulp to the side for now. You can choose to use this to make Hazelnut Bliss Balls – see recipe on page 224. We love zero waste. For grown-ups, an option is to warm some of the milk and add a shot of coffee. I love it this way, just as much as drinking it cold from the fridge with the kids.

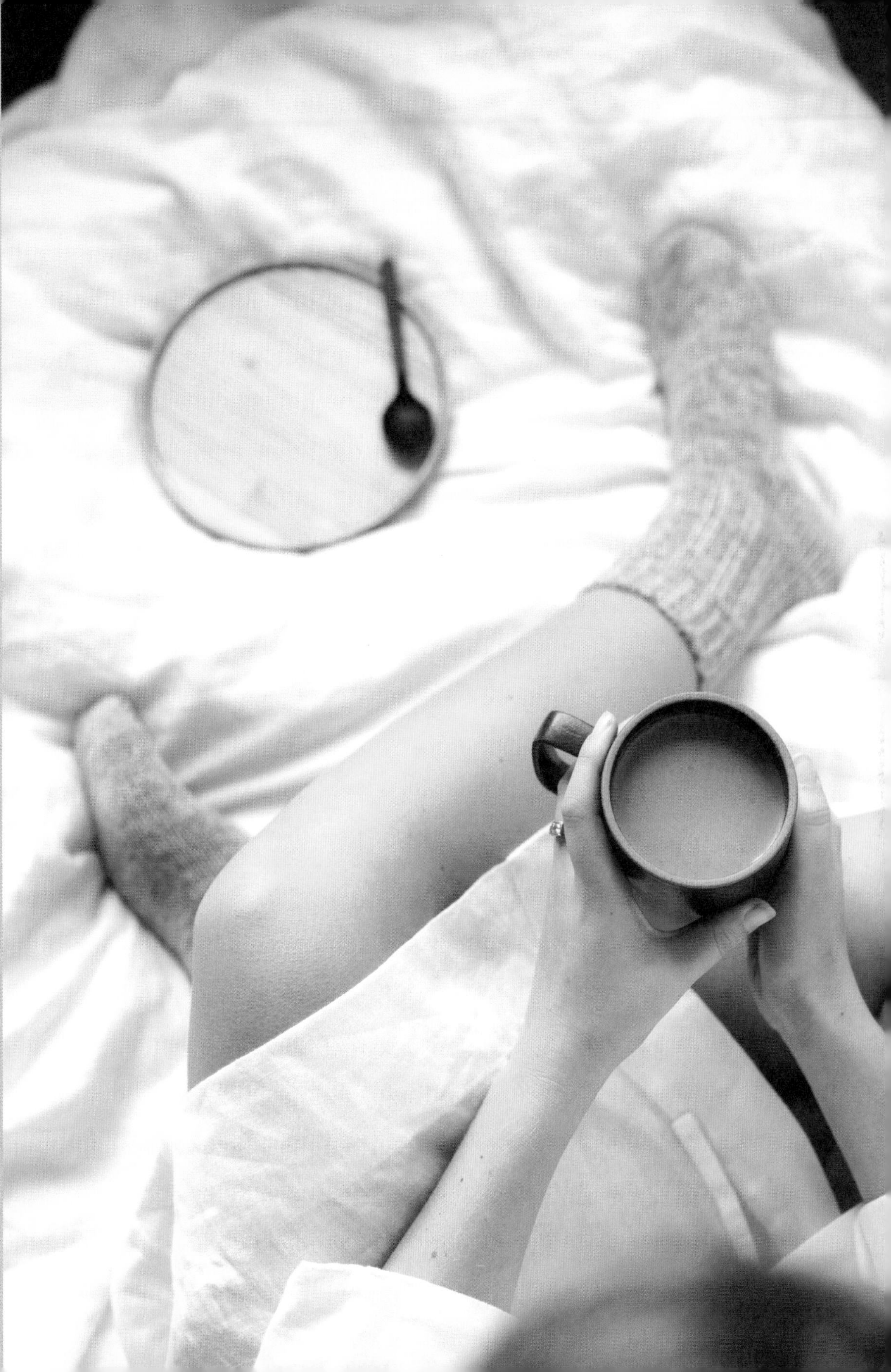

Cashew and Fig Milk

*I love whipping up homemade milks.
This one I love to drink just as it is. Or I
sometimes pour it on homemade muesli.
There's just a hint of the fig taste in this
(you could use Medjool dates if you
preferred). It's creamy and satisfying.*

½ cup **raw cashews**

2 cups **filtered water**

pinch **salt**

2 **figs**

¼ tsp **vanilla paste**

1 tsp **mānuka honey**

Soak cashews in filtered water for three hours. Then drain the water and rinse with fresh water.

Put the cashews and all remaining ingredients in a blender and blitz until smooth. It's that simple. Store this in the fridge for a couple of days (if you haven't drunk it already in one slurp). It gets thicker after a day or two in the fridge, which makes it even more yum.

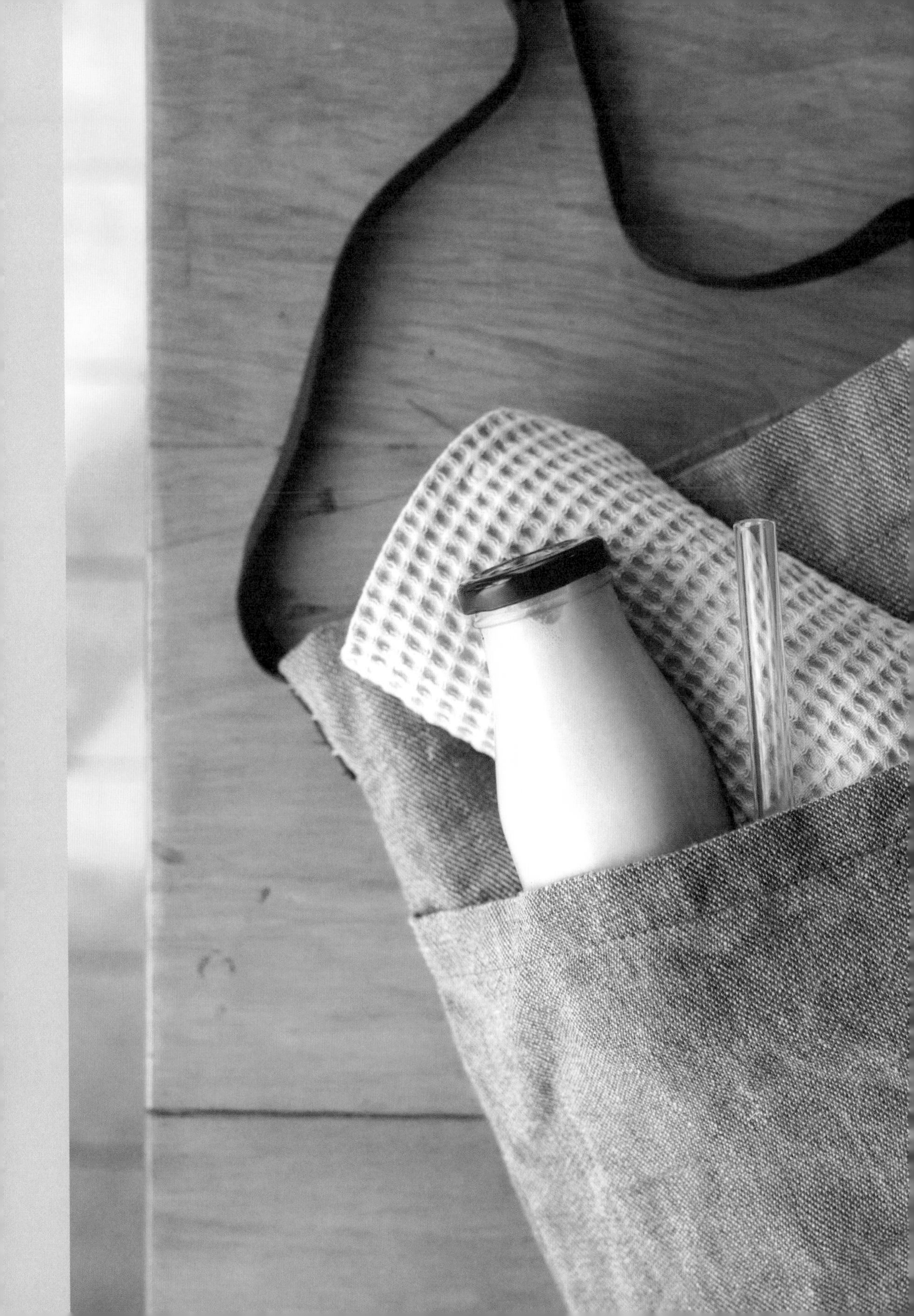

Give a stuff – give back+

Give back to others. Do it because it helps others. Do it because it's about being a decent human. Do it because it will fuel your own happiness levels too – it feels good to help others. Do it especially if you have kids. You want them to learn from your positive actions and spread more kindness out into the world.

Giving back is contagious. Share kindness and it will grow. The person who receives a kind gesture 'catches' the good vibes. They are then inspired to spread these positive feelings further.

I run health retreats, and when I inspire clients around the topic of happiness, I urge them to 'give back'. I recommend they choose a way to give back that resonates with them and interests them. This is super important. Think of a charity that interests you or something you feel happy about doing. If you love animals, then it could be an animal-related charity. If you enjoy the process, then you might want to give back more. That's why it's important to choose a charity that resonates with you. It will be more enjoyable and sustainable.

It's normal to feel cautious about lending a hand in the beginning. You may be concerned that a charity may want more time, or resources, than you wish to gift. So give back on your terms. It could be helping for an hour, for a week or on one project, or more. You decide.

Giving back is contagious. Share kindness and it will grow. The person who receives a kind gesture 'catches' the good vibes. They are then inspired to spread these positive feelings further.

But never let your motivation be that you want something in return. Giving back is exactly that: it's giving, not wanting. Remember that even the smallest gestures can mean a lot and have a ripple effect. Can you recall an occasion when someone helped you in some small way? Like offering you a seat on a bus when you were pregnant? Or giving you that extra 20 cents when you were short on coins for your coffee? This kind of behaviour can release feel-good hormones and make you smile, right?

It doesn't even need to be a charity that you help. You may choose to help a friend, a family member, a work colleague, your community, a school or even a stranger. It can be transparent or behind the scenes. That doesn't matter.

Do something just **because**. If we all do our bit with this, the world will be a better place.

Achilles and why I give a helping hand and helping eyes

I became more attuned to the importance of giving back when I became a parent. I wish for my kids to be kind. One way to teach them is to lead by example. So rather than tell my kids to be kind, I show them. My biggest wish is for them to be kind and help others in this life.

Time is precious for me – like it is for everyone. I have a young family, I've got my own health business and I have a to-do list that never seems to end. But I make time to be a volunteer ambassador for the Achilles New Zealand charity. I volunteer several times a year. This charity helps disabled athletes in running events. I'm a marathoner, and so it's about sharing the passion for running with fellow runners who need a helping hand.

I've guided blind runners in a handful of my 21 marathons. To run my own race is incredible. But to help a blind runner to achieve their dream is a soul-soaring kinda thing. It's a feeling that money can't buy. The athletes in this charity are now not only people I help. They are friends for life. We've shared something – sweat and tears.

One athlete I helped through two marathons, **Hannah Pascoe**, has since gone on to represent New Zealand as a tandem para cyclist. It was amazing to be a small part of her journey. She gave me a blessed Māori greenstone necklace as a thank you, and I'll treasure this always.

'I have a young family, I've got my own health business and I have a to-do list that never seems to end. But I make time to be a volunteer ambassador for the Achilles New Zealand charity.'

GIVE A STUFF – GIVE BACK

A lot of people ask how I guide blind runners. I use verbal cues. I tell them a kerb is coming and they need to lift their legs in three, two, one second. Or I cue, 'Duck soon, because a branch is coming up overhead.' Or I instruct them to turn left or turn right. I also talk about what I can see while we are out running, so they can imagine the experience further.

We hold a short guide rope between us. Using this, I can keep the runner as safe as possible, and they can follow my run rhythm. Guiding is harder than running my own race. I watch the blind athlete like a mother watches her toddler – like I have eyes in the back of my head. Their safety is paramount. I'm aware that one wrong cue could see them trip and injure themselves. We are often on the road and near traffic, and there's no room for inattention. So I take the role extremely seriously. But we also have a lot of fun.

When I started guiding I was terrible. Ask blind runner **Mike Lloyd**. Two minutes into the first run with him and I was describing everything around us. I commented, 'You should see the sea right now, it's beautiful!' Yeah, I needed to get my foot out of my mouth at that moment. I wanted the ground to swallow me up. But Mike laughed and remarked, 'That's such a classic first-timer's stuff-up.' He was laughing so hard he was almost hoarse. I could then laugh too, and we carried on. He was laughing at me. I was laughing at myself.

Then it was only a matter of minutes before I had my foot in my mouth yet again with Mike. I'm a bit of a slow learner. Anyway, next I described the beautiful scenery, clouds and people and everything around us. Then I remarked, 'Oh, and now it's starting to rain.'

'Yeah, I got that one already,' quipped Mike. Again, I felt terrible. I begged the ground to swallow me up. But I couldn't run away and leave Mike in the middle of nowhere! Again, he laughed and I laughed. Again, he was laughing at me. I was then laughing at myself. After that, I managed to put my thoughts into words more slowly to avoid more foot-in-mouth moments. This is a good life lesson, by the way! It's not only helpful as a run guide.

'It is a wonder to learn you can give more than one-hundred-percent and be more for having done it.'

Mike taught me how to be a good run guide. He's also an amazing marathon runner. He could teach anyone how to run a marathon. And he's super funny. He's a joy to be around. All the athletes in Achilles are awesome and inspire me, always.

The Achilles International charity is global, with a home base in New York. **Dick Traum** is the founder. I've been lucky to spend time with him whenever I've been in New York. He smiles and his whole face lights up and glows. He's also got a cheeky humour which I love.

He wasn't always disabled. His life changed on 30 May 1965, when he was 24. Someone in a car drove into him at a petrol station and that's when Dick lost his right leg. But he never let that hold him back. In May 1976, he completed the New York Marathon using an artificial leg. He was the first amputee to run such a distance.

'It's a memory never forgotten,' he wrote in his **Go Achilles!** book. 'After the race, the New York Road Runners Club had a ceremony at Lincoln Center. Fred Lebow (the New York Marathon director) handed out awards to the top 20 runners (including legendary runner Bill Rodgers). Then announcing a special award, there was a hush over the crowd. Calling me to come forward, Fred put a medal around my neck. This ignited a standing ovation from 1500 people.'

Dick, who is a very successful businessman, started the Achilles charity with an aim to change perceptions that people with disabilities are frail. He wanted anyone in society to be able to participate in mainstream events. He wanted to show they could be productive members of society. He wanted to show they could be successful too. He knew how being successful in sport powered other areas of his life. So he wanted to share this with others.

'In 1983 we had six Achilles athletes run New York. It exploded to 13 in 1984 and an astonishing 25 in 1985, including our first New Zealander, **Brian Froggart**. At that time I was worried that we had peaked. How many disabled runners could run marathons? We had over 300 sign up for New York in 2018. We also have several hundred who do other marathons.

'The vision for Achilles was a group of disabled runners in New York City. It expanded into a presence in over 50 countries and 100 chapters. This excludes 11,000 Achilles Kids in 350 schools throughout 21 states.

'My vision for the future includes expanding our Hope & Possibility race to additional cities and countries. It is a race where there are awards for different disability divisions as part of a mainstream race, including able-bodied athletes. The event, put on by Achilles, should generate income and media coverage for the chapter.'

Another focus Dick is passionate about is research concerning how running can improve physical, social and cognitive skills for people on the autism spectrum, cystic fibrosis, traumatic brain injuries and stroke.

Ultimately, his charity is here for that feel-good factor for athletes involved.

'Achievement is both addictive and contagious. Each success increases the expectations of what is possible in the future. Self-esteem improves with each triumph, as does the levels of aspiration in other areas of life – personal, professional, and physical. People who have had a significant achievement are viewed differently by others, and this makes it easier to reach future goals,' Dick wrote.

I agree with Dick. I reckon running a marathon through Achilles gives disabled athletes a superpower. I've seen lots of disabled athletes improve their confidence and go-get-'em attitude with life after achieving success in the sport of running. It's heart-lifting to witness.

I love this quote from his book:

'It is a wonder to learn you can give more than one-hundred-percent and be more for having done it. The individual recognises that the same principles used to succeed in athletics can be applied to achieve in other areas of life. Over time the athlete craves the next challenge, the next test, and the next competition. When we have passion, once a goal is met, we ask, "what's next?" and target a new challenge. We expect more from ourselves. Others see us differently. We grow and become leaders. Our passion for achievement propels us onward, with knowledge of our strengths, toward a future of hope and possibility.'

Dick says running in a group like Achilles gives athletes a support network. There's a spirit within the group that helps these athletes be successful. At first, I saw this charity as a way to help disabled athletes to achieve sporting goals. But I've seen that it is so much more. There's a real flow-on effect. I've seen lots of disabled athletes gain more determination in life. Dick kicked off a charity that has a real-heart and changes lives.

I ask Dick what his favourite race is. Of course, he picks the New York Marathon. 'It's big, it's grand and we have over 300 people signed up. Imagine someone watching it for five hours, that's 300 minutes, and seeing our 300 Achilles members passing by at the rate of one per minute. I ran my first in 1976 and my 27th NYC last year. Imagine over a million people cheering you on!

'A second favourite was in Kalisz, Poland, in 1988. At this time, other amputees were running marathons faster than me and there was no way I could beat them. My endurance, however, was pretty good. So I ran the 100-kilometre "Super Marathon" in Poland on my above-the-knee artificial leg. It took me a full day, but I finished! Not too many people running on artificial legs can top it,' Dick says proudly.

'Achilles exists for the disabled athletes. But the volunteers bring real magic to the charity too,' says Dick.

'Achilles works because of its volunteers. Every Tuesday evening and Saturday morning, dozens of volunteers join us in New York City to run with Achilles members. In the NYC Marathon, some 400 help by running as guides, at standby stations, at the start and finish lines.

'Our volunteers are the most important resource we have. Someone asked, "Why would you get up at four in the morning and spend a whole day with a disabled person running 26 miles?" The answer is heartwarming. "There is a great joy in helping others."'

New Zealand blind runner **Tamati Pearse** is one athlete I've helped. He was at high school when I first met him. We have done several marathons together over the years since. It has been heart-lifting to see him improve as a runner and also see his confidence strengthen. It has been amazing to see him go confidently into work and become a wonderful young man. He has guts and determination, and his smile lights up a room. He's another one with a cheeky and lovable sense of humour. And I always know I have to keep up with politics if I'm guiding him. He loves talking politics, and he is always up with the news he hears on the TV and radio.

During the years, I've helped disabled athletes through many events. I've helped at so many that I've actually lost count. I have a pile of race medals in a drawer by my bedside. I call these 'dream tokens'. Each medal holds incredible shared memories of struggles, triumphs and sometimes joyful tears. Memories of all those smiles at finish lines.

The charity and its members have become like a family to me. I care about everyone involved and their success in races and in life in general. And, in New York, the course is full of bright yellow Achilles T-shirts. A lot of war veterans fill the course, often with horrific war injuries. But people with disabilities flock there from all over the world. They're all there to feel included, chase goals, achieve a dream. We are all the same.

I love that the charity is inclusive of everyone, no matter what. Some members are missing limbs, others are missing sight. Others have battled things like cancer. One athlete in our New Zealand chapter lost his legs in an underground explosion. Another is bravely facing Parkinson's disease. Many of the guides who help are family members or friends of people with disabilities. I'm part of the group because it feels good to be part of something that's meaningful and I enjoy helping others run.

Life is about the journey, never the destination.
When I'm guiding, I see beauty in the little things,
beauty in everything.

I call myself a 'girl guide' because I'm a girl who guides athletes through events. From the outside, I'm the one helping someone else. But the truth is these disabled athletes help me just as much. Actually, they help me more. They're my heroes.

They show me that the only barriers you have in life are the ones you set yourself. These disabled athletes succeed despite their setbacks, and they do it with pride and a smile. They don't focus on their disabilities. They focus instead on their abilities. If they are missing a leg, then they might use the power of their arms to propel them in a wheelchair through a marathon. Or they might use a prosthetic leg to walk that gruelling marathon distance.

And, yeah, there are always tears, snot and smiles at those finish lines. Or is that just me? Those precious memories will be with me forever. Those stories, through those many miles, are magic. They lift my heart up. These are the stories I'll recall and feel uplifted about forever – even when I'm in a rest home and can no longer run.

Life is about the journey, never the destination. When I'm guiding, I see beauty in the little things, beauty in everything. I describe the pretty light on the water, the oranges and yellows of the leaves in autumn. I tell the blind athletes about all the beauty around them. It's mindfulness in action.

I became involved in this charity to help others and share a passion for running. It was an unexpected spin-off that my kids saw first-hand that helping others was a nice thing to do in life. My kids are sometimes on the sidelines of these marathons. They cheer on the disabled athletes. They hear all about the athletes' triumphs and care about their successes too.

I'm inspired by lots by people who give back. In this chapter, I'll introduce you to two inspirational people who are giving back on a whole new level. Actually, they're changing the world with their kindness. I'm in awe of what they do.

An ordinary lawyer and mother does something extraordinary

It was a newspaper article that changed **Denise Arnold**'s life. The story was heart-wrenching and sickening. It was about child trafficking in Cambodia, and it inspired Denise to do something. She has since helped many children in Cambodia, and she's also changing the country on a grander scale.

Denise sits down for coffee with me in a café in Auckland. She looks like Princess Diana, in a way. She's petite with blonde hair cut short, kind blue eyes and refined, pretty features. She talks a mile a minute, laughs lots and has a kind smile. Her enthusiasm is infectious. She's also very, very funny. Her wit is sharp and clever.

She starts our conversation by telling me, 'I'm just an ordinary lawyer and mother. I'm just one person who felt compelled to do something.' But I beg to differ. While the rest of us gave that newspaper article two minutes of our attention, Denise decided to act.

Denise is no ordinary lawyer and mum. She's like New Zealand's own version of Mother Teresa. She will absolutely hate me for saying that. But her giving back is on such a grand scale. Denise's determination is as strong as steel. I don't think an army tank could slow this woman down. But her voice is soft and almost has a fragility to it. She talks quietly, but there's nothing stronger than her will. Get out of her way if there's a wrong that needs to be made right.

'Her kindness made my face a wet mess, twisted my stomach into knots and sunk my heart deeper into my chest.'

I first met Denise and heard her speak at the worldwomen17 conference. She's a lawyer in Tauranga, a tiny city by the seaside. Denise told the story of how she came to start up the Cambodia Charitable Trust. This trust provides free education to vulnerable Cambodian children – especially girls. This is because girls are the most vulnerable there. And, yes, that is for some of the worst reasons you can imagine. Think sex slavery, trafficking and living with huge, unrelenting poverty.

It is Denise's view that, through education, the charity can be a powerful lever for social change in Cambodia. The trust's website sums up the mission best: 'Education breaks the poverty cycle, protects girls from sex slavery, boys from slave labour and opens the door to a bright and purposeful future for each child.' The trust works alongside families and communities to access good teachers and resources and ultimately provides hope for a brighter future.

At the conference, Denise almost had a whole audience of a thousand women in tears. I'm sure it wasn't only me that had water escaping from my eyes and dripping down my nose, cheeks and lips. It wasn't the horror that she described that got me in that teary state. It was her compassion and kindness. Her kindness made my face a wet mess, twisted my stomach into knots and sunk my heart deeper into my chest. I'll never forget how she described reading that newspaper article. It must have been only about 400 words. 400 powerful words that changed someone's life path and that had a ripple effect for tens of thousands of children's lives.

When Denise read that newspaper article about children in brothels, she was sick. She was nauseous. She felt helpless. But when she tucked her own small children up in their safe and warm beds that night, she decided to do something. And she hasn't stopped since.

'I decided that I didn't have to solve everything. I just had to do something. **Mother Teresa**, after all, said if you can't feed 100 people, just feed one. I took a giant leap of faith, and I just got started. I decided that by not acting, I would be letting evil flourish.'

'I decided that I didn't have to solve everything. I just had to do something. Mother Teresa, after all, said if you can't feed 100 people, just feed one.'

So she started to do something and now can't stop doing more and more and more. And now her family and friends and lots of strangers have joined her to do good too.

Sitting with Denise in the café, I ask her how she had the powerful drive to decide to help children in Cambodia and actually put it into action.

'I grew up privileged, happy, became successful and knew there was more I could give in life,' she says. She tells me that, at first, she decided to go to Cambodia to talk to people there about what was happening. She didn't even know how she could help – or if she should – in the beginning. She hopped on a plane in 2007 to spend three weeks in Cambodia. She needed to see things first-hand. She saw unrelenting poverty. Everywhere. She saw starvation and extreme deprivation. And she heard about the vulnerable children and the real-life horror of what was happening to them.

'There was fear at the start. Some of my fear was of my insignificance. That I'm from a small town in a small country and I'm in a big world. In a way, you could think, who am I to try and take this on? What right have I got to be meddling? Then, I thought, how could I not?

'I was overwhelmed. I was stuck, because it was a huge challenge, and it remains a huge challenge. But I decided to look, keep an open mind and see what my heart told me. I felt terrified that I might fail, that I might be ridiculous. I think my biggest concern was that many people set out to do good and inadvertently cause harm. The question for me was could this cause harm? If I felt it wasn't going to cause harm, then I would support it.'

While in Cambodia, she asked someone she felt she could trust, 'How can I best help the children?'

'I was told we just need to get these kids to school. That made sense to me. I trusted him, and I was right to trust him. Education was key to helping the kids and their families and to reviving communities. Education would give the children and families the smarts to know how to not be trapped into handing over their children for trafficking. Schools would give the communities hope.

'When I first headed to Cambodia, I was terrified that I would want to bring the children home. But I don't believe that this is the right way to help them. They should stay in their own community, be supported and grow up within their own country.

'I see things that are really sad and could bring you to tears. I made the choice not to work in the area of rescuing children from brothels. I made the choice to be the fence at the top of the cliff. So whenever I see something sad or heartbreaking, I want to know how we fix it now or stop it from happening again.'

Denise is a problem-solver. She gets to the heart of problems and solves them one tiny piece at a time. Here's an example. She asked one girl, 'What's your biggest struggle?' The girl explained that getting to school on time was hard. She didn't know the time, because she didn't have a watch. So Denise bought her a watch, which cost only a few dollars. Then, Denise bought her a bike (which cost $80). She bought the bike after the girl told her how long it took to get to school: hours. The bike saved her having to spend hours walking to and from school. This, in turn, left the girl with more time to care for her disabled sibling. Denise then bought that girl a chemistry book and a $2 calculator she needed for her schoolwork. The girl is now able to flourish at school.

Denise says she can cope with solving practical problems.

'I can't necessarily look the sadness in the eyes. I have to deflect – to look instead at how I solve problems. I made a decision years ago that I don't want to sit down amongst the children and cry. That's not my role. My role is to lead them. To try to lead them forward and to keep paving a pathway for them out of the despair. Also, it's not my role to be a friend or someone placed on a pedestal. It's my job to be their leader and figure out as much as I can.'

Denise now leads a charity that helps many children in Cambodia. She helps 19 primary schools, four secondary schools and 18 teacher-training colleges. (That was at the last check.) A staggering 100% of proceeds raised goes to the project. She pays for her own flights to Cambodia. Every cent raised for the kids goes to the kids.

I ask Denise how hard it is to juggle the charity work with her already busy life. After all, she has a husband, two daughters and a loving extended family and works long hours as a partner at a law firm.

She tells me a few years ago she dropped back her work hours as a partner in a law firm. The charity takes up too much of her time for her to be a full-time, focused lawyer, she says.

'The charity takes up a lot of my life, but I love it.'

I ask: How many hours?

Denise tries to fob me off without answering.

I ask again. How many hours?

'A lot,' she says. 'I don't watch TV and I don't vacuum my cars. There are things that have been let go,' she quips. 'I used to do a lot of handcrafts because I'm such a fidget, but now they are just in the cupboards.

'I find the Cambodia project like blue-sky thinking. There's so much opportunity to transform lives from hopelessness and despair to a pathway through to independence and empowerment. It's so precious to be part of that. I find sometimes when I'm in Cambodia that I get this shock and ask myself, "How did I come to be here?" Every now and again, I get a wake-up moment on what the charity has achieved. I still struggle to realise how this all happened.

'I get an enormous amount of satisfaction from being able to dream up ways to change people's lives and implement them. I think that's incredible. I don't think I could have stayed in my outwardly successful life without contributing to something that is bigger than me.

'Many of these children won't know me, and yet we will leave a lasting gift for the rest of their life, which is their education and a sense of belonging, and I think that is amazing. If I pass away, then nobody can take that off those thousands of children.'

Denise says many people ask her why she decided to help that day after reading that article. Her response: 'Why wouldn't you?'

She admits the charity work is tough. It is not without cost. There's a financial cost to Denise. A physical cost. There's an emotional cost. There's a time cost. Over the years, the many fundraising projects have impacted on family time. She admits it is hard to go on holiday because she constantly needs to be across any emails. She may get an email from government level that could need her urgent attention.

'I do get really tired. I find it hard to turn the brain off at night,' she admits.

To keep balance in her life, she cycles, does Pilates and walks with friends. She loves to walk

To keep balance in her life, she cycles, does Pilates and walks with friends. She loves to walk around Mt Maunganui, which is a 30-minute walk by the seaside near her home.

around Mt Maunganui, which is a 30-minute walk by the seaside near her home.

'I love my Pilates two days weekly. If it wasn't for this, I would probably seize up. I know, physically and mentally, I would pay a price if I wasn't doing that. The walk around Mt Maunganui is my favourite place in the world. I love reading, and I like cooking.'

Denise credits the other charity members for the extent of its success – people like high-flying New Zealand businesswoman **Theresa Gattung.**

'I'm fortunate to have the backing of people like Theresa. She's so busy and committed to other projects as well. Every time I've needed her, in terms of things like, "I need to know how to cope with this," she will always contact me back. I don't take that for granted. It's a huge privilege to have her wisdom there to help me when I get stuck. Her way of seeing things is clear and concise and comes from that heart position. I follow her advice to the word.'

I comment to Denise that it's amazing to hear that even a smart and wise lawyer still needs a 'wise tribe' to surround her. 'That tribe is a part of me not falling over,' she says. She says it is important to have others to step in when you need them, and Theresa is just one of this amazing tribe.

'This charity takes up a lot of my life. But I love it. I feel enriched by it. But I am very conscious of the backup that I have from others.'

I ask Denise about the joy this charity gives her.

'I'm just lucky to be part of it. I feel fortunate to have found my place, my thing, and to be able to impact on thousands of little children is a privilege. So I don't get the whole accolade thing. Giving time, money, effort, skills ... you are giving, but you get so much back. I get back a sense of purpose. Somewhere to pour my passion and energy that is meaningful. I get to connect with amazing human beings who are givers themselves, and I have met people who I would never have met who have enriched my life hugely through this. So I'm really honest when I say that I have received back tenfold what I've put in.'

She says over the years, her girls have had to understand when the charity has been her top focus.

'It was one of my daughter's birthdays, and I had to have a function with the charity. I felt so bad about it. I couldn't do much about the date, and she had to consider that there was something bigger than her at play.'

Denise says family helped her with her girls when she first visited Cambodia. Any time she was away from her daughters when they were young, they were looked after by her family with love.

There were also deeper teachings at work. She explains: 'I wanted to show them a mum with another pathway, a mum with a sense of purpose and who is being, in a way, brave. I was still scared. I hope I taught them more than I could have taught them had I been with them 24/7.'

Denise's daughters are now in their 20s and passionately help the charity too. Denise tells me proudly how her daughters sponsor a child each now. She's proud too that her daughters have since 'become champions in their own way'.

'Tegan is passionate about plastics in the ocean and trying to get us all to change our behaviour, while Emily cares about honest storytelling through her video work.'

I remark to Denise that there's a ripple effect at play here. She has inspired the next generation on kindness and giving back. She's quiet for a moment and looks suddenly overwhelmed, and I notice her voice becomes a little shaky.

I next ask her who inspired her kindness. She considers this question for a moment, pauses and them beams the biggest smile. The penny drops that she learned giving back at the dinner table while growing up. The modelling came from her mum, a former public health nurse.

'She worked once in the lower socio-economic area of society, dealing with babies, young children and parents. She had harrowing stories about some children at the dinner table. She constantly fought for her clients. She would get them to the police if they were being abused. She was a constant champion for women and children. She then retired with all of that bottled up inside of her. Now she has poured this same passion into the Cambodia charity.

'I guess I've learned how to be an advocate for others through my mum and listening to her at the dinner table. The strength that she showed and the determination she had ... this got embedded into my DNA, I suppose. I hold her responsible!' says Denise, laughing and laughing.

Denise has to leave our chat because she is on her way to do a presentation at an exhibition fundraiser for her charity. I attend this too and watch Denise stand before a room packed full of people. She tries hard to hold back tears as she explains the charity's work and the need to fundraise. I note the eyes of everyone in the room – all watery and wide open.

Kindness matters

Orly Wahba doesn't just have the coolest name on the planet. She's also making kindness trending.

She's the author of **Kindness Boomerang.** This book gives inspiration for each day of the year, with different ideas on how to be kind.

Orly is known for an online video that became a viral sensation, watched more than 25 million times by people around the world. The video shows how even simple acts of kindness can make someone's day and inspire them to 'pay it forward'. So then the kindness goes on and on and on, eventually returning to the person who started it. It comes full circle.

Orly also runs the non-profit Life Vest Inside. This organisation has a mission to make kindness trending, based on the idea that our ability to overcome our hardships, to make it through tough times, is an internal life vest. Through giving kindness and, in turn, getting it back, we can better stay afloat.

She believes that giving kindness can be a 'lifeline' when we go through rough times.

'Kindness can help us rise after we fall,' she tells me as we Skype. She's in Boston. I'm in Auckland.

Orly, who has a deeper, huskier voice than normal because she has a cold, says, 'Please excuse me, but I'm still in my PJs!'

'Kindness can help us rise after we fall.'

I tell her I love that she's still in her PJs. The last Skype chat I had, doing an interview for this book, saw me in my PJs. This was while the person I was interviewing was in a beautiful black dress with perfect hair and make-up. I tell Orly I was her last week, and we laugh.

Orly is down-to-earth real. She's super passionate about this topic she writes about.

As Orly and I chat, she tells me she has recently tried yoga for the first time. She saw on my website I was a yoga teacher, and she wanted to tell me about her first yoga session.

'I'm the least flexible person on the planet. But I ended up loving it. It was so restorative. I love the self-care element of yoga too.'

I tell her yoga is actually built on kindness. It's not just about being kind to your body. It's about uplifting others. I tell her that yoga is actually built around giving back, community and kindness. The movement side of yoga is merely one aspect of the practice. I tell her she is a master in yoga already without realising it. Living a mindful life and being kind is at the heart of yoga. This is yoga.

I ask Orly what kindness means to her.

'Kindness is infectious. We pass it on and it keeps growing. When we give kindness, then our self-value increases. It can also be an antidote to depression, as kindness boosts serotonin.'

Orly says the mission of her organisation is to inspire kindness. But, also, it's much more than that, because 'inspiration fades'. She wants people to go from inspiration to action. She aims to inspire, engage, educate and connect around kindness. She wants people to believe in themselves and humanity again. She does this through social media and films.

'I want people to know they are enough. And, when we feel enough, then we can impact change. External things are not important. So things like money, fame, how many friends you have on social media, to name some.

'And kindness does not equate to being a doormat. Kindness needs to come from the right place. And that starts with loving you.

These things do not contribute to your internal happiness. They trick you into thinking that you are happy. Because these things give instant gratification. But instant gratification is not sustainable or lasting. You take a shot of adrenalin, but you crash right after. Sustainable happiness comes from kindness. And when you give, then you are valued for the right reasons.'

Orly says in today's society, people are lonely and isolated. So kindness matters more than ever. 'People are looking to connect.'

She wants to inspire people to give back in tangible ways, 'on their own clock', and 'to find their own path'.

'Kindness can be simple. It can be just in the way that you talk to people. How you greet someone who opens the door for you. How you connect with your family. Those are the things that make you kind. Even how you look at people,' she says.

Orly says trust is needed in order to be kind. 'Be courageous with this.' She adds that you should never give if that kindness is a sacrifice, otherwise you may come to resent it.

'And kindness does not equate to being a doormat. Kindness needs to come from the right place. And that starts with loving you. You can be firm. You can be kind. You can stick up for yourself. It just comes back to the words you use, the tone you use, the responses that you give, the communication you have. That will determine whether it is kind or not kind. You can still come off as the kindest person saying no.'

I ask Orly, 'Is it hard being kind all the time?'

She says there are times when it is difficult. Yes, some people have tried to take advantage of her. She will always reply with kindness, though, she says. But if some people really push the boundaries, 'then that's really hard'. She notes that sometimes other people's actions can be outside your control.

Lastly, I ask her for her most powerful kindness wisdom. She says, 'Kindness begins with you. Then, being kind can help you to see the beauty in yourself. And the more you see the beauty in you, then the easier it is to love others. Being kind to others is easy. It's being kind to ourselves that's hard. You need to recognise that you are an important piece of the puzzle ... each person matters just as much as the next. That's the way we create impact. Kindness comes from within.'

Live epically.
Live for a powerful purpose+

Are you living for a powerful purpose? Or only a pay cheque?

Are you living a life that lights you up? Or living a beige-walled and pristine kind of existence?

Are you grimacing and trudging your way through this world? Or are the outer corners of your mouth lifted up?

Do you wish you could live as the best version of yourself? Or does fear hold you back from breaking out of your hard-shelled existence?

Realise the brevity of life. Life is about the important stuff. It's not about more and more stuff. It's all about the people you care about and experiences that light you up. Stuff the baubles. Give me adventures instead.

I've now learned it's okay to walk away from people and places that don't have my back. If you surround yourself with positive people, they will propel you forwards. If you stay in a space that sucks the life out of your soul, you'll feel suffocated and remain small.

Have a hunger to live your best life. Chase your dreams – even if it is a tiny piece at a time. Keep striving. And don't forget to give back to the world along the way. You don't want to celebrate your success in a majestic palace, alone.

Have a hunger to live your best life. Chase your dreams – even if it is a tiny piece at a time.

Living an epic life starts with loving yourself. It's not selfish to embrace self-care. Do things daily that lift your energy levels. If you look after yourself well, then you can help serve others better.

I'll never forget being at a health retreat many years ago. I was sitting in a room with 15 women, all aged in their 40s and 50s, but I felt like I was with just one person. It was like being in one of those mirrored rooms in a museum where the same person is reflected a hundred times. There was a theme with all these women that smacked me in the face hard. Almost every woman in that room regretted who they were. They were caring and kind mothers who had lifted up everyone else in their lives. But they had forgotten someone along the way: themselves. They had merely existed.

None of these women had taken time for themselves or put themselves first. Their kids had flown the coop, and they were now lost and disoriented and didn't know who they were or what to do. They all wished they had looked after their health and happiness more. They were trying to work out who they actually were. They were miserable, regretful and tearful. They served their loved ones in an honourable way. But this important motherly deed didn't have to be at the expense of their own identities.

Life is about balance. Loved ones need to be loved and propelled forwards. It's important. But please know that you deserve to live, love and thrive as well. If you do things that make you happy, then your brain functions at a higher level. This makes you shine bright.

Don't wait for that near-death experience to realise you forgot to live. No one ever wishes they had worked more when they are gasping for breath on their deathbed. They wish they had lived every important moment more. They wish they had realised that happiness was part of the journey, not the end point.

There's a reason why mindfulness is trending. We live on a planet that is getting faster and faster. We need to slow down, pause and celebrate now. You can't wait to be happy. You need to choose to be happy now. Notice the little things and the magic in the every day. Know that today is a gift.

Look, no one does everything on life's journey perfectly. I definitely get busy and then have to stop myself, pause for a moment and register what's important. Life is like a see-saw. It goes up and down often. You don't want your life tilted only on one side. You want to try and get it level as often as you can. Keep striving for balance.

Happiness is not dependent on your genes

One of my favourite books on the planet is **The Happiness Advantage: The Seven Principles of Positive Psychology That Fuel Success and Performance at Work** by **Shawn Achor**. He's a happiness researcher, speaker and Harvard-educated guy based in Dallas, Texas. His words are pure research-backed wisdom.

He's married with two precious children. He's real too. Despite being a happiness researcher, he has spoken publicly about overcoming depression. So he knows how valuable positive psychology tools can be: life-saving.

The Happiness Advantage features seven principles that fuel success and performance at work. But these principles can fuel success and happiness in your everyday life too.

I love this book so much it is hard-worn. Many pages are marked.
Many pages are folded over and read so much that it looks like a dog has
chewed the edges. I'll often open it and read a few paragraphs at night.
This book is like a bible to me on how to live. It's based around positive
psychology. Yeah, I used to raise my eyebrows and yawn over that term
too. But research shows it works. So sit up and soak up these words below.
Shawn changed my life by speaking to me via the pages of his book.
Can you imagine how much air guitar I did in my hallway at home when
he agreed to be in this book? Yeah, it's kind of embarrassing, and thank
God no one saw me, right?

Shawn talks in his book about happiness fuelling success, not the other
way around. This is because happiness can rewire the brain. Dopamine
floods our learning centres. If we are happier, then we can be more
productive. Then, this affects performance and success.

Shawn says it is common for us to think we will be happier if we have X
amount of money. Or we will be happy if we get married. Or we will be
happy when we pay off the mortgage. Or we will be happy if we go on that
tropical holiday.

But waiting to be happy is such a waste of precious time. We all have the
ability to adjust our mindsets so that we can feel happier right now.

There are a ton of research-backed tools available to boost our happiness
levels.

In one of his Shawn's TED talks online, he recommends 'raising your
positivity in the present'. The idea that reaching success makes us happy
is a 'broken' idea. We have to instead learn to be happy now, in the
present. This is because happiness can, in fact, lead us to be successful.

'I think that living with purpose is
making our definition of success
and happiness not just about us.'

Back to my chance to connect with Shawn. He agrees to answer some emailed questions as he has a young baby around the time I approach him.

First, he congratulates me on writing my book – and also having three kids. 'A full life!' he exclaims. I want to respond, 'Yes, full and I'm so grateful, but also full of chaos!' But, of course, I don't. I think that in my head. Of course, my kids make my life 'full'. They are the biggest gift, and they are what I am most grateful for in this world. Their happiness is a big part of my purpose. But, of course, I do wish I could post them to their grandparents during those teenager 'moments'.

Anyway, my first question is how can people live their most epic life, and does this relate to living their purpose?

He says, 'It would be pointless to live a grand life and travel all over the world or become rich or famous or be one of the most successful people you know if it didn't bring you and others happiness and meaning. So I think that living with purpose is making our definition of success and happiness not just about us. This is actually the thesis of my book **Big Potential:** the only way to see our full potential is to make others better because others make us feel better.'

My next question to him is how can people choose happiness? I love his response: 'Most people think that their happiness is dependent on their genes and their environment. So we become victims to both. But when we did the research, we saw a very different picture. When people made conscious positive habit changes to their life, it broke the tyranny of genes and environment over their happiness. The key is creating a mindset change AND a behavioural change.'

Then comes my third question. By now, I feel like I'm being granted three wishes from a genie. After all, happiness is the most valuable thing on the planet, right? My last question is what are your personal daily happiness habits? Or your best lessons learned?

He responds: 'I write down three new things I'm grateful for each day. I journal about the most positive experience of my day and keep a picture

'Most people
think that their
happiness is
dependent on
their genes
and their
environment.
So we become
victims to both.
But when we did
the research,
we saw a very
different picture.'

Shawn Achor

'I write down three new things I'm grateful for each day.'

of it in an app called Day One. I exercise, and I meditate for five minutes. Those are the base habits that we have researched. But I also go on a walk each day with my wife and son. I read for fun each day.

'Best lesson learned is that depression is not the end of the story; change is more possible than we imagine.'

Shawn's responses make me reflect on things that boost my wellbeing. As well as the things I already mentioned in Chapter 1, i.e. sleep, play, healthy food, exercise and being in nature, they include (in no particular order):

· Happiness is seeing my kids healthy and happy and succeeding in things they wish to do well in.

· Smiling at strangers. I love seeing the warmth of their smiles in return. It's uplifting.

· Meeting new people and hearing new perspectives. I want to keep evolving and challenging everything I view in the world.

· I've learned not to say 'yes' to everything (because this can spread me too thin). But I support friends whenever I can, because they deserve my support.

· Mindfulness and yoga are tools that powerfully uplift my soul. The philosophy that underpins these two things is a good guide for living. I keep distance from people who don't cheer me on. But I don't fully walk away from anyone unless they are very toxic. I'm a yogi, and I don't expect everyone to be on the same path as me at exactly the same moment. It's called tolerance. But I'm also not a doormat and can sense people's intentions.

· I seek out the sea. The cold rush of the waves invigorates me and reminds me I'm alive. The beach, with sand in between my toes, watching my kids build sandcastles, is my happiest place. Away from work, I think I'm most mindful of the beauty of the world and the beauty of everything in my world: family. And, of course, they annoy the heck out of me in real life, when they squabble. But without those 'downs', I wouldn't fully appreciate the 'ups'.

- Noticing the little things uplifts me too, particularly with nature. At home, I have a giant tree outside my bedroom. Every morning, I note the beautiful changes, from when the leaves fall to the new buds appearing. I love watching the leaves change colour over the seasons. I rejoice in new flowers blossoming every spring. That tree gives me so much happiness. Sometimes I lay in bed and watch the branches swaying in the wind. It's calming.

- My garden blooms with fruit, vegetables, flowers and herbs. I grow walls of edible flowers. Eating the edible food from my garden is nourishing. Actually, it's time in the garden that is the answer here.

- But there's a balance to all this too. For example, too much time in nature at one point in my life made me realise I'm also a city girl at heart. I love my work, I love learning, I love striving, I love growing. I get a kick out of the rush of my work success. So a bit of nature time and city time are things I try to balance.

Blissology and badass huggability

A love of nature is also a passion for yoga teacher **Eoin Finn**, from Vancouver, Canada.

His job title is blissologist. He has about 30 years' experience in yoga and meditation. He travels the world teaching the physical and spiritual aspects of the practice. He is often a headline act at Wanderlust yoga festivals around the globe. He has a passion for surfing and looking after our oceans.

Eoin is an ocean activist. He's driven to raise awareness for the world's imperilled coral reefs. He wants us all to take better care of our precious reefs.

I've met Eoin several times and interviewed him for magazine articles. I've attended his yoga teaching events in Australia, Hawaii and, several times, New Zealand.

He looks like a classic surfer dude – ruffled hair, tanned, strong – and he has an ease in how he moves. He's grounded, relatable and real. And he likes hugs. Eoin hugs everyone. He loves connecting with others. Connection with others is central to yoga.

He has a wonderful presence. So when I think of Eoin, I think of connection, saving the oceans and his badass huggability.

Actually, when I met him for the first time, he hugged me the same way he has hugged me since. He uses both arms and wraps them around you tight. Then he squeezes. It's a proper two-arm job. He then holds you tight for longer than a few more seconds. It's real awkward the first time. I blushed until I turned crimson and didn't know which direction to look. I froze to the spot.

That first hug was like watching a cup of tea warm up in the microwave; it seemed to take ages and ages and ages. But that was because I was so darn uptight. That hug taught me that it's nice to feel the warmth of another human. I also remember that in one of the first yoga classes of his I attended, he made the entire room of yogis hug. I was mortified and felt like running from the room. But my feet were kind of glued to the yoga mat. I could barely breathe, and, again, I didn't know where to look. I knew I'd

'That first hug was like watching a cup of tea warm up in the microwave; it seemed to take ages and ages and ages. But that was because I was so darn uptight. That hug taught me that it's nice to feel the warmth of another human.'

look like a dork if I scarpered. But after you've hugged several people in an awkward manner, then you get used to it. Well, at least, I got over myself, and I can now hug with a bit more ease. Learning to hug is a lesson in learning to embrace others metaphorically, too, I reckon.

I'm not saying we should all go out and hug strangers. Ask first! But it's about connecting well with others. That's the point. Go on and try it. Hug another human genuinely, warmly and authentically for longer than a minute. It will make you uncomfortable. Then it will make you smile.

I ask Eoin what blissology is. What is a blissologist?

'I recall my first bliss moment. I was six years old and in the wilderness in Canada. I remember the stillness, looking up at the night sky and feeling the warmth of a campfire. I was filled with this deep sense of awe, joy, gratitude and reverence that nature opened up in me. Blissology is really a movement based on explaining what happens in these moments,' Eoin explains.

'My mission is to help others tap into our wisdom centre. We use the wisdom of our hearts to guide our relationships with ourselves, our communities and with nature. To access our heart wisdom, we must get back to nature. Seek solitude in nature and your deepest heart becomes clear. A mantra I share with others who want to experience this is, "The beauty I see lives in me."

'The experience of blissology is the heart of the mystical experience. A feeling that all of life is a profound miracle, that there is a force that binds our hearts, that we have a calling to share this love with others fearlessly.'

Eoin tells me the ocean lights up his soul. It's here that he feels he has superpowers. With no malls or parking lots in sight, just blue sky above, water on his skin. He unplugs, is away from 'conquest actions' and can 'just be'.

It's here that he has a still mind. It lights a fire within him being here, and he says 'if we can light a fire in our own hearts, then we can light a fire in others' hearts'.

He tells me that being in nature helps us find our bliss, our purpose. 'Pausing, noticing the small and beautiful things in this world like the light in the trees. Or the patterns of some ants on the dirt. Being in nature is a fundamental thing for your health. It's a spiritual experience.'

He quotes **Albert Einstein**: 'There are only two ways to live your life. One is as though nothing is a miracle. The other is as though everything is a miracle.'

Eoin says someone questioned him recently: 'But who has time for that?' He laments that values have changed so much around the world. 'Now we are more likely to not blink about waiting in line to order a doughnut. Yet we protest that we don't have time for nature?'

He says one secret to living an epic life and finding your purpose is simply to enjoy your friends and family.

'Slow down. Pause. Find a way to push the reset button. Laugh. Hear music. Relish art. Be in nature. We treat people like ghosts in the way we live. We can go on without making eye contact with another.'

Eoin implores everyone to slow down and to connect more. 'This opens us up to love. Slowing down makes us kinder. Slowing down makes us happier.'

We need to be prepared to pay attention to our relationships too. He likens this to 'watering a plant'. This is required in order for it to grow.

Eoin wants us to make 'love' a central value in our culture. 'We have an infinite source of love inside us.'

He jokes that some people who attend his yoga classes 'look like they are getting a tax audit'. What he means is they are unaware of how they present themselves: 'Often unsmiling. Stressed. Disconnected. Not present.'

So I guess what he means here is we should tap into more awareness in ourselves. When we pause to sit under a tree and consider life, then we can consciously choose how we want to show up.

'Slow down. Pause. Find a way to push the reset button. Laugh. Hear music. Relish art. Be in nature.'

Eoin says we should be clear on what our purpose is

'Get to really know, ultimately, why you are on this planet and what your gifts are to share. For me, my mission is to be a conduit for love.'

He jokes that you should adopt a short life mission – 'that's even shorter than Twitter'.

'Each one of those words becomes a mantra, a powerful vibration, a powerful reminder of the direction you should be taking in life. It's a good compass, of course, to know if you have gone off course. So even though my mantra is short, it's really understanding what each word means,' he explains.

'Love is a big one in the sentence of his mantra,' he says. He laughs and says 'we only have one word for love, while the Inuit people, who inhabit the Arctic regions of Canada, have many words to describe it.'

Eoin says you need to get clear on what love is.

'We use "love", like, "I love chocolate", "I love life" … For me, love is what life is all about. It's a force that blurs the line where you end and another begins. A lot of people think of romantic love. That's one type. But there's universal love too.'

Eoin says he is being the most epic version of himself when he is teaching yoga. He feels joy and love and knows this is his purpose. He says by knowing this purpose, he can create projects and goals around it.

'Of course, there's reality as well. I have to balance out my dreams and my passions from my deepest heart from reality. And I also need to be able to balance the spreadsheet,' he says, chuckling.

'But you can tell when people are too concerned about the spreadsheet. There's never the same warmth when you come across those interactions. There's definitely an art to balancing our calling and the spreadsheet.'

Eoin says everyone knows their powerful purpose, but sometimes it can be 'a little bit fuzzy'.

'I say it's like digging a well. Just keep moving the sand and dirt until you get to the water. You know it. It's the thing that lights you up the most. When you talk about your life mission, you become animated, engaged, more physically present and in love with life. If your friends observe you when you talk about it, they can tell you are passionate.'

Eoin recommends that if you don't know your purpose, you should think about peak experiences in your life. 'Ask yourself, "When was I my highest vibrational self?"'

He says when he takes action on the reefs that are dying, he feels in service of others. 'At that moment, love comes through me, not from me. Love is not about when I'm the doer – it's about when I'm a conduit.'

Eoin recommends that people not be too specific with their own life mission. 'For example, don't say, "I want to open a retreat centre in a specific place." Because what if you fell in love with someone who lived somewhere else?'

If other people tell him, 'I want to be a conduit for love too,' he replies, 'That's great!'

'If people have a similar mission, that's cool. They will have different ways of expressing that. I actually never get depressed about, you know, oh my gosh, someone's stealing my thing. I instead think, "Isn't it so awesome that we are so similar and that others want to be conduits for love?" If you have a similar life mission to someone else, then celebrate it.'

Eoin says he has a 'test' for when he is his 'most likeable self' in this kind of situation.

'My definition of greatness is seeing the greatness in others. When I am my most likeable self is when I see the greatness in others. On the other side of it, when I'm feeling jealous and angry for comparing myself to other people, then this is the test. I know then that I have completely lost the plot.

'Ask your friends and family. But you are probably not very likeable in those times when you don't support others.

'So by being jealous, I'm actually giving myself an ingrown toenail. And do I want to walk with ingrown toenails?' He laughs. Loudly. 'When I feel like I have ingrown toenails, then I question myself: "How do I want to vibrate, really?"

'That's my personal take, anyway. I'm not perfect. There's a lot of love in the yoga industry. But it's a competitive way to make a living, you know. There's definitely a spreadsheet to take care of. I'm not a perfect person who feels no jealousy of other people, but I check in with myself when I do feel that. When these feelings come up, I have a conversation with myself.'

That's when Eoin tells me he gets back to nature. Nature helps his mental, physical and spiritual health feel in balance. Nature helps him to be quiet and present and connect back with love.

'We can get into our ego stuff. But when we are in nature, the lines blur between ourselves and things that are outside ourselves. We feel intimately connected to the trees, animals, the ocean. We feel connected to all life. We feel that beautiful sense of joy, love and peace, and, yeah, that's how nature can help us get unstuck. And from connection with others comes love.

'When we are in nature, we can be happy. And I don't mean on our phones at the same time and talking to people about gossip, work or relationships. I mean when we are really out in nature and unplugged. When we can pick up the signal of love. There's actually a vibration of nature, and it's pure love.'

Eoin says there are different ways to experience joy. For example, kids are happy and a definition of love and joy. But they are not exactly peaceful, sometimes, he says, erupting into laughter again.

Surfing brings joy for him too but in a different way. 'I lose track of time, then. So surfing can become transcendental. Time disappears. I don't feel the pressure of time. There's gratitude. Awe. So much passion. At that moment, I don't know who or what God is, but I want to cosmically high-five him or her,' he jokes.

Eoin's last lesson is not to be afraid of pain. 'Recognise that life is going to have painful moments and challenging moments. It's not going to be all sitting in a hammock, drinking Coronas [beer] and watching the sunset. There will be moments of that, but there will be sad, challenging moments also. That's the flipside of love.'

'Recognise that life is going to have painful moments and challenging moments. It's not going to be all sitting in a hammock, drinking Coronas [beer] and watching the sunset. There will be moments of that, but there will be sad, challenging moments also. That's the flipside of love.'

LIVE EPICALLY. LIVE FOR A POWERFUL PURPOSE.

Happiness flavours and rewiring your brain

World-renowned neuroscientist **Dr Kerry Spackman** is the author of **The Winner's Bible: Rewire Your Brain for Permanent Change**. This is a science-backed guide to help you to rewire your brain and transform in order to live an epic life.

Kerry has worked with world champions over the years. This includes Formula 1 racing-car drivers and Olympic teams. He has even worked with New Zealand's globally renowned rugby players, the All Blacks.

Kerry specialises in optimising performance, or, rather, propelling people towards greatness. In other words, he helps people to live epically on a world-stage level. But what he teaches in his book, and often speaks about at events, is tools that can help anyone to live an epic life. His advice is not just for elite athletes.

In Kerry's book, there's a chapter called 'Show Me Your Friends'. He asks you to list the six people you chose to spend the most time with over the last month. Then write down four adjectives that describe each of them. These adjectives will tell you a lot about yourself.

What he is getting at is that who we surround ourselves with helps to shape who we are. So analyse your friends, business partners, loved ones, everyone. They have more of an impact on shaping and influencing you than you think.

I did the exercise, and I found it revealed a lot about me. Some of it was confronting! Some adjectives made me laugh and, of course, described me exactly. I recommend you do this test too.

I meet Kerry at a café in Auckland to interview him for this book. I've interviewed him several times over the years and seen him speak at events. Every time, he is warm and welcoming. He takes the time to ask questions about me and although he doesn't give lots of time, he gives his genuine presence. He knows the art of connection.

As we sit in the café, I ask him, 'How can people live an epic life?'

He takes a sip of his tea and then talks fast: 'It's one thing to have goals, a strong belief in yourself and a positive attitude. But you've got to understand too about what's going on in your brain to really get ahead. To strengthen your mind, firstly ask yourself what truly drives you and who are you really? Then drill down into your history, psychology, physiology and philosophies [what he calls the four pillars] and examine where you sit in the universe. Then examine your goals, passions and self-beliefs.

'Once you have crystallised a passion or mission, then audit your strengths and weaknesses and then work on what you need to strengthen. An independent audit will help. This is because how you view yourself can be different to how others view you. Working hard is key too.'

Kerry uses that well-known term 'carpe diem' – meaning 'seize the day' – in his book to inspire. 'I don't know anyone who has a gold medal who hasn't worked their butt off,' he quips.

I take him back to placing your friends under a microscope to see if they are good in your life. Kerry says choose those who are close to you 'very wisely'. 'Their thoughts will influence and shape your thoughts and every aspect of your life. Their behaviours, how they spend their time, their ethics, dreams and desires will mould you more than you think. You also want to be able to rely on some of those close to you to lift you up in life when you fall. And we all fall sometimes, so you need people you can count on.

'So for each friend, knowing the inner character, inner beauty – their soul – is most important. Ask yourself if you can count on them to be there when you might need them the most. Do they care deeply about you?'

Kerry says there's an old saying, 'Show me your friends and I'll show you who you are and who you will become.'

I ask Kerry, what if you have 'low-value friends'? That's the term Kerry uses in his book. 'You can change them,' he says bluntly and without hesitation.

LIVE EPICALLY. LIVE FOR A POWERFUL PURPOSE

'There's an old saying, 'Show me your friends and I'll show you who you are and who you will become.'"

He reasons, 'Sometimes you might accumulate friends but grow and move on. Change requires work, but it's worthwhile,' he adds.

As we sit talking over a cuppa – herbal tea for him, a latte for me – he talks about a piece he loves by **Albert Einstein** called 'The World as I See It'.

In this piece, Einstein writes: 'The ideals that have lighted my way, and time after time have given me new courage to face life cheerfully, have been: kindness, beauty and truth. Without the sense of kinship with men of like mind, without the occupation with the objective world, the eternally unattainable in the field of art and scientific endeavours, life would have seemed empty to me. The trite objects of human efforts – possessions, outwards success, luxury – have always seemed to me contemptible.'

Kerry says this article is essentially a one-page summary about 'what's important'. He tries to live life in part by this summary. And he starts his days with gratitude.

'Every day, I wake up and think to myself and think of all the people who helped me to get where I am. I am here because of the efforts of hundreds of people I have never met, and so I'm reminded of, "What can I give back?" In the modern world, we are very egocentric. How can I do more, be more? Sometimes having an exocentric view and thinking outward is more satisfying and helpful.

'I like Einstein's focus on kindness, beauty and truth. Truth is really important. Beauty, then, comes in many forms, like poetry, music, people, landscapes, etc. We talk about mindfulness, but what about beauty? That third word is the nicest: "kindness".'

'Think of the rocking-chair test. When you are sitting on the rocking chair when you are 95 and rocking backwards and forwards, you think, "What was important, really?"' He says remember too that life is brief.

Kerry tells me he doesn't focus on the word 'love', because he believes love can be 'quite selfish'. He rather focuses on kindness, because that's all about giving back.

Kerry ponders further the question of how to live a meaningful life. He offers this idea: 'Think of the rocking-chair test. When you are sitting on the rocking chair when you are 95 and rocking backwards and forwards, you think, "What was important, really?"' He says remember too that life is brief.

Kerry next tells me that happiness comes in 'many flavours'. 'There's the superficial happiness. It's the latest bauble, the latest entertainment, the latest thing that tickles your fancy.' He says the Greek word is best: 'eudaimonia'. This means happiness or welfare, or 'human flourishing'.

Kerry recommends 'taking that big helicopter view. That's important. Not looking at the end of your nose.' He says you can tell when people have a warmth and contentment about them and don't have an agenda. He feels these people are closest to finding eudaimonia.

'They're doing something worthwhile, they're at peace with themselves, they're good people. This just oozes out of their pores,' he explains. 'I don't think real success rules our happiness, and I also don't think we can buy happiness. It's about the inner purpose.'

He says it helps too to have 'good life skills'. For example, being resilient. He says this skill can be learned if you were not taught this in your upbringing. Lots of skills can be taught to help you live a better life and view the world in a better light. You can rewire your brain.

Here's an example Kerry talks about from when he worked with the top New Zealand rugby team, the All Blacks. In a game of rugby, things often go wrong, and this can easily spiral downhill quickly.

'The question is how do you stop that?'

One of the tools the players used was to ask themselves the question, 'What colour hat am I wearing?' He explains: 'You have two hats, a red hat and a green hat. With the green one, you think positive thoughts, while the red hat is all about thinking negative thoughts.'

So he asks the players, 'How much of the game do you have a green hat on?'

'I worked with them on how to get the green hat back on.'

What about money? I ask.

Kerry replies, 'Money gives you lots of options. But, above a certain level [at which your health, living conditions, etc. are met], any more probably doesn't buy happiness. It just buys options.'

Kerry then shares an anecdote that lights this example up beautifully.

'I was on a mega-yacht which is unbelievable. Then I flew home and got off the plane and went to visit my mum in Royal Oak [a non-flashy suburb in Auckland]. I parked outside the dairy, and there was this beaten-up Ford Falcon ute, and on the back was an aluminium dinghy with a little outboard, and this fella and his son had big beaming smiles.

'I asked him, "Did you catch any fish?" I think the whole thing [car and boat] would have been worth $2000 yet they had been out on the Manukau Harbour and had an absolute ball. You could tell by the look on their faces that they had had fun. I contrasted that to being on a mega-yacht earlier, where some people were not happy.

'So there's this guy with his dinghy on the Manukau Harbour, with a couple of snapper fish, who had had a happy day. While, on the super-yacht, there were oysters being served and nothing that money couldn't buy and there were still people who were not happy.'

Over the years, Kerry has worked with lots of successful people. This includes academics in universities, government officials and globally renowned sporting champions. He reckons he has noticed a theme amongst those who are very successful. He calls this 'the charm factor'. This is at the heart of the 'good life skills' he was mentioning earlier, which help people to be successful and happy.

Kerry says consider this idea: 'Would you do business with someone who is fun, enjoyable and charming? Or would you do business with someone who isn't nice?'

I nod, as I see his point.

'Successful people also have good decision-making skills,' he remarks. 'They have the ability to sacrifice the short term for the long term. They rationally look at decisions. Successful people tend to make better decisions. There's luck. But there's hard work too.'

He then tells me a story about Olympic gold medallist rowers **Eric Murray** and **Hamish Bond**. They are both famous New Zealand blokes. Kerry remembers going out on the water one day to watch them and analyse data around their rowing. This was on Lake Karapiro, on the Waikato River, in the North Island.

'Successful people also have good decision-making skills,' he remarks. 'They have the ability to sacrifice the short term for the long term. They rationally look at decisions. Successful people tend to make better decisions. There's luck. But there's hard work too.'

'It was a miserable day, blowing 100km an hour, freezing, raining, and no one else was on the water but Murray and Bond. We were on a chase boat chasing them [to watch their performance]. They were in their singlets and shorts. When they came in from rowing, Eric Murray remarked, "That was a championship row."'

Kerry asked him, 'What do you mean?'

'He said, "Everyone else was in the gym doing squats and legs and whatever because it was miserable out there. We could have done that. But we did something that was nasty and hard, and, you know what, if the Olympics are in 100km/hr winds, then we will win."

'And so that's what a champion does. They go the extra mile,' says Kerry. He says the difference between a champion and everyone else is 'everyone else has an excuse. Champions never have an excuse.'

Before Kerry finishes his cup of tea and dashes – he's working on some projects with billionaires and big corporates – he leaves me with a final piece of advice. He seems passionate about this being integral to living an epic life. He says this with raw, heartfelt emotion.

'You have to forgive people. Remember this person has this fault and that's okay. Realise you don't have to fix it for them, but be aware of it. Then remember that you do not have to be like that.'

I love this quote.

I haven't told Kerry this, but one of my favourite lines from his book is this: 'Life is a process of becoming.'

I like the idea that we can always strive and work to become our best selves. We can all work on brain rewiring. We've just got to be willing to be aware and do the hard work to polish those bits of us that don't shine bright.

Challenge yourself, change yourself₊

Don't be a dreamer. Be a doer.

You need goals to move you forwards. But so many people just don't know where to start with health and fitness goals. They feel overwhelmed and almost paralysed to start. Another big issue holding us back, often, is wanting to do things perfectly. If we can't be perfect, we give up and walk away.

I want you to focus on progression, not perfection. Choose something you want to achieve, and then choose to believe in yourself. Change your thinking from 'I can't' to 'I will' and 'I'm willing to do the work'. Then you need to take action.

I tell people I coach, or my yoga students, 'All you have to do is show up.' That's the hardest part. If you show up, then you get the work done. And no one ever regrets taking a healthy action!

It has taken me a lot of time to realise that you get better when you practise. Repetitive actions help us to change. Start with action, then repeated actions become your behaviour. After a reasonable period of being consistent with our behaviours, this becomes 'a lifestyle'. So if you want to be a runner, then just run regularly each week. Want to be a cyclist? Cycle regularly. Want to become a skilled yogi? Just practise, practise and practise, and you will get there.

I tell people I coach, or my yoga students, 'All you have to do is show up.' That's the hardest part. If you show up, then you get the work done. And no one ever regrets taking a healthy action!

It's like when I learned the saxophone. I had to start by learning the notes, then read music and then get the tempo right and accentuate the right notes. It took time and practice.

I always tell runners I coach that you can't go out and run a marathon overnight. Well, maybe you could, but it would hurt! And it's likely you can't touch your toes overnight as an older yogi either. It will take some stretch practice.

What I'm getting at here is that you have to be okay with being bad at something and willing to practise getting better.

My dad always told me, 'If you know what you want, then you are halfway there.' He's right. All you have to do is solidify a goal that you are passionate about and then go for gold. And stop holding yourself back!

Yes, pain and frustration and likely even boredom are part of the process. But know that things you want are worth the work. They are worth fighting for.

Often, we have hopes and dreams, but without plans and action, we have nothing. We stay glued to the same spot.

Get some people to cheer you on. Tap into the support of people who care about your success. Tell them your goal, and this will make you accountable, and then they will be a cheerleader when you are successful, every step of the way.

You deserve that support. You deserve to achieve your goals. You matter, and your goals matter. Don't let anyone else tell you otherwise. Stay away from people who want to hold you back.

Then reduce any barriers in your way to achieving your goal.

For example, if you like drinking on Friday nights, then don't plan your run for Saturday. That's going to be an uphill battle if you feel hungover! Schedule the run instead on Sunday. It might set you up for success better.

If you are a parent, remember you influence your kids with every action. If you want your kids to be fitter and healthier, then you need to walk the talk.

Let's put that word, 'influence', under the microscope for a minute. It's actually pretty powerful. We are influenced by our friends and people we love and admire. We influence others too. So make sure you are influencing others in a way that's positive. You want to be a good role model. How can you expect your kids to be healthy eaters if they've never been shown what to do? Take responsibility for your actions and realise there is a real ripple effect at work here.

I'm a marathoner, but I don't expect my kids to be runners. I just hope that they see that my regular actions with fitness make me happy and that this is a 'normal' part of my life. My biggest wish is just to inspire them to be healthy and happy in a way that resonates with them.

How can you expect your kids to be healthy eaters if they've never been shown what to do? Take responsibility for your actions and realise there is a real ripple effect at work here.

I won't have absolute control over that. But I can do my best to influence them in a positive way.

If you feel lost when it comes to aiming for goals, and you can afford it, then get a personal trainer or coach. I'm not just saying this because I am one. It's proven to help people achieve their goals smarter and faster.

And quit the negative-self-talk stuff. Find confidence to believe you can achieve goals. If you don't believe you can achieve a goal, then you are never going to get there. It's called self-efficacy. It's your belief in your ability to succeed or not. You need self-belief to achieve.

Consider what stage you are in. Are you contemplating change, in the planning stage or acting with change? Awareness of where you are at is golden.

I have a client who rang me up and said, 'Rach, I'm going to run.' She may as well have told me, 'I'm going to be a nun.' I never thought she would ever do this. I was so excited and blown away that I almost fell off my chair. I couldn't have talked her into this goal – she used to roll her eyes at me whenever I mentioned that word previously. I get it. I had to wait until she felt ready and inspired to start. I'm so proud of her. And, yes, I was exactly like her several years back.

Now she has the desire, I'm equipping her with the skills and a safe plan and support to achieve her goal. She's doing great.

If you want to get healthier or fitter, then focus on the outcome: for instance, having more energy or feeling and looking healthier and less stressed. These things are worth working for.

If you can't afford a coach, then stick to SMART goal-setting. The trick is to break goals down into bite-sized pieces. Be precise with goals, and set milestones, timelines and deadlines. Goal-setting works backwards.

Here's how SMART goal-setting works

S **SPECIFIC**
It must be a specific goal that you want to achieve and that is important to you.

M **MEASURABLE**
You must be able to measure if you have achieved it.

A **ACHIEVABLE**
It must be within your grasp and reliant only on you to be achieved.

R **REALISTIC**
It should be a challenge but not something impossible.

T **TIME-SPECIFIC**
This sets a clock and an urgency on your getting the work done.
It gives you focus.

Sometimes the hardest part is pinning down specific goals that matter. That's where a coach like me is great. We know how to break down barriers to help you achieve success in a sustainable way.

Remember small steps can lead you to your bigger goal. And celebrate all those wins along the way.

I love setting big goals, because they allow me to focus on where I want to head. These goals help me to grow, expand, learn and thrive. I need a game plan for my life. If I set targets that are within arm's reach, they won't mean as much to me as bold and meaningful goals that require grit and discipline. In a way, I'm constantly designing my life. Years ago, I stumbled through it!

One goal I had years ago was to start a run journey. I had a bucket-list thing to do a half-marathon one day – even if I just crawled through it. It was about doing it.

I started with a walk/run routine twice weekly for three months. Back then, I was so unfit that I'd puff pushing my toddler in a pram on the school run. My face was crimson. It hurt. It was hard. I hated it. It would have been easy to give up. But after a few weeks, I noticed I was getting a little better and there was more running and less walking. Then, months later, I joined a run club for more motivation. I told a coach back then that if they helped me to run a half-marathon, they wouldn't be a PT (personal trainer), they'd be an MM (miracle-maker). I slowly built up the kilometres over 12 months, and then I conquered my first half-marathon. I was ecstatic because I achieved a dream goal – and I even managed another goal of doing it in under two hours. By just showing up and committing to that goal, I got there. Eventually. And all that hard work paid off and felt unbelievably amazing. I achieved something I never thought I could up until my 30s. Achieving that was empowering. It made me immediately think, 'What can I try and conquer that feels scary next?' Sports goals can help to fuel life success. I'm a firm believer in that.

After that half-marathon, I planned my next goal: a marathon. This scared me like crazy. But having a trainer and run friends who believed in me propelled me forwards.

So my running dream started small and ended up growing, bit by bit. Fast-forward to today and I'm a multi-marathoner. Running has become my moving meditation. I feel free, find flow and feel amazing now as a runner. But it took time, hard work and perseverance to get to this place!

Anyway, back to choosing goals that motivate and inspire you. Think of things that give you a fire in your belly. If you work hard at them, then you'll feel empowered. Set short-term goals but long-term ones too. Consider what you want in five or even 10 years. The first time I did that long-term goal-setting exercise, it was scary. It's overwhelming to consider where I might be in 10 years, but it's a crucial plan to pin down. Don't go through your life letting everything happen by chance. Are you jealous of people who have successful lives? Do you think they are just lucky? They likely had a plan and worked hard to achieve their success. As **Kerry Spackman** says, 'There's luck. But there's hard work, too.'

Consider goals around areas such as your health, education, fitness, work or something personal. Just choose something that resonates with you and makes you excited. Really know your life vision. Then believe that you can achieve and work hard towards what you want.

You can drink beers and still lose weight

Artist **Simon Richardson** proves if you have the right mindset, you can achieve incredible weight-loss and fitness results.

He didn't even use a gym and still drank beers!

Simon is one of the superstar clients I coach. He's a multi-award-winning painter. He exhibited last at the Southern Gothic exhibition at Dunedin's Milford Galleries. He exhibited works alongside fellow high-profile artists Jeffrey Harris and Grahame Sydney. Simon has been in the media limelight lots. He has won multiple awards and scholarships. He gained notoriety early on over painting former All Blacks rugby player Anton Oliver in the nude. Simon and Anton became friends many years ago after Anton bought one of Simon's paintings of a cup of tea and piece of toast for $10,000. You need around $15,000 to $20,000 to afford one of his works these days.

Back to Simon and his coaching. When I first started coaching him in February 2018, his goal was to lose 9kg to reach his goal weight, 79kg. The only exercise he had done previously was running. But he was losing the love for this sport because he constantly had sore legs.

'I can fit all my jeans again!'

I coached Simon remotely via phone or Skype. I'm in Auckland; he's in Dunedin. I put Simon's nutrition, fitness and lifestyle under a microscope. I checked in with him weekly to update his plan. I gave him new tips weekly that were achievable, relatable and sustainable. I made sure his plan always aligned with his goals.

Simon can't access a gym as he lives on a remote peninsula – in a blissful spot overlooking the sea. So I got him doing body-weight training and cut his run days in half. I forced him to have a rest day weekly for recovery.

Simon loves his celebratory Friday night beers, and so I kept these in his plan. I believe in sustainable lifestyle changes and loathe deprivation.

After six weeks' coaching, I got this text from Simon:

'I can fit all my jeans again!'

I was blown away by the exclamation mark as Simon is usually a very quietly spoken and reserved kind of guy. I knew he was excited. I then felt even more excited than him. As a coach, it's a buzz helping clients reach their goals. Helping others is a heart-led thing.

Within two months, Simon reached his goal weight. He is also stronger, fitter and running faster. When I look at his before and after photos, comparing his body transformation, I can see the muscle definition in his back particularly, his much leaner middle and even a beautifully improved posture. The exercises I've given him have helped to correct his posture so he is less hunched over. This is a common thing for most people, as a lot of us sit at a desk all day. For Simon, he paints many hours in this position. He looks more upright and confident now. The best ripple effect of his journey, from my perspective, is he is sharing his newfound nutrition knowledge with his family. There goes that theory in action that if you inspire one person then they inspire others around them too.

I still coach Simon. I credit his ongoing success to his incredible determination. I was merely a guide in the process of his reaching his goal weight.

I ask Simon some questions about his health journey.

What has been the hardest part of the journey?

'Nutrition! I had to learn to be disciplined.'

What do you love?

'The variety of CrossFit-style exercises I get to do.'

What helped you on your journey?

'Having a coach. It was great to have someone telling me what I should be doing. I found that fantastic and really motivating. I also really enjoy the fitness programme.'

What do you love about your transformation?

'Having muscles. I've never had that before.'

What's your advice to others wishing to be fitter or healthier?

'You shouldn't give up on yourself if you get to your 40s or 50s. Look after your body!'

Fitness and goal-setting tips

(1) ABANDON THE ALL-OR-NOTHING ATTITUDE
For example, if you want to start running, just start with a walk/jog routine. Then gradually increase your steps and then distance over time. Building your fitness slowly is smart. If you start slow, this stops you from feeling overwhelmed. Getting started is usually the hard part. Once you've started, it can generate the momentum to keep going. Over time, your fitness routine will eventually become a habit.

(2) LEAVE YOUR SHOES AND FITNESS GEAR OUT THE NIGHT BEFORE
This will help to set you up for success. Setting up your environment can really help on those days when your willpower is missing. We all have days like that, by the way.

(3) JUST START
Know that it's going to be hard some days, and suck it up. Stop scrolling on your phone and looking in magazines constantly for inspiration.

(4) HANG OUT WITH PEOPLE DOING INSPIRING FITNESS STUFF THAT INTERESTS YOU
You'll get swept along with their enthusiasm. They will positively influence you and propel you forwards.

(5) VISUALISE YOURSELF AS THE FITTER YOU THAT YOU DREAM OF BEING
Own this new identity, and tell others you are committed.

(6) KNOW THAT PAIN IS PART OF THE PROCESS BUT IT WILL GET EASIER OVER TIME!

How to get a healthy high

Exercise is fun and good for your body, but it's also powerful for your brain. I interviewed **Toby Mündel**, a Senior Lecturer in the School of Sport, Exercise and Nutrition at Massey University in New Zealand, for a newspaper story about the science behind the buzz when you exercise. He teaches a paper on 'the exercising brain'. If I can't convince you to move your body for the body benefits, I'm hoping Toby's scientific view will be more persuasive.

'The exercise high does scientifically exist,' he says. So how do you get that healthy high – you know, that buzzy feeling of euphoria? 'You have to do prolonged exercise, like running, swimming or biking long distances. This will take you beyond feeling pumped, which is something a weightlifter might feel after a short and intense workout.'

Toby says part of the exercise high is due to an increase in brain activity (increased pressure and blood flow to the brain).

'It's like shifting up through gears on a car,' he says. 'Men and women also experience an increase in different hormones [for men, it's adrenalin; for women, it's oxytocin] in response to stressful situations, of which exercise can be seen as one, that puts them in a different state.

'Both sexes also release endorphins, which scientists once thought were solely responsible for the high. But further tests in animals show endorphins don't easily pass the blood/brain barrier and so cannot be the only reason for euphoria.'

'The exercise high does scientifically exist.'

Toby likens endorphins to a type of 'morphine', which 'numbs pain and creates a euphoric state': our internal opiate. 'The body releases something similar to cannabis and gives you that euphoric feeling,' he says. 'This may sound daft, but it's true.'

He says that relatively recent research shows that another area too is responsible for this euphoria, called 'the endocannabinoid system', which essentially modulates sensations of pain and mood in the brain. Prolonged exercise also raises serotonin and dopamine – neurotransmitters that send messages around the brain – to increase feelings of 'reward' during prolonged exercise, much like many get from drugs, alcohol or sex.

However, the exercise high is not the same experience for everyone. 'People get different levels – or, rather, respond differently to it. Just like how some people might respond differently to smoking actual cannabis,' he says.

And he also warns that more exercise does not equal a greater high.

'The same dose of exercise does not give you the same "hit" all the time, and, typically, the more you do something, then the less the high might become.

'Chasing too much of a high can also become addictive, with people exercising more and more to try and feel the same way they once felt. Exercising for five hours is not usual for non-elite athletes,' he says.

He adds that most people just want to lose weight, look good or manage stress – like him – and the exercise high might make them feel floaty now and again.

So make sure you don't push yourself too far.

Failing to plan for your wellbeing? Then you are planning to fail.

I want to challenge you to change yourself for the body and mind benefits. But if I need to, I will scare you into action.

A lack of exercise, too much food and chronic stress can snowball. These issues can spiral out of control and result in hypertension, heart disease, diabetes, depression, anxiety, cancer and even death.

Failing to plan for your personal wellbeing is planning to fail to stay 'well'. It's crucial to fit smart fitness, health and nutrition solutions into your lifestyle – for anyone of any age.

Degeneration with age is actually minimal; degeneration with inactivity is immense. You have to be personally accountable for how you are showing up in the world in how you look, what you say, how you act, everything.

How you move and fuel your body influences how you think, feel and perform. It also influences how you sleep. Stress levels play a major role too. These things affect the chemistry of your body and your entire being in more ways than you can imagine.

Please prioritise your health. Health is your true wealth (so the saying goes, but it's so true). If you don't prioritise healthy living, it can lead to alarming consequences. A lack of exercise, too much food and chronic stress can snowball. These issues can spiral out of control and result in obesity, elevated blood pressure, heart disease, diabetes, depression, anxiety, cancer and even death.

Let me put high blood pressure – a silent killer, often with no warning signs – under the microscope for an example. Hypertension results in damage to blood vessels. In a very serious scenario this could lead to heart damage.

Now, let's look at obesity, which is, sadly, an epidemic. We focus often on the aesthetics and forget about the unseen damage:

- Excessive joint stress (which can lead to painful arthritis)
- Elevated blood pressure (which can harm your heart)
- Sleep apnoea (which leads to tiredness and lack of concentration)
- Low respiratory function (which affects how you live every moment of every day)
- Lowered self-confidence (which can spiral into serious mental health issues like depression, which is another epidemic)
- Cardiovascular issues, diabetes, arthritis, cancers and many more health problems

I teach a yin/de-stress style of yoga, meditation and mindfulness to a lot of people battling stress. I've worked with executives, lawyers, partners in firms, entrepreneurs, teachers, chiropractors and mums. I teach them how to use quick techniques to calm their nervous systems (these tools are science-proven). I also educate them with wellness wisdom every session relating to how movement and their mindsets shape the lives they live.

Through my work as a magazine wellness columnist, I've interviewed lots of top experts globally. I've interviewed researchers, professors, wellness gurus, nutritionists, neuroscientists, psychologists and happiness researchers. I've also interviewed and met lots of wellness gurus in New Zealand. I know the strategies that they use themselves (because these strategies are science-backed). And they all care about what they eat and how they move and are aware that a healthy lifestyle is crucial for living a good life. They all know that healthy lifestyles can lead to more happiness. I think maybe there's just too little education out in the world to make people fully realise they can be on a fast road to death if they don't care how they live.

My wonderful friend **Jo Thomson** is a nurse. I love chatting to her about how to uplift the health of the world. She is looking at how health professionals have those conversations around weight with clients. But the health problems of extra weight are often not discussed with people, maybe due to fear of upsetting them.

'Discussing in a non-judgemental way how eating healthier and exercising regularly can be fitted into their life can help people to make changes for the better.

'Research has shown that using terms such as obesity makes people feel judged. Showing people where they are on a chart is a good way to open the conversation.

'Health care professionals can empower people to make changes, such as increasing vegetables on the dinner plate, reducing carb serving sizes and being more active each day, so that they and their families can slow or stop weight gain,' she said.

Perhaps we need to say more frankly, if you don't eat well, fail to exercise and are overwhelmed with work stress, then this can have a ripple effect.

Incidental physical activity

If you don't know how to get fit, start with making sure you are getting enough incidental exercise. Years ago, our grandparents didn't 'plan' exercise; it was all just part of their day. Now, we plan our exercise because we don't get enough of it.

The key is to keep moving your body. Movement keeps you strong, sparks brain activity and helps boost mood and energy levels. Physical activity helps you ward off issues like obesity, diabetes, depression and hypertension.

Here are 10 of my beginner fitness tips

1 WALK WHENEVER POSSIBLE
I inspire (bribe) my kids to walk to the local park or to visit friends. I make my kids walk to school every day – it's a ritual to spend time with them, chat and make sure they move their bodies to kick off the day! My youngest son is not always happy about this. But I explain that he needs to walk to school because I love him and I care that he is healthy and happy. Cue groans from the little chap. But after a few minutes, he is skipping down the road and happy to be on his feet.

2 USE SCOOTERS OR BIKES FOR THAT FUN FACTOR
Use whatever excites kids to get active.

3 USE TV-WATCHING TIME TO DO HOUSEHOLD CHORES LIKE FOLDING WASHING OR TO STRETCH

4 STAND INSTEAD OF SITTING
It burns more calories and helps to keep your muscles working. If you are on the phone or reading, stand. Stand while you are on your computer or while doing hobbies like painting or mindful drawing. Stand while watching your kids play or swim or while you wait for a taxi or bus.

5 USE THE STAIRS INSTEAD OF A LIFT
Every bit of exercise is a bonus.

(6) WALK A DOG – YOURS OR A FRIEND'S
It makes the movement fun and the focus goes on walking the pet rather than having to get out for exercise. The dog can be a terrific distraction.

(7) SIGN UP TO PARTICIPATE IN A FUN COMMUNITY EVENT TO KEEP YOU MOTIVATED TO TURN UP TO FITNESS SESSIONS
I tell clients this 'scares you into action'.

(8) SEEK OUT NATURE INSTEAD OF BEING ON TECHNOLOGY
Beaches, bush walks, lake swims, or walks to a park. This will uplift you.

(9) DO BODY-WEIGHT STRENGTH EXERCISES AT HOME OR AT A PARK
Google workouts to do on your phone or just make them up. Or simply do things like lunges, push-ups, squats, knee-lifts and stretches. This will get your heart pumping and is so darn good for you.

(10) PUT MUSIC ON AT HOME AND DANCE
My youngest son loves this! You don't even have to be good at dancing in order to reap the wellbeing benefits. It's a good way to exercise, boosts brain power and is a brilliant way to interact with others.

'Humans are not meant to be sitting. We are meant to be standing up and moving. It's in our genes.'

Dr Borja del Pozo-Cruz, Senior Research Fellow in Active Living at the Australian Catholic University, says that the message to the general public is to endeavour to exercise for roughly 30 minutes daily. However, he reckons it should be changed to striving to be physically active throughout the day.

'Humans are not meant to be sitting. We are meant to be standing up and moving. It's in our genes.'

He says moving constantly helps sparks brain activity, improves physical health, makes us stronger and helps people to cope better with everyday life.

Exercise in disguise

Make sure you dance – even if you are no good at it (like me).

Not only is dancing good exercise, it also boosts brain power and is a brilliant way to interact with others and to feel a sense of togetherness. You can do it when you are a toddler or aged over 100.

Plus, if you're older, dancing can be protective against dementia – because you have to 'exercise' your brain to dance.

So says **Carlene Newall de Jesus**, who is working in the Dance Studies department at the University of Auckland. As part of her doctorate, she's working alongside the university's Centre for Brain Research (CBR), researching what it is specifically about dancing that gives the significant cognitive benefits. She is looking at different dance activities to try to find out which types work better for different people and therefore what kinds of activities produce the best outcomes.

Her research will investigate the benefits of dance for people with dementia, which is a global problem on the increase with ageing populations. Currently, around 50,000 New Zealanders suffer from dementia, and that figure is set to increase to 170,000 by 2050, according to the **Economic Impact of Dementia** report commissioned by Alzheimer's New Zealand.

According to the Alzheimer's Disease International website in the UK, the global stats are on track to reach 75 million in 2030.

If you're older, dancing can be protective against dementia – because you have to 'exercise' your brain to dance.

Carlene leads hip-hop classes for kids who are mental-health patients in Auckland city's Starship Hospital and instructs dance in retirement homes. She's a passionate choreographer and dancer, loves to practise contemporary dance and hip hop and is even a circus aerialist.

She says significant research overseas already confirms that frequent dancing is beneficial for individuals. 'It may help to delay the onset of dementia.'

She says to try and reduce the chance of dementia, you can do several things like exercise often, engage in recreational activities, continue to use your brain in new ways, socialise with lots of people and do things that are creative.

'Dance is a beautiful combination of all of those things. Dancing is physical, cognitive, a new creative thing you can do with other people, and that's what gives it such a unique potential.'

She says it doesn't matter if you have danced a lot in your life or not at all; you can keep modifying any kind of dance to keep it 'new'.

'Modifying dances in small ways is all you need to do. Dances can be modified really easily, and dance in itself uses memory a lot. Think of a normal dance class – it's usually geared towards learning and remembering something. I fit this into teaching older adults,' she says.

Asked to describe the joy she gets from dancing, Carlene says, 'It's that state where you are so immersed in the music, the movement, you are with other people, you are all connecting together in a way that you don't even have to consciously think about. It can become second nature. You can release another way of being that lets out your personality and your style, and an inner version of yourself gets to come out and play. Play, by the way, is something that we don't do enough as adults.'

I ask Carlene if this means that you can dance anytime, anywhere, in your jeans or PJs, in the dark, literally however you like.

'Yes! Some people think there is this invisible door to dancing and that there is a technique that you have to have. But, actually, anyone can dance. It's just moving to music in a way that you like, and there's no wrong way or right way of doing it.

'There can be no rules. Make it just moving to music. You can move your head. You can dance with your fingers. You can dance sitting down or standing up. I think people mistakenly think that there are too many rules that they don't know. They say they "can't dance" and "I don't know how to dance". But, actually, there are no rules, and that's the beauty of it.'

So dancing like a kid or a grown-up, jumping around and not caring what you look like seem to be key here, I remark.

Carlene laughs and says, 'Yeeeeeeees!'

She adds that dance can be intergenerational, as well.

'There's no reason why a seven-year-old can't dance with their 70-year-old grandmother, because it is something that transcends generations.'

So go on! Dance like a kid. Jump around. And don't give a stuff how you look.

The moment of truth

If I can't inspire you to move after telling you I was once an unfit mum and am now a marathoner, then I know a story you won't be able to ignore and that still inspires me profoundly.

New Zealand radio newsreader **Niva Retimanu** is famous and multi-award-winning for her incredible voice on the radio. She's also a friend of mine, she was a yoga student in my classes for several years, and her journey from unfit to fit will astonish you. This girl has been through it all.

As Niva sits in my kitchen ready for this interview, she tells me, 'We can't start the interview yet. I'm missing something!' She then dives into her handbag, pulls out a bright red lippy and sweeps it over her lips. 'I talk better when I have lipstick on,' she quips, then erupts into laughter.

I love Niva's laugh. It uplifts my heart. It's loud, and all her friends tease her that we can hear her laughter miles away. We always know if she is close because we can hear her – often before we see her. That's Niva, always roaring with laughter, louder than a lion.

Niva is a friend who 'gets' me. And when a girlfriend gets you, they're gold. When we get together for a chat, it is actually a 'talkathon', usually at one of our favourite cafés in Mt Eden Village, near where we both live. She's one of the few people I know who can out-talk me. Just.

I often forget Niva has celebrity status. To me, she's my mate who laughs loud, wears large hoop earrings and loves loud lippy. Niva loves all her friends fiercely. She's one of those people who peels the layers off you,

'The moment of denial had stopped. I could hear my raspy breath, and I thought, "If I carry on like this, it's not going to be good.'

like an onion, until she finds the real you. She's real and authentic, and she cuts through anyone's crap. Niva is what I call a glue-girl. Everyone loves her. She's friends with everyone, and she can bring diverse friends together in the same room.

As we sit in my kitchen, my British Blue cat, Hermione, does crazy somersaults on a clothes rack. We laugh. Then Niva starts to tell me her story.

I encourage her to share her real journey, from how really hard it was to how really awesome she is now.

'Don't worry, girlfriend, I'll have you crying in no time!' she quips, then unleashes that infectious laughter again.

'Oh, crap. You're gonna have me in tears for sure,' I say. 'Actually, wait a minute, then, until I get my lippy on too.'

I ask Niva to start by telling me what inspired her to transform.

'I call this the moment of truth. I remember when I decided to go from being fat to fit,' she says frankly.

It was on a day in spring when she had that moment of truth that shocked her into action. She explains: 'I reached a point of no return, really. That moment was when I bent down to tie up my shoelaces. I could barely see my feet, and my stomach was piled over. Something as simple as that, while I was getting ready to go to work …

'I was in floods of tears. I was by myself, and the flood of tears came. It was an amazing release for me. It was sad but also a release. The moment of denial had stopped. I could hear my raspy breath, and I thought, "If I carry on like this, it's not going to be good."

'I thought, "I've lost two parents, and if I continue going down this road – living on takeaways, smoking, doing no exercise and drinking – I'm going to

"I've lost two parents, and if I continue going down this road – living on takeaways, smoking, doing no exercise and drinking – I'm going to be six feet under." That's what hit me. It was life versus death.

be six feet under." That's what hit me. It was life versus death. For me, it was never about looking beautiful or to get back to a smaller size. My decision to change was about life versus death.

'I decided enough was enough. If I'm going to be brutally honest, I had hit a really dark, dark stage in my life and I was depressed but probably didn't know it. I didn't like myself. I was big, and I couldn't fit my clothes. I was in denial, and I didn't know anything about healthy eating. I was living off takeaways and was very lazy. I didn't do any form of exercise. I was a heavy smoker at the time. I was having over a packet of cigarettes a day, and I was drinking alcohol, and that was getting out of control.

'At the basis of that depression was the loss of my parents. I hadn't dealt with the losses at that time. That's when I thought, "I've got so many issues, so many problems." At the same time, with all of this happening, I was also dealt some news. I learned I had two uteruses, one kidney and two bladders. That wasn't a death sentence, but it was something unusual that I didn't have my parents to talk to about. Now, I feel special because of this. But at the time, I thought, "Oh my God, I'm a freak of nature. I'm not dealing with anything."

'I had been in denial for a long time, even though clothes couldn't fit me. What hurt me the most was that as a baby, child, a teenager and in my 20s, I was actually quite slim. I was always size 12 to 14. I was never obese back then. But the weight exploded over my 30s to 40s. That was the decade. I knew what I looked like before, then I came to this.

'I was depressed, and that whole dark cloud was over me. I hadn't actually seen how bad I was. Even though I couldn't fit clothes, I didn't look at myself in the mirror. So I was doing everything I possibly could to stay in denial.'

Niva says she would buy size 22 shirts and take the labels off but never really considered how she looked. It was all about avoidance over that decade of the downward spiral.

Another thing that sparked her change was seeing others struggling with health issues. She wanted to be a positive role model, particularly for others in her culture, she explains.

'I'm a Pacific Islander, and it doesn't take a rocket scientist to know the statistics. Also, with being in the media, I thought, "Who am I to judge others? I'm supposed to be a role model as a newsreader."

'I'm a newsreader in the mainstream, and I thought, "I need to get my shit together." And even though I don't have my own children, I have lots of nieces and nephews. I wanted to be active with them.'

Niva decided to prioritise her health that spring day. Once she made that decision, she did not know where to start. So she went to her local doctor to ask for help.

'I told the doctor, "I've got all these issues, and I don't know what to do. What do I deal with first?"'

The doctor advised her to start by quitting smoking – the most serious issue first.

'I was terrified if I did this that I would put on weight. But she said, "You have to stop the smoking, and then we'll deal with the obesity."'

It was then that Niva knew she had to quit seeing some friends who liked to party – at least for a while. She knew if she drank alcohol then this would lead to smoking. And then her life would spiral further out of control.

'So I quit my social life. I thought, "That has to go first." I made an announcement to my friends. They were gutted, because I was their free entertainment,' she says, chuckling.

What kept Niva on track was thinking of that shoelace moment, that moment of truth. And also remembering the loss of her parents – her dad from cancer and her mum from heart disease – at such a young age. She decided to adopt what she dubs 'a steely determination'.

After stopping the binge drinking, eating and smoking, Niva was ready to try to exercise. She was also seeing a counsellor to heal some of her sadness. She needed to heal unresolved grief from the loss of her beloved parents. She needed to accept she was an orphan now, she says. The counsellor helped her to accept what had happened and move on.

Next on her journey, boot camp beckoned. 'That was scariest part – turning up to that boot camp. I was worried I would be the only one over 100kg and unfit. I didn't like my body. I couldn't fit any of the gear. I lacked confidence. I had a fear of going to gyms. I couldn't fit any clothes. I purchased XXXL clothes. I wore black, because it was slimming, from head to toe, and I looked like a burglar!' she says, laughing her beautiful, bold laugh.

Niva drove 30 minutes to attend a boot camp with other Pacific Islanders, where she felt comfortable. 'I knew I would be with other big people, so I would blend in. Here, I could see others that could feel my pain. There were others who were overweight and smokers too.

'The boot camp got me out of bed in the mornings. This helped with the non-drinking, because I couldn't have got out of bed if I was drinking.'

Niva found the boot camp a battle. Her words: 'Bloody horrible.' She had aching muscles that had laid dormant for years. But being out in the fresh air helped her. She noticed after a few weeks that she could breathe more easily, after smoking for 25 years. Gone were the huffing and puffing and laboured, loud breathing.

Niva says her goal started small. 'My short-term goal was to get up and go and survive the day and see if I could get up tomorrow. My goals have always been simple, and that has been a key to my success. Living for that day and just for that day. The bigger picture ... I just couldn't think too far ahead.

'It was a slow process, and that's how I got through it. I never tried to do all five or six problems at once. I did it over a six-year period. You do have to be patient through this process. You have to be ready. You can't tell someone to change – they have to find their time to change.'

Niva says it was not until her 40s that 'the penny dropped. I finally got it.' That was when she had her moment of truth and was ready to transform. No one could have persuaded her to change before that time. 'I thought, "One day, I won't be able to tie those laces," and that was it.'

After two years of boot camp, Niva needed a fresh challenge. She knew the importance, by this time, of setting fresh goals. Next on her health journey was learning to run. Niva was inspired to run by a famous friend on radio, **Kerre McIvor** (then Woodham), author of **Short Fat Chick to Marathon Runner**.

I interviewed Kerre for a magazine article when she wrote that book. It's as inspiring as Niva says. Kerre has inspired thousands of women and men to run from scratch. I've been lucky enough to do several events with her since, and she continues to be an inspirational runner.

'I thought, "If Kerre McIvor can do it, then I can do it!"' says Niva, chuckling. 'If someone can run and they're short and fat, then there's a chance for me.'

So Niva started walking, then jogged, and finally started to run. She has since conquered lots of marathons throughout New Zealand, Rome, Chicago, New York and Beirut, to name some. Running doesn't come easy to her, she says, then jokes, 'I run because I'm not good at anything else.'

She has literally come last at some events and taken up to eight hours to finish some marathons. But her journey has inspired many to become fitter, healthier and happier. She's a run legend now, just like Kerre. In Niva's book **Leading from Behind**, which was released in 2016, she shares her health journey and adventures. This book has inspired many couch potatoes to change their habits, and she's proud.

Niva says her most important life change came last. This was learning about nutrition. Learning about the health benefits, or hidden sugars, of some foods was a revelation, she says. This knowledge is now something that's second nature and informs all her food choices. She doesn't always make perfect choices, she says. But she knows now that she can have some bad days but choose to get back on track again.

Over the years, Niva has lost 30kg. She says every time she runs a marathon, she thinks about how far she has come. Not just the miles of the race. But how far she has come on her life journey. Every marathon reminds her of that 'moment of truth', and she remembers her beloved parents too. She used that pain to propel her life forwards. You can too.

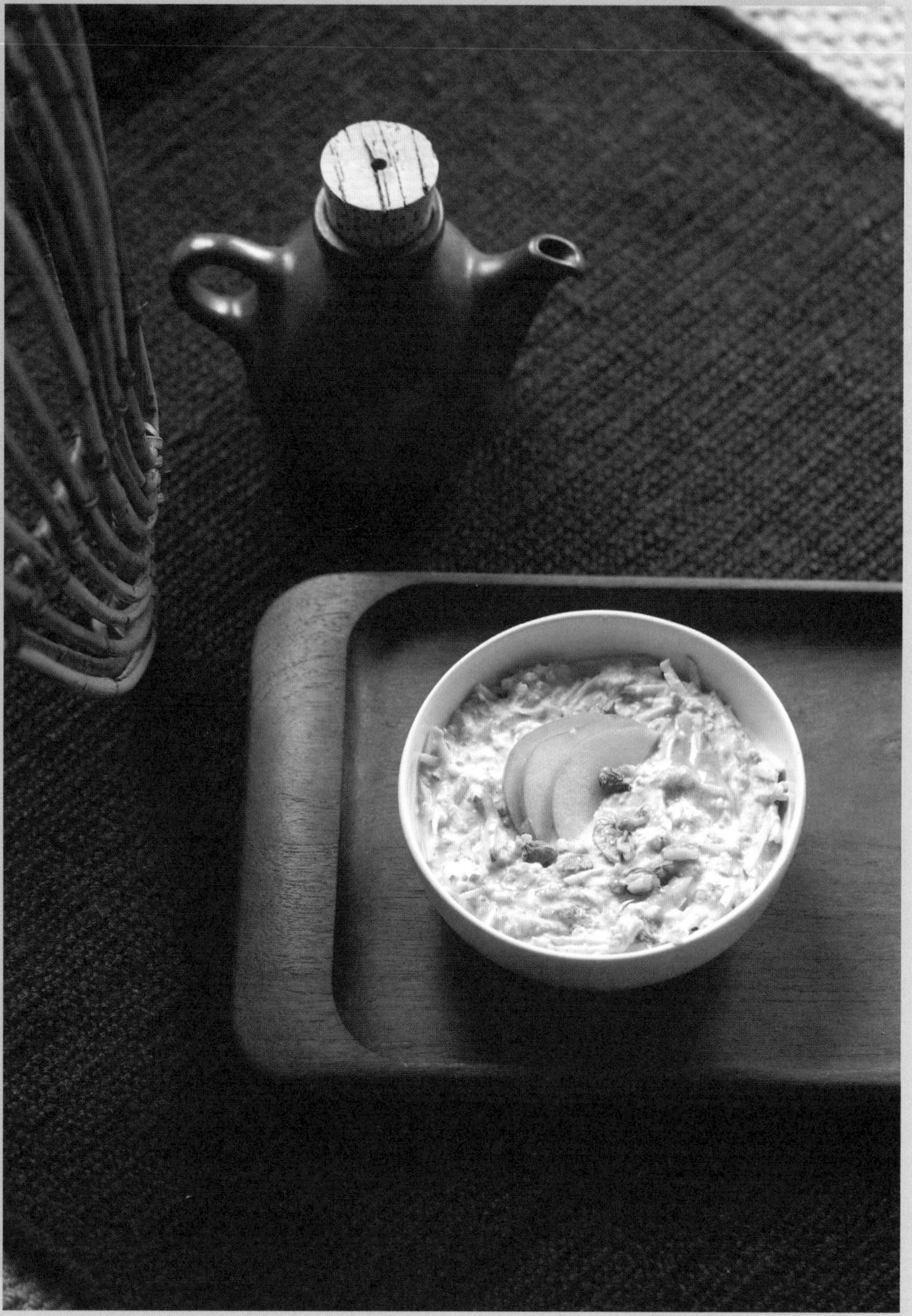

Breakfast Bliss+

Breakfast is the first opportunity in the day to fuel your body well. It's my favourite meal. I'll often have a smoothie bowl with granola on top, or slices of avocado on buttered ciabatta toast (just add lemon, salt, pepper and chilli flakes). When I have time, it's scrambled eggs, salmon and lots of salad - which is a great way to inject greens into the start of the day. The latter option keeps me full for a long time too, which is a bonus. Here are some other favourite breakfast recipes I love to make.

Gluten-free Coconut Pancakes

Coconuts are such a favourite in my household, and in this recipe, they show up in one of the flours that I use as well as the cooking oil I like using. Did you know coconut can be good for the outside of the skin? Coconut oil can be used as a moisturiser. Use it too to bring shine and lustre to your dry hair. It can be used as a make-up remover and also for cooking and baking, of course. Unheated, I love using it in bliss balls. Yeah, I'm personally in love with the coconut flavour.

I also have fond memories of being on holiday in Fiji, where the beautiful islands are covered in tall, swaying, green coconut trees. The beautiful local boys taught my kids once how to retrieve and open up coconuts – to drink the coconut juice and eat the coconut flesh. The locals shared their time and skills and connected with my kids, which was heartfelt. That's the ultimate way to share food: pausing and savouring the moment, and sharing it with new or old friends. Time and connection with others are the most precious gifts.

1 cup **rice flour**

½ cup **coconut flour**

½ cup **chickpea flour**

¾ cup **organic coconut sugar**

2 tsp **baking powder**

pinch of **salt**

3 **eggs**

2 cups **milk** (any milk you choose)

Sift the dry ingredients into a bowl. Then add the eggs and milk. Blend all ingredients until you have a smooth mixture. To cook, turn the cooktop on to a medium heat. Melt generous amounts of coconut oil in a frying pan. Then pour a spoonful at a time of mixture into the pan to make small pancakes. Wait until each pancake bubbles in the middle and then turn over. Cook until lightly brown.

These are topped with coconut yoghurt, strawberries, honey and bee pollen. But choose whatever topping you love which is seasonal and at hand! My kids will top them sometimes with maple syrup or golden syrup.

Tip: Keep adding more milk to the mixture for a really smooth consistency and to make the portions go further, if you wish.

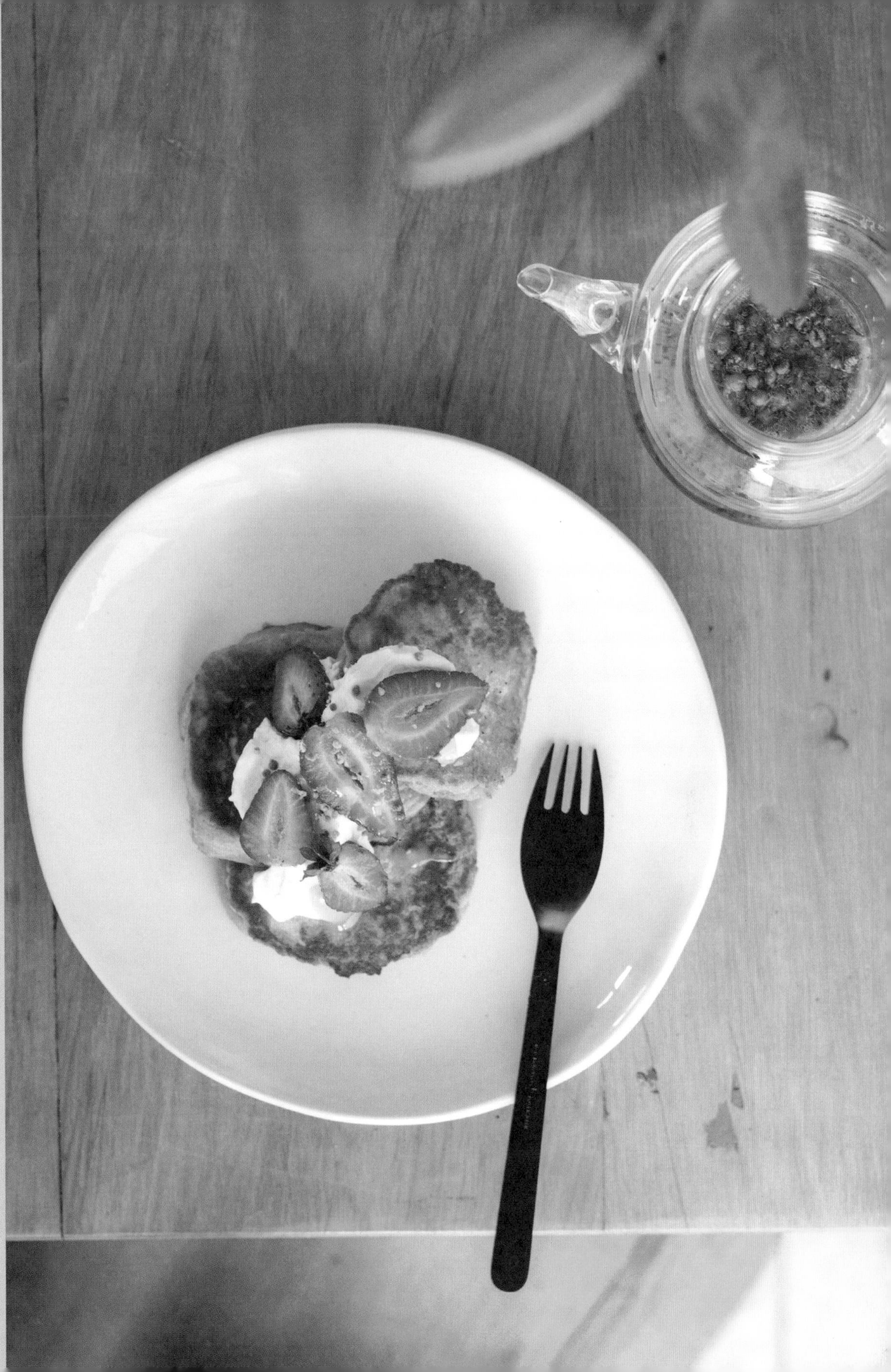

Power
Your Day
Porridge

Porridge is a favourite breakfast of mine. Pair it with fruit, such as blueberries, and some yoghurt. This can power my running well. This gluten-free porridge is creamy and yum. Use this as a base and then change up the toppings daily to vary your nutrient intake. I love the creamy flavour and spice of cinnamon.

½ cup **amaranth flakes**

½ cup **cashew milk** (to make this, I soak ¼ cup of cashews for two to three hours, drain the water, add enough new water to make up ½ cup of cashew liquid, and blitz it in a blender until smooth)

½ cup **coconut cream**
(or use normal cream if you prefer)

½ tsp **cinnamon**

1 tbsp **fine coconut**

Place all the ingredients into a pan and heat until warm and smooth. Place in a bowl and top with whatever your heart desires. This one was topped with coconut yoghurt, sliced pear, a drizzle of maple syrup and some roughly chopped pistachios. But other days I'd choose toppings of blueberries and cream, or whatever seasonal fruit I have in the kitchen bowl. Another favourite topping is grated apple, shaved coconut and nut milk.

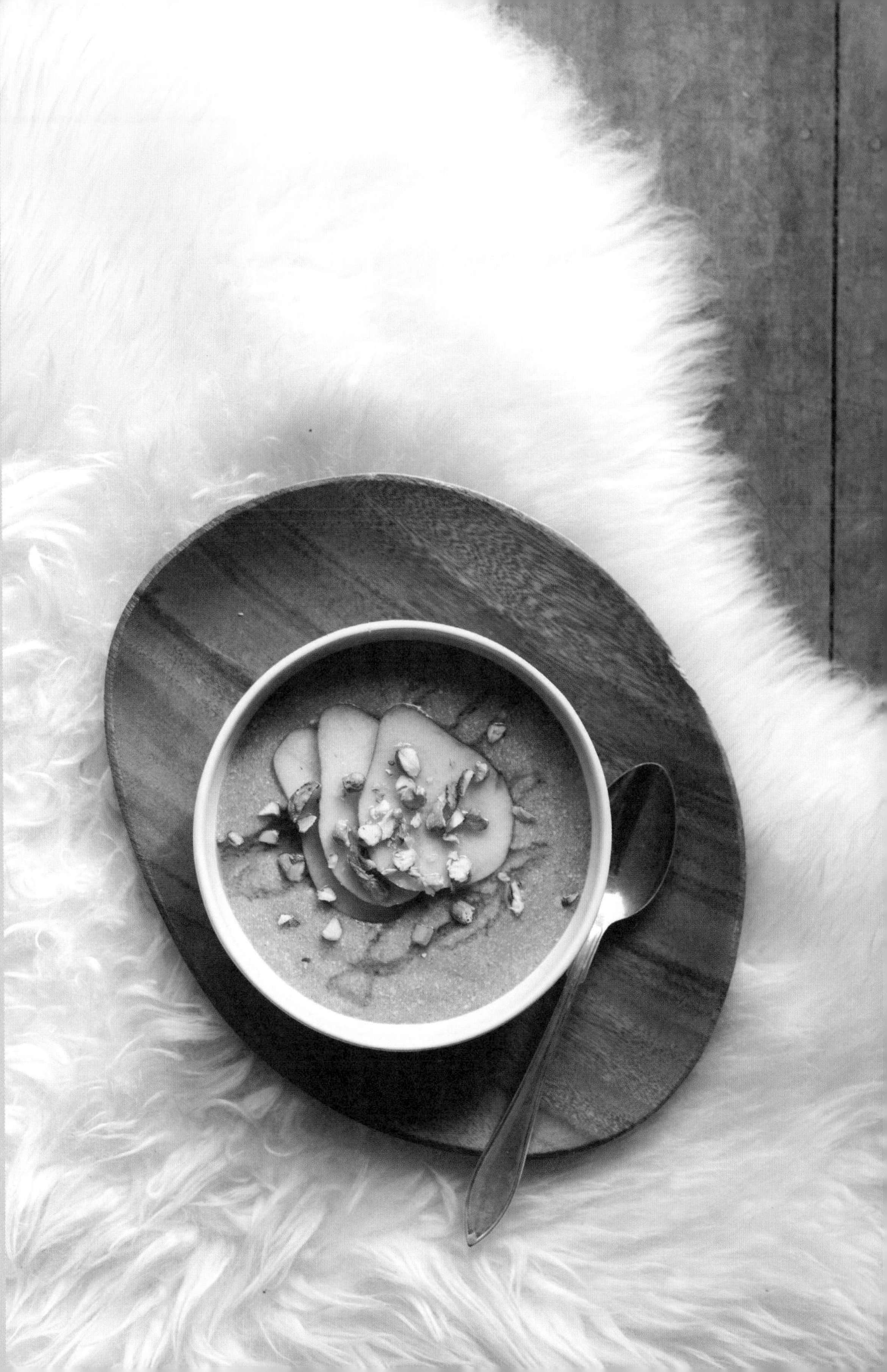

Ginger Coconut and Nut Muesli

I love muesli for breakfast. I even reach for it sometimes as a snack if I'm ravenous around that mid-afternoon time. It can save me from hitting those sugary snacks. I usually pair this muesli with yoghurt and either blueberries or raspberries. Or here I have it with cashew milk and fresh strawberries. The nuts I've used here can be changed up; for example, if you love cashew nuts then use more of those and less walnuts. I love the strong coconut taste in this recipe and there's enough ginger to give it just a subtle flavour.

1 cup **pumpkin seeds**

250g **coconut chips**

1 cup **sliced almonds**

½ cup **raw walnuts**

½ cup **raw cashews**

½ cup **black chia seeds**

2 tsp **cinnamon**

3 tbsp **coconut oil**

2 tbsp **rice malt syrup**

3 tbsp **freshly grated ginger**

Put all the ingredients on a lined oven tray and mix together using your hands. Bake at 130°C for 20 minutes (until the coconut goes crunchy). Remove from the oven and leave to cool. Then store the muesli in glass jars, place a ribbon on the top and gift it to someone you love (with a smile). Or keep it and scoff it yourself.

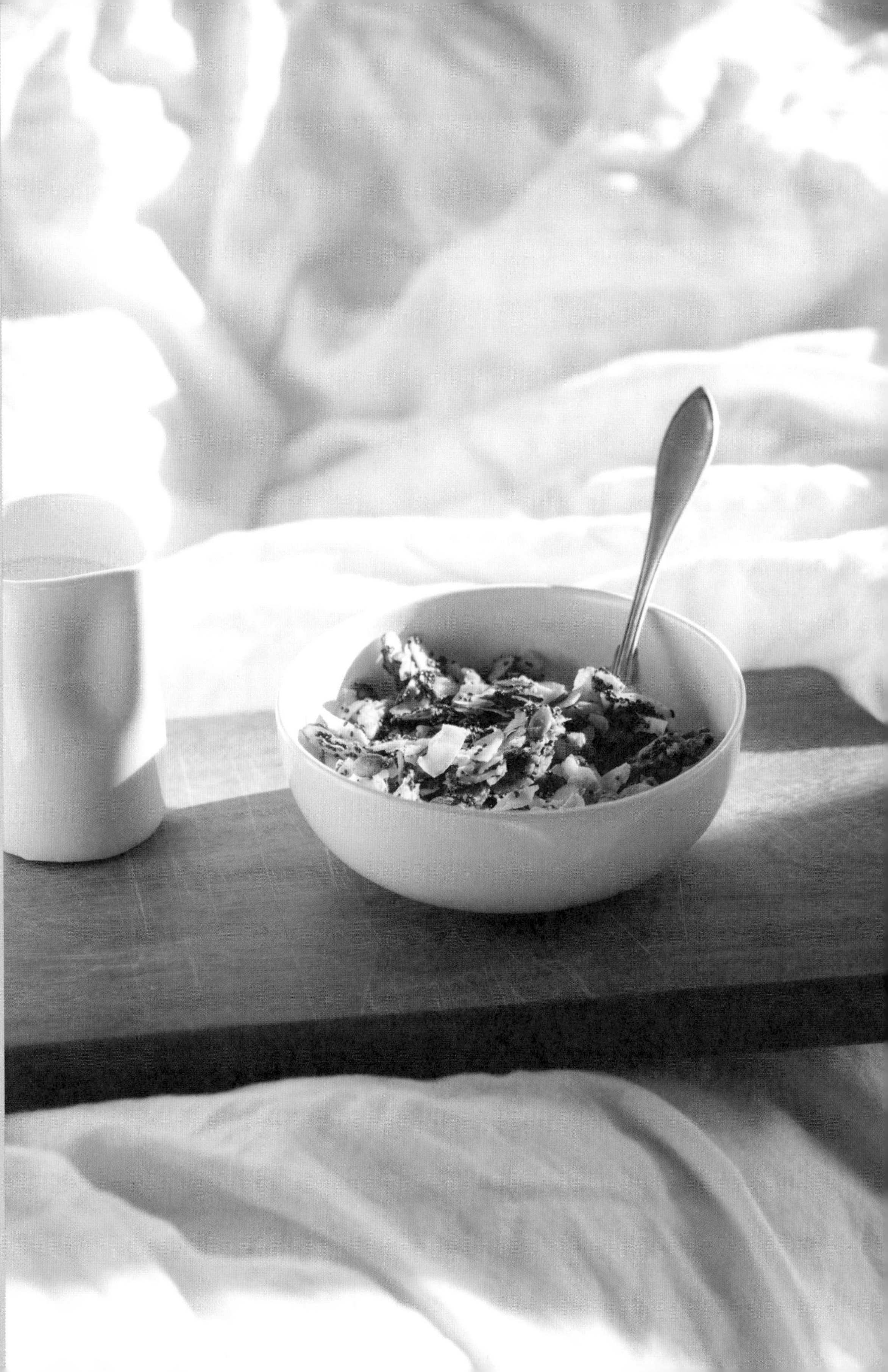

Bircher Muesli

This is a go-to for me to power my day. I've had it before I've run a few of my marathons. I love Bircher. There are so many flavours in this and it gives me awesome energy.

½ cup **wholegrain oats**

½ cup **coconut cream**

½ cup **water**

1 tsp **mānuka honey**

2 tbsp **sultanas**

½ tsp **cinnamon**

1 small grated **green apple**

1 tbsp fine **coconut**

Put all the ingredients in a jar and then place in the fridge overnight to soak. The oats grow overnight, and they are delicious to eat in the morning. It's also a quick breakfast to have in the morning because it is already made and ready to go. Perfect for being on the run. Literally.

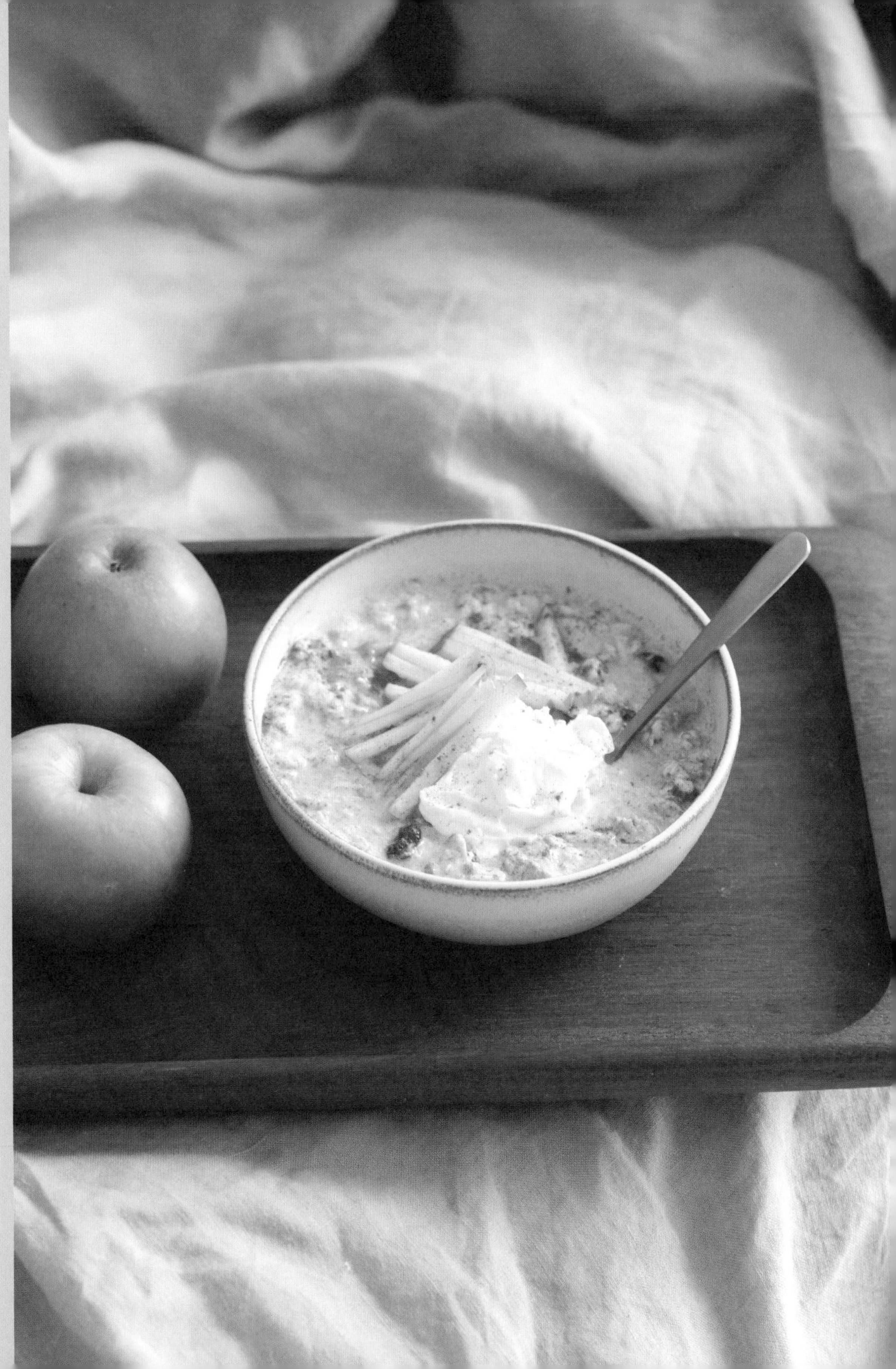

Building resilience and happiness+

Don't let the rotten, tough and ugly times define you or drag you down.

If you slip up or stuff up, embrace your vulnerabilities. Carry on. Be resilient. Also, have people around you who give a stuff about your success. And seek help if you need it.

We can all fall down in life. Often. If not physically, then at least mentally. We can lose our jobs. Miss out on promotions. Get sick. Lose loved ones. Feel emotionally bruised.

Life is a rollercoaster; it's full of ups and downs. It can be easy to go into shock when tough things happen, give up, be afraid to carry on and feel helpless. But if you can pick yourself up quickly and carry on, or find another way forwards, you'll thrive. Resilience is crucial to our happiness levels and wellbeing.

The word 'resilience' makes me think of my youngest son, Finn, when he was aged six and doing his school cross country. He fell over at the very start of the event on a muddy, freezing winter field. The right side of his face, body and leg were muddy. But, mostly, he was mortified.

He looked up to hundreds of spectators. Everyone could sense his gut-wrenching distress. The next few moments felt like minutes. Finn froze on the spot. You could see him gazing at all the other kids, now far ahead.

You could sense he felt like giving up. You know that raw feeling that you've lost before you've even started?

At that moment, Finn's brother Lachie, then aged 10, stopped being a spectator on the sidelines. He raced across the field to help. He told Finn, 'Don't give up!' Lachie promised to run with him. With that support, Finn decided to run, and the crowd cheered loudly. At the finish line, the two boys got the loudest cheers. Finn finished second to last, smiling.

He finished, and I'm so proud.

It was also a valuable lesson he learned that day in how to get up when you fall down. You get up, with support if you can, and carry on.

Next time you feel paralysed by failure, pick yourself up and carry on with a smile — like my kid did. Also, think of someone you can help today like a brother might. It might propel them forwards. Oh, for the record, my kids aren't always perfect or always happy siblings. But I celebrated the power of that magical moment, like any parent should.

In this life, you have to choose to be resilient. I use the word 'choose' on purpose. You need to choose to rise up and focus on positivity. Choose to look at a new way ahead. Don't choose to freeze and go into woe-is-me mode. Focus on forging ahead in a new direction.

None of us are robots. We all freeze and feel sorry for ourselves on occasion. We all mentally fall down. But the quicker you can pick yourself up, the better.

If we choose to interpret adversity as something that is temporary, then we can look at lifting ourselves up. Life is not linear; there are bumps and ups and downs along the way. Life is a rollercoaster, remember. But the downs can help you to appreciate the ups.

If you can find that positive pathway forwards, then you can learn, grow and flourish from your struggles. Rise up. Let those learnings bring layers, understanding and a richness to who you are. After all, who likes to be around someone who is bitter, twisted and stuck on a downward spiral all the time?

A term for rising up is 'adversarial growth'. Ultimately, you get to choose how you live every moment of every day. You don't get to choose what happens to you sometimes, no way. But you always get to choose how you respond and experience all those ups and downs. Just don't stay too long on the dips of your own rollercoaster ride.

Master your mindset. Make your life unfold in the fashion you work hard at weaving.

I've been personally working on this. A lot. I used to be terrible at it. I'm not perfect at it, and some things still tick me off or wound me deeply, and I stay too long on those rollercoaster dips. But I'm increasingly choosing to be less of a victim and instead focus on the good in life and ignore the stuff that doesn't serve me.

It's okay to feel down some days, that's normal. But when you can never see the positive in anything, it becomes soul-destroying and self-fulfilling.

This more positive pathway is making my life richer. After all, you can become twisted and tortured by tough times and let them freeze your life in misery and pain. Or you can seek out the

> Master your mindset. Make your life unfold in the fashion you work hard at weaving.

good, the light and the kindness and not only bounce back but actually propel yourself forwards. I promise you that rewiring your outlook on the world to make it a happier one will be the best thing you can do.

Adversity helps us to reach our greatness. Failures are just part of the process. And everyone goes through a truckload of failures on this life journey. Life in general, school, work, business, friendships, marriage, kids, every kind of relationship you have will never entirely be plain sailing.

When it comes to kids, let them start learning life's hard lessons early on. They need to be strong and independent. It will be one of the best things you can teach them.

I'm actively teaching my youngest son at the moment that it is okay to fail. Trying your best is what really matters. Trying, trying and then trying again is how you learn and think of new ways to expand your thoughts and views.

For me, being more positive doesn't mean I'm a tree-hugging hippie, some kind of 'yes' robot or, worse, a walkover. It just means I'm trying to practise patience, tolerance and all that stuff better. I think we could all do with more tolerance and seeing things from another point of view.

One of my biggest battles through a big portion of my life was letting people hurt me. I've become more assertive. I had let other people hold onto the lever of my happiness for far too long. I think I stood still, frozen by sadness, unkindness and bitterness a lot. What a waste of energy and time, looking back. I can now better catch my thoughts before they cascade down into a destructive path. I also don't focus on conjuring up catastrophes like I used to. I no longer focus on what-ifs but rather on what is actually real.

I think we should be teaching kids more skills around emotional intelligence earlier on. I wish I had strengthened these skills while younger. Intelligence is something we focus on at schools, but I think emotional intelligence is crucial also. Why do we care more about maths then a healthy mindset? This is madness. And, yeah, maybe the hard times in life

> **Hatred kills creativity and doesn't help you to lift your life up and forge ahead. So don't let terrible times cripple you from feeling free and happy. Just choose to move on.**

that we all go through are a lot harder because we don't have these skills embedded.

Pause for a moment and consider whether you are personally holding on to hatred or hard times in your life. Please acknowledge these thoughts and then be kind to yourself.

Hatred kills creativity and doesn't help you to lift your life up and forge ahead. So don't let terrible times cripple you from feeling free and happy. Just choose to move on.

Energy flows where energy goes. So I try and focus my energy on good people, good thoughts and good actions. Again, I'm far from perfect, and I will trip up now and again. But at least I'm more mindfully aware than I used to be and working hard on this.

Sitting in a local café the other day, I was reminded how you can work yourself up into a cycle of hatred. I was sitting near a girl in her 20s who was droning on and on about someone she had 'blacklisted'. I had to eventually move and sit at the other end of the café. Her toxic words were unrelenting and dragging me down. She was corroding my insides, and my anxiety levels were skyrocketing. As she spat out more and more words of hatred, she got uglier and uglier.

I wanted to walk over to her, hug her and then shake her. I wanted to tell her to focus on building her own life up, not tearing others down. But then I remembered she was young, she was just learning. I felt relief I was no longer that girl and paralysed by a washing-machine-like cycle of hatred that went around and around and around.

Happiness has a bad reputation

Robert Isler is the President of the New Zealand Association of Positive Psychology and an Associate Professor at the School of Psychology at the University of Waikato.

He says when people experience trauma, it can go two ways. Some people feel defeated and down, while others can realise how to improve things.

He says working on professional and personal development can help strengthen anyone's resilience.

'About 40% of resilience comes down to a genetic component, while 60% is up to individuals to create a good and happy lifestyle. It's all about the way people perceive and appraise situations and ultimately think about them,' he explains.

This brings him to cognitive behavioural therapy (CBT), which is an evidence-based practice for improving mental health. It focuses on developing personal coping strategies to deal with unhelpful thought patterns, behaviours and attitudes. It helps with ways to change how we self-regulate when we become emotional.

'CBT is about being critical of your own thinking, because very often it is not helpful and can even make you mentally unwell and lead you down the wrong pathway,' says Robert. 'Many people think themselves sick.'

'Flow is when you are completely immersed in a situation, in the moment, that you are completely focused on. There's no mind-wandering, you're just totally happy with what you are doing.'

He recommends that people put time into consciously creating 'positive emotions'.

'Create three positive thoughts for every negative emotion. The advice is that negative emotions come for free. You don't need to put effort in for these. So putting triple the effort into positivity for every negative emotion will "broaden and build" your cognitive processes and help you see the bigger picture, according to positive psychologist **Barbara Fredrickson**.'

Another way to feel happier is to find 'flow', which is a state of heightened focus and immersion in activities that bring about happiness, he says.

Positive psychologist **Mihaly Csikszentmihalyi** has contributed pioneering work around this term and sees flow as the secret to a life worth living. It's a way to find authentic happiness.

I ask Robert to explain that term, 'flow', further. He says, 'Flow is when you are completely immersed in a situation, in the moment, that you are completely focused on. There's no mind-wandering, you're just totally happy with what you are doing. You have lots of ideas to keep going and do the best you can do at that task.'

I tell Robert I find flow through running. I now have a strong skill set in this, and it's while running that I feel lost in the moment, lost in the act of 'doing'. When I'm running, I feel an incredible reset in my body and mind. I'm on a natural buzz too at this time, created by endorphins, the body's own morphine!

You can find flow through activities like work, play, music and art, to name some things.

Robert says resilience is strengthened by 'living in the present'.

'Resilient people don't worry about the past, realising that's gone and you can't change it, and they don't worry too much about envisaged future events, because they might be an illusion and not eventuate.

'The only real thing is the present moment. If people can learn to consciously focus on the present moment in a non-judgemental way [being mindful], then this goes a long way to combat negative emotions like anxiety, stress and depression,' he says.

Mindfulness is an evidence-based tool that helps people to become more aware of how they think, feel and act. They can then acknowledge unhelpful thoughts and calmly accept them without being influenced by them. So, rather than reacting on impulse and intrusive, negative thoughts, you can learn how to respond more mindfully.

Robert says being mindful is an important skill to work on. 'It's about becoming aware that every situation can change at any moment, which should create optimism and hope. This is exactly what depressed people are lacking – hope in the future. Everything looks bleak and dark,' he says.

He explains that the founder of positive psychology, Martin Seligman, used the term 'learned helplessness' for those people who get in a situation where they lose control, become helpless and feel they can't do anything to get out of that situation. The good news is that optimism can also be learned – counteracting learned helplessness. Martin is behind what's called the PERMA model, a scientific theory of happiness.

PERMA stands for:

P **POSITIVE EMOTIONS**
Being optimistic and positive leads to creativity, perseverance and thinking broadly to see alternative solutions.

E **ENGAGEMENT**
Being engaged in activities like learning an instrument or doing a sport, so we are immersed in the task and flow, stretches our skills, emotions and intelligence and increases happiness.

R **RELATIONSHIPS**
We need to connect with others to feel happy and supported during tough times.

M **MEANING**
Purpose helps to give us fulfilment and life satisfaction.

A **ACCOMPLISHMENTS**
Goals drive us to thrive.

Robert says good-quality sleep, exercise and good food are prerequisites of PERMA. He adds that doing things like watching a lot of negative TV in a passive way can pull people further away from achieving PERMA components. However, negative emotions can also keep you 'down to earth'. It's just that positive emotions help us to move forward better.

'What about stress?' I ask. He says, 'Acute stress can be good if you make it your "friend" and use it to do important things that give you a sense of achievement. Stress can inspire you to get somewhere. It's only a problem if you let stress become chronic and overwhelm you.

'Positive and negative emotions can have a direct effect on your genes. They can switch health-related genes on or off. The field of epigenetics is looking at interactions between the environment, psychology and your gene expressions,' he adds.

Stress can inspire you to get somewhere. It's only a problem if you let stress become chronic and overwhelm you.

He points to research by US scientists Elizabeth Blackburn and Elissa Epel, who have found that it's possible things like stress can influence how we age at a cellular level.

This is to do with our telomeres – the structures at the end of chromosomes in the DNA which keep them protected. In a nutshell, the shorter your telomeres, the more at risk you are of illness and other diseases. Being happier, healthier and less stressed can be linked to longer telomeres.

'When you are stressed, those protectors [telomeres] can get shortened and the DNA is more vulnerable for problems. Ageing decreases the length of telomeres. Stress and bad experiences and trauma can have a direct effect on those biological markers,' Robert explains.

He says doing things like practising mindfulness can help telomeres to lengthen. 'There's evidence that good health, lifestyle and happiness have a huge effect on the biology of your body.'

Robert is passionate about educating children on the true effects of a positive lifestyle, based on kindness and compassion for themselves and others. He wants people to be more armed with knowledge and practical skills for creating a good and healthy lifestyle to help them flourish.

It seems that the high school curriculum needs more than the traditional subjects like maths, history, English and science. Teenagers could do with some help when it comes to positive psychology – learning things like better impulse control and how to relate to other people and be kind, compassionate and empathic to themselves and others. These are things that will help them navigate through a socially more and more complex world.

Robert says changing habits is, however, easier said than done.

'When you build a habit over many years, it is what comes easy. Changing a habit is very hard, and you often slip back to the old habit. It's all about building resources and changing your mindset,' he says.

He gives an example of this. 'Most people know that exercise is good for you, and there are lots of positives that come with it. But motivation can be tough. When you really hate doing exercise, there's almost no chance that you will keep doing it. There needs to be a mental change.

'For example, people generally don't want to walk for half an hour per day, and they think it is boring or simply too hard to build into their daily routines. But if they have a dog that enjoys going for a walk and expresses this vividly, then suddenly walking is a much more appealing proposition.

'Regarding diets, you need to see the bigger picture, the good things in changing eating habits, and not just focus on losing weight. Because by itself, eating less is no fun and not a good reason for doing it,' he explains.

He also talks about there being a huge difference between pleasure, on the one hand, and meaning and engagement, on the other.

'If people just want to have instant gratification and pleasure, then that can have negative psychological effects if they don't also have meaning, engagement and accomplishment in their lives.'

He adds that short-term pleasure can be fun, 'but there's no future for that'. He views this as 'Hollywood happiness'.

'If you consider meaning and engagement as being a cake, then pleasure would be icing on the cake. It can look quite beautiful, but icing by itself on a plate will look ridiculous. Sensation-seeking as a form of instant gratification is not healthy either and can also be risky,' he says. 'Just consider speeding and dangerous overtaking when driving.'

Robert reckons people shouldn't be seeking happiness but should instead create an environment that is likely to foster contentment and wellbeing.

'So, again, sleep and eat well, do exercise, create meaning and engagement in what you do and celebrate accomplishments and having good relationships and good networks. That's what it's all about.'

Be raw, real and among soul sisters

'I've cried three times alone in my office at work.'

This is how **Theresa Gattung** began her speech at the worldwomen17 conference in New Zealand in 2017. There were 500 women in the audience, including me. Her speech started the same way it ended – with 1000 hands together in a thunderous applause. There was even a standing ovation at the end.

The conference was held by Theresa and some friends. The purpose was to share knowledge and wisdom, raise issues and inspire others to create meaningful change on a global scale.

At that conference, I expected Theresa to talk business, but instead she spoke of tears. She revealed how she had become more resilient over the years.

I had always viewed Theresa like some kind of bulletproof businesswoman. To hear her real and raw vulnerability was refreshing. It was a reminder to me that we are all human.

Let me give you some context here. Theresa is one of New Zealand's best-known business personalities. She's the co-founder of My Food Bag (a successful meal-delivery service), but she is well known mostly as the former top boss of a telecommunications company worth billions, formerly known as Telecom but now named Spark.

When I was a girl in school, she was one of the most well-known women in this country for her leadership. I remember the newspaper headlines well. She was New Zealand's first million-dollar woman. This title was given to her for being the first female in this country to earn that mega amount of money for being the head of a top company. Back then, that was a lot of cash to earn in a year for someone high up the business ladder.

She was truly inspirational to me because she came from the same tiny place on the map that I did – Rotorua, a small city in the North Island.

Back then, Theresa wore a business suit and spoke only in a business-like way. She appeared unbreakable – like so many people in power do.

Theresa spoke at the conference about 'the elephant in the room'. The elephant she was talking about was how some women's career paths were blocked by other women. 'You know, the Queen Bee Syndrome,' explained Theresa.

She revealed that during her career she had been reduced to tears thrice – including twice by women.

According to Theresa, the first situation was when a female colleague took her idea and claimed it as her own. Theresa went to her boss about this and was told abruptly: 'Put your big-girl's pants on.' It left her – understandably – in tears.

'I swallowed it and adopted a male way of doing business,' she said.

Another time she cried was over another top-level female colleague who constantly 'tried to make life as difficult as possible'.

'Every week, 10 minutes before an important meeting, this woman would email about things that had "gone horribly wrong" on my watch,' said Theresa.

She spoke about how women can sense the intention of this kind of behaviour, while 'men can miss it'. Theresa knew exactly what was going on.

Theresa then remarked to the room full of women at that conference that when faced with these kinds of situations, we should try not to pull other women down too.

'It's how we are that will shift that energy,' she said.

She had observed that women liked to be liked, in general, while men 'don't worry about that. They just want to be respected.'

She spoke about how it was difficult to have a public profile, be a leader, be respected and be liked. 'I like to be liked, but it doesn't get in the way of what I want to do in the world.'

She encouraged women to be true to themselves, and, on that topic of likeability, she reckoned if you lived from your truest self, 'you will become radiant'. This is important.

She told the conference-goers to try and communicate from 'a heart level'.

After that speech, I interview Theresa for this book. I ask her what she learned through those times of tears. She says she now knows how powerful it is to have a tribe of women around her to help keep her strong and feeling supported. She wishes that women would stand together more, collaborate and help each other to grow stronger.

'Support from another woman or women can be the glue that holds things together,' she says.

She also wants to empower women to walk away from 'toxic situations' if they need to.

'Don't think you can necessarily change this. Sometimes you just have to do something else. You don't have to put up with it. Choose your environment,' she says.

I catch up with Theresa again a few months later at her modern Auckland home, which has lots of glass and a giant swimming pool. She loves to swim every day. It's a powerful daily ritual for her wellbeing. She admits to loving food, and she believes that is her downfall, wellbeing-wise. But she has always kept active with her love of swimming, and she's proud of this wellness ritual, which she never forgets to do. It's how she starts every day.

There's no business suit in sight when we chat. Theresa is in a colourful, feminine outfit with lots of red. She's wearing bright red lipstick and bright red nail polish, which match her red sports car.

Sitting in her bright red chair, with me on a bright green sofa, Theresa talks about how you need positive women in your life to lift you up.

She also opens up about a time that changed her and tested her resilience more than ever. She bravely reveals what helped her to get through this testing time.

As she talks, she strokes her fluffy grey one-eyed cat, Ollie. Her fluffy orange cat, Archie, is by her feet. They were given to her when their owners went to live overseas. (Theresa has a love of animals, and for much of the last decade she has been heavily involved with the Society for the Prevention of Cruelty to Animals (SPCA), including chairing the Wellington SPCA and being on the national board. She helped raise over $1 million for the new Wellington SPCA centre.)

Theresa says it was in February 2016 that her best friend of three decades, Margaret Doucas, died unexpectedly after an operation.

Theresa was devastated and admits, 'I didn't deal with her death well at all.'

It threw her into grief like she had never experienced. She went into the mode of helping and helped to organise the funeral. On reflection, she can see that she 'bottled things up' and didn't process the grief well.

One day, months later, Theresa woke up not feeling like herself.

Theresa spoke at the conference about 'the elephant in the room'. The elephant she was talking about was how some women's career paths were blocked by other women. 'You know, the Queen Bee Syndrome'.

She ended up in hospital. Doctors didn't know whether it was a leg infection or whether she had a heart infection. After five days in hospital, she was mostly better.

Months later, though, Theresa was still not quite herself, and her friend Barbara Garbler recommended a counsellor. Barbara felt Theresa would benefit from processing her grief.

Theresa immediately agreed. She had previously viewed counsellors as something she would never need. She was a strong woman with lots of support and couldn't imagine needing to be on a counsellor's chair getting help.

'It was brilliant. It helped me release a lot of emotion,' says Theresa. 'I cried a lot.'

After three counselling sessions, she felt so much better. Her message is that you can be resilient, but there will be times when you fall down and need help to feel truly better. And Theresa says no one should ever feel bad about going to a counsellor if they need to. She would do it again 'in a heartbeat' if she felt she needed it, she says. She now feels more resilient than ever and learned tools to cope that were really valuable through those sessions. 'I highly recommend it.'

She has also learned to value every precious day she has on the planet. Losing her best friend suddenly has changed her outlook on the world profoundly.

Meals, movement and mindset

Luke Hines is a healthy cook and author based in New South Wales in Australia. He was on the high-profile television show **My Kitchen Rules**. He has a holistic approach that is all about eating nourishing wholefoods.

He reckons to live your best life you need the right synergy between your meals, movement and mindset.

I could have put Luke in the nutrition chapter of this book, because I love the paleo, ketogenic and low-carb recipes from his latest book, **Smart Carbs**. Those chocolate recipes are off-the-scale amazing! But, instead, I chose to put him in this chapter because I felt he had some powerful things to say around mindset. He shares some things that have helped him to be more resilient.

Luke is tall, broad, muscle-bound, tanned and blond and has piercing blue eyes. His eyes are that light blue of a perfect ocean vista, like you might find on a remote Fijian island. Yeah, I won't hold back – the bloke is beautiful. But he's beautiful on the inside too.

I meet him in a café in Auckland for his latest book promotion, and I am inspired by his outlook on the world. I love his openness about how he has learned how to be stronger from within.

He tells me that 2017 wasn't his year. I love one of his Instagram posts on this, which reads, 'I had my own Britney circa 2007 moment, and although I didn't shave my head and go on umbrella attacks, I was pretty damn close.

> 'Don't ever feel like you can't turn things around. I had a jelly belly and an unhealthy mindset. But I'm now back on track and loving myself as I should. I feel confident in my own skin. We all have ups and downs. It's about how many times you get back up.'

'I was struggling. I felt lost, scared and like I was surrounded by darkness. It played havoc with my anxiety and I wasn't loving myself at all. This lead to the over consumption of potato cakes/scallops (the jury's still out on what they're actually named), lack of movement and extra doses of stress hormones, putting my mind and body into havoc.

'Fast forward to now and I got help, made some positive changes and most importantly started believing in myself again when I had stropped. I became my biggest cheerleader instead of being my worst critic.

'Don't ever feel like you can't turn things around. I had a jelly belly and an unhealthy mindset. But I'm now back on track and loving myself as I should. I feel confident in my own skin. We all have ups and downs. It's about how many times you get back up.'

I tell Luke I loved that social media post and ask him what he did to get back that powerful and positive mindset.

'I stepped back. You need to keep boundaries with your boss, colleagues, friends and family so you can protect you. I started turning down opportunities for work. I cleared my calendar.

'I can't emphasis enough how much more you will be motivated if you look after yourself well. I go to the gym, walk every day with my dog on the beach. I also make sure I have a treat daily. I have nutrient-dense wholefood treats that I make.

'I also have technology-free time.'

In other words, Luke learned to slow down and say no to things that didn't serve him well – otherwise, he'd burn out.

He tells me that having a strong mindset and being resilient are as important as getting enough movement and eating the right meals. All these things help you to stay strong and happy.

On that note, I ask him about how he moves and eats in a typical day.

He says he rises at 5am to exercise with his dog on the beach at his home in New South Wales. He has a cooked breakfast like eggs, chilli, avocado — and maybe some carbs if he has trained that morning. This meal keeps him full for a long time and his blood sugar levels, well, level.

A few hours later, he'll have a 'power-up coffee'. This is a double-shot long black with grass-fed butter and coconut oil, which keeps him feeling full 'for a long time'. He then typically has an early dinner of something like lamb curry. This is full of coconut cream, peanut butter and chilli, teamed up with oven-roasted cauliflower. This dinner is high in protein and low in carbs and helps him to feel full.

Being around Luke is uplifting. Reflect on how your mindset, movement and meals philosophy can propel your happiness levels too.

Staying positive through a double whammy: breast cancer and redundancy

Karen McMillan is a bestselling author who has a loyal following for her engaging novels, which often tug at the heartstrings.

It was her non-fiction books that captured my attention when thinking about people to interview for this book. She has tackled some difficult life topics – eating disorders in **Feast or Famine** and facing cancer in **Unbreakable Spirit and Everyday Strength** – all of which had a genesis in the life struggles that have come her way. But through her struggles, she has learned how to build resilience in her own life.

She was diagnosed with breast cancer in 2011. It's a moment she will never forget.

'It's terrible to hear that you have cancer. But I found I had reserves of strength and resilience that I wouldn't have thought were possible.'

'I was lucky to catch my cancer early by being vigilant about my health checks, and going into cancer treatments my prognosis was very positive.'

She believes some of her resilience came from a place of knowledge. 'When I was in my 20s, both my parents had cancer and died young, and I nursed them through their final days with the help of hospice.

'Through that experience, and from writing books on the subject matter, I had a good understanding of not only the medical language around my diagnosis but also the real-life experience of having met so many people who have faced cancer.

'There is always the fear that cancer might be a death sentence, and it was truly devastating to see my parents die at such young ages. But I was lucky to catch my cancer early by being vigilant about my health checks, and going into cancer treatments my prognosis was very positive, whereas from the get-go both Mum and Dad were fighting a losing battle.'

Karen has also drawn strength from the many positive people she has met over the years. So she went into her cancer treatments with clear strategies to help her cope.

She says she deliberately paused after being diagnosed with cancer and then she discussed with her husband how they were going to tackle the time of her cancer treatments.

'It's up to people how private or public they want to be when facing cancer, but I decided that being open with people would be the better way to go for me and also for the people who care about me.

'I actively thought about how people could help me through this time, in many practical ways, to ease my stress. It's easy to try and be stoic and soldier on without help, but I know from life experience that doesn't work very well and can leave you feeling lonely and isolated, on top of the original problem.'

While positivity is important, Karen believes it is more important to keep things real but to employ strategies for the days you feel down too.

'Of course, being positive in any crisis is going to be a much better space to be in than being negative, but it would be pathological to be constantly happy when you are experiencing something scary and life-changing like cancer.

'I think it is more important to feel whatever you feel but look at strategies to pull yourself out of a dark hole when you need to.

'It's okay to have a good cry when you feel the need. But you should be kind to yourself and allow people to help you during your time of crisis. And you need to take advantage of the many things for you to boost your spirits on a difficult day.

'When I was battling cancer, I found that simple things like sitting in the sun and short walks on the beach in the fresh air boosted my spirits.

'I tried as best as I could to eat food that was nutritious, as there are plenty of studies that show that eating healthy food not only fuels the body but also improves your mood.

'I didn't do as much exercise as I should have because I was too exhausted, but when I did manage a little bit it helped me feel stronger in body and spirit.'

Karen says she was very fortunate that she could draw on the strength of friends and family and was able to talk about what she was going through with them.

'It's amazing that the simple act of talking makes such a difference, but in my case, it helped how I felt emotionally about the situation.

'I delegated as much of my normal life to-do list to trusted people, and that enabled me to have some pamper time. Just reading a book or listening to music was a balm for my soul – and having a cuddle with our cat was a great tonic too!'

For the first time in her life, Karen kept an occasional journal when she was going through her treatments, and she believes it helped to put her thoughts down on to paper. And a huge thing for her was planning for when the treatments were going to be over. Of course, not everyone has a good prognosis when facing cancer, but she was in the fortunate position of being able to plan an overseas trip with her husband for the following year.

They got advice from her doctor about what was realistic and then set about planning. 'Having that trip to look forward to made a massive boost to my wellbeing.'

Even though the treatments for cancer are much better than they used to be, Karen says they are still tough. She doesn't want to scare people, but she says, 'You do have days where you feel very ill and exhausted and down in the dumps, and you wonder if you will ever get back to normal.'

Recovery from cancer treatments can often take longer than the treatments themselves, and Karen was only just recovering from her cancer ordeal

'It's okay to have a good cry when you feel the need. But you should be kind to yourself and allow people to help you during your time of crisis.'

when she was dealt a double whammy. She was made redundant from her job in publishing.

'The news came as a thunderbolt for me. I guess, in hindsight, the signs were there, but I hadn't seen them at the time. I was concentrating on working and getting my health back again. It was a huge shock, and it was upsetting to think that not only was I leaving a job that I thoroughly enjoyed, but I was also worried that I would have to leave the industry that I loved so much. I love working in publishing, and I love writing books – I'm just a book geek, and this is my happy place.'

Karen chose not to take her redundancy personally. This is something that helped her through this tough time.

'There can be a tendency to let something like this get on top of you, so you feel that this latest crisis is heaped on all the other challenges you have been through, and it ends up being this insurmountable, ugly pile of compost in your life.

'It is easy to take something like a redundancy too personally, when the reality in my case was that most people in the company were axed – I was one of the majority.

'It would have been easy to think that it was so unfair that I'd only just battled cancer and now I had another life challenge to contend with so soon. But I never felt that way. Instead, I tackled everything proactively, and instead of looking at all the negatives, I choose to embrace the positives.

'Being made redundant means you can shout from the rooftop that you need a new job, rather than having to be discreet. I quickly updated my CV and wrote to everyone I could think of that might have a job or know of someone who might have a job.

'My main fear about being made redundant was that there would be no jobs in publishing, and, of course, there is always the financial insecurity that goes with losing your job.

'But I was incredibly fortunate. Within a week, I had some freelance work lined up, and within two weeks, I had a completely new way of looking at things.

'My husband was on a commission-only job, so I'd had tunnel vision thinking that I needed another salaried job, but suddenly I was in a position where I could freelance.

'Five years on, I can look back at being made redundant as a blessing. I now have a wonderful lifestyle with much better life/work balance, and I have much more flexibility managing my author duties with my job in publishing, working with other authors.'

With her cancer diagnosis and redundancy now in the past, Karen is full of gratitude for her life.

'I can testify that my life on the other side of these challenges is even sweeter and more precious than before. I've learned I am more resilient than I would have thought, my relationships are stronger, and my passion for life is undiminished.'

I ask Karen what three key things she would suggest to others facing challenges in their own lives and how they might be more resilient.

'Kindness is a key thing,' she says. 'People are often kind to other people but not very kind to themselves. In any crisis, there should be some acceptance that you are going to need help to get through and that it's okay.

'I can testify that my life on the other side of these challenges is even sweeter and more precious than before. I've learned I am more resilient than I would have thought, my relationships are stronger, and my passion for life is undiminished.'

'Through my cancer treatments, I felt I could physically feel the love from people, as well as appreciating all the practical support. And when going through being made redundant, it was friends' introducing me to other people that resulted in the wonderful work I now enjoy. Having this cocoon of support helps you to find your reserves of resilience, so, like a plant that flourishes with sun and water and good soil, you are nurtured in this way. So be kind to yourself and allow other people to help you.

'My second tip would be to try and be proactive about how you might fix the problem you are facing, and stop, pause and think before taking action. It's helpful to consider what solutions there might be, what help you need and what will work for you and your personality. Of course, you might be upset and emotional at the time of finding out unwelcome news, but if you can start putting together an action plan – one that you feel comfortable with – then you are going to be in a better position than just hoping your problem will go away by itself.

'I'm not saying that all problems can be fixed, by any stretch of the imagination, though! I was lucky to have a good prognosis with my cancer diagnosis, and I got work after my redundancy very quickly, and not everyone is that fortunate. But it is likely that even if a problem can't be completely fixed, action can be taken to make things more bearable. I guess that is one of the main philosophies in the book **Everyday Strength**, which I co-authored with chef Sam Mannering. We aren't trying to cure cancer, but, instead, we are providing practical tips and recipes with the aim of making every day a little better for a cancer patient. Sometimes a small improvement in someone's day at a time like this is invaluable.

'Finally, your emotional and spiritual self needs to be actively nurtured during the challenging times in life. You need to feel whatever it is you feel but look at all the many ways you can pull yourself up and find some light in the darkness. So don't ignore your spiritual side and the power of prayer and meditation, or the many small things you can do to lift your spirits. And it's important not to give up hope.'

Karen says after her second parent died, her beloved mum, she became clinically depressed. She thought she would never get out of the big black

'It's the wonderful but messy tapestry of life that I embrace. It grows a little more each day, creating a unique and sometimes unexpected pattern, and is ultimately my life's legacy.'

hole she felt she was in. She got the medical help she needed to help her through, and she got back to her usual happy and positive self. But after going through that dark time, she feels more self-aware, and she thinks that this built resilience in her life.

'If I ever face something in my life that is negative and challenging again, I know I can employ strategies that I have used before to get me through. Because life can throw many unexpected challenges at us at any time. It's not the tough times that define us but how we handle the grim times that is the key test of our character.

'It would be wonderful to go through life where it is all sunshine and rainbows, but the reality is the human existence is fraught with uncertainty, and illness, accident or loss could be part of anyone's future.

'But I try to embrace each day with an attitude of gratitude, and if one of those nasty curveballs of life comes my way again, I've already discovered I am more resilient than I would have thought, so I welcome the future – the good and the bad.

'It's the wonderful but messy tapestry of life that I embrace. It grows a little more each day, creating a unique and sometimes unexpected pattern, and is ultimately my life's legacy.'

BUILDING RESILIENCE AND HAPPINESS+

Never allow what you cannot do to stop you from doing what you can do

When I think of resilience, I think of my friend **Ian Walker**. He was an inspirational marathoner when he could run on two strong legs. And he remains an inspirational marathoner now as a paraplegic. He instead uses the might of his arm muscles to power himself on a three-wheel hand-cycle through marathons. He focuses on what he can do to get through a marathon, not what he used to do.

He's inspirational to watch on wheels. He is speedy on flat stretches of roads, while he has to slow for corners and uneven surfaces. It's a sport of speed and precision, and when he reaches that finish line, his face glows with both sweat and joy. He loves the adventure, challenge and thrill of marathons. And the training to do this sport keeps him goal-focused and fit.

Ian has always loved the thrill of completing that 42km distance. He ran 10 marathons when he was able-bodied. His fastest run time was 2 hours, 37 minutes in Buller in 1999. If you aren't familiar with marathon times, I can assure you this is a very speedy time. He was darn good at this sport. And he's darn good at it on wheels too.

The moment Ian's life changed forever was 7.30am on a bright, sunny, ordinary day on 6 December 2006. He was cycling over a bridge on the Napier–Hastings highway, going about 50km, when he went headfirst into the back of a truck. The injuries were devastating and included a spinal-cord injury and concussion.

> The moment Ian's life changed forever was 7.30am on a bright, sunny, ordinary day on 6 December 2006. He was cycling over a bridge on the Napier–Hastings highway, going about 50km, when he went headfirst into the back of a truck.

'The helmet saved my life. I was lucky,' he says.

In everyday terms, Ian has no feeling from the chest down and requires a wheelchair for mobility. He does have some movement in his left foot, and he is working at building up the muscles around the left knee, so he is able to step with his left leg and then hitch up his right leg to get around with the assistance of a frame.

'For some time, on reflection, I felt quite bitter about the accident. However, I've come to accept it was an unfortunate set of circumstances that culminated in a devastating conclusion.'

Ian spent months in the Burwood Spinal Unit in Canterbury recovering. That's where he first saw the words that he has since adopted as a life motto.

Those words, which were on a plaque in the kitchen, read: 'Never allow what you cannot do to stop you from doing what you can do.'

Ian wishes he could reverse that devastating day, rewind the clock, freeze that moment in time and change it somehow.

'Not a day goes by where I don't wish I could walk. I'm 6ft 2 and I can't reach stuff on the tops of shelves at the supermarket. It's the little things that are so hard. But I live with acceptance better now.'

It has been a hard road to recovery, including nine major operations, pain medication therapy, physio and regular medical checks. But Ian can do everyday things. That includes powering his hand-cycle at speed. He just found a different way to keep doing the sport he loves.

'Life can get tough physically for me at times. But you've got to persevere,' says Ian. 'The secret is to keep trying and never really give up.'

BUILDING RESILIENCE AND HAPPINESS+

He has conquered several New Zealand events on his hand-cycle as well as competing twice at the New York Marathon in America.

He spends a lot of time training for events. He also goes to the gym and swims (using an inflatable belt around his middle).

His work now is being a motivational speaker through his company, BMotiv8d. He credits his partner, Louise, as his anchor and 'constant in life'. 'Without her, most of what I do and achieve wouldn't have been possible.'

Speaking of that word, 'possible', Ian says he hopes to show others with disabilities that events like the marathon are possible to take part in.

'I want to show that being in a wheelchair doesn't mean the end of getting out and being involved in the community and being involved in events like this. It's for runners, walkers, everyone. We are all there for that finish-line feeling.'

Another strong reason that Ian has never given up on his marathon dreams is acceptance. He explains, 'It's about being accepted – accepted as part of the community. I want people to know that being in a wheelchair shouldn't make me less of a person and that I shouldn't be treated any differently. I guess what I'm trying to say is I'm no different.'

Are you anxious?
Or are you James Bond?

Social anxiety is something we all experience. It's actually normal. But it can be problematic when it escalates into panic attacks or phobias and holds us back.

So says **Dr Eric Goodman**, author of the book **Social Courage: Coping and Thriving with the Reality of Social Anxiety**. I recommend parents read this book. It will help them with guiding their kids through tricky and prickly emotions. Better still, a precocious 12-year-old or older child could read this book themselves. It's full of exercises and strategies to help you cope.

Speaking via Skype from California, Eric beams into my New Zealand home. He is down to earth, relatable and like you'd imagine a doctor to be – kind, articulate and reassuring.

I tell him that his book is so insightful. While reading it, I realised I had felt anxious in so many situations.

'Do many people tell you this?' I ask.

Eric remarks that only psychopaths never experience social anxiety. 'Or if you are a paragon of social sophistication, like James Bond,' he quips.

I'm not James Bond and, thank God, I'm not a psychopath. Phew. I'm glad about being anxious sometimes now! It's comforting to know I'm like

I'm glad about being anxious sometimes now! It's comforting to know I'm like almost everyone else on the planet. We all worry – to varying degrees. This is human nature.

almost everyone else on the planet. We all worry – to varying degrees. This is human nature.

Eric says in America alone, about 30% of people will have an anxiety disorder at some point in their lives, and about 10% will have a clinical level of anxiety. Those in 'more communal cultures' suffer less with this. So support clearly helps.

He says we all feel scary thoughts, shame, awkwardness, rejection, failure, embarrassment. We all sometimes feel like an outcast or inept. Along with these emotions, we can sweat, blush, get a racing heart or feel numbness.

All this is normal.

For instance, it is normal to feel anxious if you are going to a party where you don't know anyone. It's normal to feel anxious if you are about to give a speech in front of a large audience. These feelings do not mean we are a failure. It's all about how we view all that 'brain noise'.

Eric believes feeling a constant pressure to be perfect does not help. He also believes that social media is driving social-anxiety statistics higher.

'Modern technology is a huge issue. A lot of people are staring at their devices rather than at each other,' he says. 'I've been noticing this more and more over the past 10 years.'

He says we can't change the reality that social anxiety thoughts will continue to show up from time to time, but learning to accept this brain noise as part of life can keep us from following these thoughts down the rabbit hole while giving a talk, being out on a date or hanging out with friends. He recommends 'accepting what you can't change and changing what you can.'

Examples of things we can do to help ourselves feel more in control include getting good sleep and nutrition, using mindfulness and avoiding substance abuse.

Eric recommends learning to live with 'social grey areas' too. What he means is that things are not going to be perfect. It's okay to allow events in life to be 'good enough' rather than 'perfect or awful'.

I love this quote from his book: 'Freedom is accepting that social anxiety is a normal human experience.'

He says you can't cure social anxiety; you live with it and can work on your ability to cope. For example, you may be anxious about public speaking. A great way to get better with this might be to have a goal to do it more. You might also do a course to become more skilful. 'Just turn problems into goals,' he says.

He says anxiety is on a spectrum, anything from 'feeling mild jitters' to feeling terrifying panic attacks. He recently saw a 30-year-old client who didn't leave his home because he got too anxious.

'People think this guy is shy and anxious. But it's absolutely debilitating for him,' Eric says.

He explains what it can be like for someone to experience a panic attack. 'They're hyperventilating and feeling like they're going to pass out. They want to flee the situation. It's that rollercoaster-ride feeling in their body, but they are just in line at the grocery store.'

He explains these emotions were around in, for example, Ancient Roman times too, but back then people were more likely in really dangerous situations.

Below are some common types of irrational thought patterns (cognitive distortions) you might relate to from the book. There are so many more! I can relate to these examples, but I've become much better at coping with a lot of them since learning to recognise that they are brain noise. Mindfulness has also helped me see clearly the difference between facts and thoughts.

Do you recognise any of these?

- **Mind-reading:** Thoughts about what other people are thinking or feeling about you, e.g. 'no one likes me'.

- **Fortune-telling:** Negative predictive thoughts about your future, e.g. 'no one will like me at the party'.

- **Catastrophising:** Predictive thoughts that are cataclysmic, e.g. 'if I get rejected, I will be utterly destroyed'.

- **All-or-nothing thinking:** Or black-or-white thinking, e.g. 'I'm either the life of the party or a dud'.

- **Unfair comparisons:** Thoughts that compare you to an extreme. Then when you don't match up, you create thoughts that you aren't good enough, e.g. 'I must be as smart as the smartest person in the class'.

Fuel yourself for happiness+

I wasted my 20s asking myself, 'Does my bum look big in these jeans?'

When I thought of food intake years ago, I would always focus so much on the aesthetics and relate it back to my weight. Now I view food as a way to fuel my happiness too. It's a game-changer.

Seek out foods that support your health, energy levels, mood, beauty and longevity. Food is a crucial piece of the puzzle when it comes to your health – and happiness.

Certain foods can help to fuel a good mood, while others can send your energy levels crashing. Some foods support immunity and can help with weight loss. Some foods, or drinks, can end up ageing you faster or sending your body into an obese and potentially diseased state.

Eating has become confusing, and people are right to feel overwhelmed. But it should be simple, really. Just eat real foods that grow in the ground or on trees. Add some meat if you are not a vegetarian. Some processed things are actually okay, like tinned tomatoes, for instance, but stay away from the highly processed stuff as much as possible. You don't need to be a rocket scientist to know that too much sugar and alcohol is not ideal.

Being mindful of the quality of food you eat is one thing. But remember that how much you eat, and what you eat, depends on the individual.

It can be built around an 'energy in' (food you eat) and 'energy out' (how much you exercise) equation. For example, if you are really active, you can eat a bit more than if you are sedentary, i.e. sit at a desk all day.

You can use calorie calculators on a lot of apps as a guide, which can work out exactly how much you can eat for your level of activity and your weight etc. But I just eat mindfully, these days, eat all things in balance and consider how full I feel. I don't eat by the clock anymore. If I'm not hungry, I won't snack for the sake of it just because it's 3pm.

There are so many diet fads. Thankfully, one old approach – where you just count calories and ignore the overall nutritional benefits of your food – has been ditched. I reckon be cautious of the super-fad diets. I mean, how can you possibly sustain these in everyday life for a long time?

I don't really buy into a single line of thinking. I just look for the trends overall on what experts tend to agree on. Most experts agree that vegetables are king, for instance. It's up to you whether you think the Mediterranean way of eating serves you better than, say, the paleo approach.

Meanwhile, there's also the planet to consider, and pesticides, organic choices, sustainability issues, food miles, supporting local businesses, paying farmers fairly ... but just figure out what's important to you while eating real, local, sustainable food whenever you can.

One thing I do really back is the Blue Zones. This is a handful of regions where people generally live longer, happier lives, like Okinawa in Japan. Some common themes in the Blue Zones are a high ratio of plant materials to meat, quality clean air, locals live an active lifestyle, i.e. move lots, and there are wonderful social support networks.

Ultimately, no single diet will suit everyone. Eat what fuels your body (and mind) for optimal performance. Some people can tolerate foods that might give another individual an allergic reaction, for example. Take my husband. The poor bloke has a dairy and wheat intolerance, so drinking cow's milk and eating wheat-based bread leaves him ill. It makes him literally bend over in pain, while I can tolerate small amounts of these foods absolutely fine. Sometimes what we can eat is determined by our bodies and what signals they give us.

Remember that chewing your food slowly is important. This aids digestion and will help you to realise when you are full (and so hopefully avoid overeating).

My approach is that I eat by the 80/20 rule. I eat mostly good, nutritionally rich, plant-based foods that fuel my body and mind. I eat some meat, fish and dairy, but I opt for the vegan options sometimes too. I'm not afraid to have some treats occasionally – a favourite is chocolate – and the very occasional glass of wine to celebrate with others when I'm a social butterfly. I'm a real kind of girl who lives life in balance rather than striving for some unrealistic 'perfection' when it comes to eating.

My approach might change as more science comes to light in different areas. But, overall, I'm not perfect with my diet; that would be boring and annoying. I care about buying local and buying foods that are in season because they are fresh and not crazy expensive. I grow lots of vegetables, fruits and herbs in my own garden in the Auckland suburb of Mt Eden (which I nickname my Garden of Eden). Most days, I'm out in the garden picking a bunch of greens and herbs to add to my family's meals. You can't get any fresher than that.

I refuse to remortgage my house to buy expensive superfoods like goji berries, which are about $10 for a small packet in New Zealand – especially as my youngest son can swallow a handful of them in a single gulp! I do buy them sometimes, though, for styling food and to give that fancy wow factor to recipes I design for magazines. But at home I generally prefer to use more affordable 'superfoods' that are in season, have the same nutritional benefits and don't have to travel from another continent to get to my plate.

What are superfoods, anyway? I think we've lost perspective with this concept. Most fresh, natural foods have their own nutritional profiles, and there are super benefits from eating humble cabbage in a meal. Yeah, chia seeds are all the rage now, but blueberries in season are amazing too. I even use frozen blueberries when they are not in season, if they are affordable. Each vegetable tends to have something valuable to offer in terms of different mineral and vitamin profiles.

Another tip is to mix up the foods you eat so you mix up your nutrient intake. One mistake I made in the past was eating the same foods day in, day out. I had a thing for oat porridge years ago, and then an expert advised me to change things up. So now sometimes I have eggs, salmon and salad for breakfast (which keeps me fuller for longer), while other days I'll have amaranth porridge with blueberries and yoghurt and a drizzle of mānuka honey.

I tend to drink water or good medicinal-grade teas, rather than reaching for sugary drinks that have zero nutritional benefits. It's something that I've just got used to, and this is normal for my kids too – well, most of the time but not ALL the time. Like I said, my family lives in balance, and we all enjoy treat foods sometimes.

Oh, and when it comes to coffee, I love it. I have one or two daily and feel amazing. Again, it's up to the individual. Some people feel it makes them too anxious and so should avoid it.

When my kids are invited to birthday parties, I'm sometimes approached by parents worried about my food philosophy, given I'm a wellness writer. They are sometimes worried I might look down my nose if they serve up some sugar-laden treats and cakes on the table.

I tell them, relax, I don't mind! My kids can eat whatever they like on these occasions, and I want them to enjoy being part of the fun. I'm not the food police. Being isolated with a plate of celery, carrot sticks and hummus and sitting alone in a corner would not be fun for them or anyone.

My son Finn boasted at the table the other night that one of his friend's dads is so cool because he is the boss of a pizza company. He loves pizza! I laughed and joked with a friend that I guess my kids will not have any bragging rights about their mum being a wellness geek. By the way, our family eats pizza regularly. It's all about balance, remember. Ours is usually homemade, full of real food and actually reasonably nutritious, but I don't skimp on the cheese. It's mozzarella all the way.

What to eat for glowing skin

I recommend you sleep well, avoid stress, use sunscreen during the day and remove your make-up before bed as a good base for your beauty regime.

For recommendations around what foods to eat to help your skin glow, I asked **Nadia Lim**. She's a mum, **MasterChef New Zealand** winner, dietitian, cookbook writer, and co-founder and frontwoman of My Food Bag (a successful meal-delivery service).

She has gorgeous glowing olive-coloured skin and is model-like. Her smile always lights up any room. Here are three of her top tips to get glowing, healthy skin:

Vitamin C-rich foods like citrus fruit, strawberries, kiwifruit etc. Vitamin C increases collagen production. Collagen helps keep skin supple and plumps it up, giving smoothness and support. As skin ages, it loses collagen.

Omega-3 fatty acids – contained in the likes of oily fish such as salmon, flax seed and walnuts. Skin cells are surrounded by a layer of fat, and it's important to get enough healthy fats to nourish your cells. Having a diet high in omega-3 fats helps your skin look radiant and adds softness to your complexion. Nadia says, 'I know this from first-hand experience at university, when we were all part of an experiment and I was assigned to the group that had to take fish-oil capsules every day for a few weeks. I really noticed a difference – my skin had never felt so soft and smooth.'

Have foods high in vitamin E like avocado and almonds. Vitamin E is a powerful antioxidant and helps to protect against skin oxidative damage from pollutants and other free radicals.

> 'I was assigned to the group that had to take fish-oil capsules every day for a few weeks. I really noticed a difference – my skin had never felt so soft and smooth.'

If the kidneys are weak or overloaded, then they cannot detoxify properly, and this can put a burden on the skin to release these toxins instead.'

What to drink for glowing skin

I connected with **Sandra Clair** on this topic. She is completing a PhD in health science at the University of Canterbury. She is based in the city of Dunedin. A highly qualified, Swiss-trained medical herbalist and medical anthropologist, she's best known as the mastermind behind the traditional plant medicine company Artemis. This company uses medicinal-grade herbs for its medicinal tea blends.

Here are her three top tips on what to drink to help your skin glow:

1. It's smart to drink a healthy dose of nettle each day. It strengthens the 'elimination organs', particularly the kidneys, which release toxins from the body. If the kidneys are weak or overloaded, then they cannot detoxify properly, and this can put a burden on the skin to release these toxins instead – often in the form of pimples or acne. Nettle also helps to eliminate puffiness and water retention, making the tissues look trim and toned.

2. Drink two litres of water daily. We are made up of 75% water and need this hydration for healthy skin and our body. Drinking medicinal teas counts towards this, but coffee, regular teas and soft drinks do not.

3. Drink herbs that are good for the liver like St Mary's thistle, globe artichoke, dandelion root, peppermint and calendula. Liver detox teas, when prepared by a qualified medical herbalist, are one of the quickest ways of triggering the elimination processes of fat-soluble toxins and improving digestion. The liver works in tandem with the kidneys, and together they provide essential detoxification for healthy, glowing skin.

Nude food and Nadia's fave foodie things

I catch up with **Nadia Lim** at her bungalow in Auckland. I see her on her birthday – literally the only afternoon she had available on her calendar at the time. This shows how hard-working she is.

As I arrive at Nadia's house, her husband, Carlos Bagrie, is heading out the door with their young son, Bodhi. They have two children. This couple juggles parenting and working full-time on various businesses and projects. Nadia is as big as celebrity foodie **Nigella Lawson** in New Zealand. She's a total star.

Nadia greets me at her door dressed casually in jean shorts and a baggy T-shirt and barefoot. She's not wearing a hint of make-up. She looks like a supermodel without having to try hard. She's a natural beauty.

Looking at Nadia's flawless, glowing, healthy skin, shiny eyes and luscious hair, I immediately think to myself: I want what she's having. She's stunning – on the outside and inside. She's super laid-back and really lovely.

As Nadia makes us a cup of tea, I ask her about her food philosophy so I can share her secrets on how to look so youthful and healthy with readers. She laughs and thanks me for the compliment.

'It's hardly a philosophy – it's common sense, really,' she says. 'People want something prescribed. You need to be able to trust your instincts and think, "Am I hungry? How does it make me feel when I overeat? Do I really need food right now? What's my body telling me I need to eat more of?"

'People need to rely on their intuition, rather than someone giving them a prescription.'

Nadia is an advocate of wholefoods.

'I like to call it nude food. It's about eating food that comes from the ground, the sea and the sky and less out of the factories. That's it in a nutshell.

'Eat more from nature. Food that has not been intervened with. Another way of putting it is eat less processed food.

'I believe in cooking more. The more you cook, the more you are in control of what you eat, obviously, and what goes into your food. If you are in control of that, then you don't end up putting anything dodgy into it.

'I also really believe in making sure you enjoy your food. That is the most important part of your relationship with food. Enjoyment, having a good time, and feeling good and being happy through what you eat.

'I think that's the most important thing for your heath. When you feel healthy and happy, you laugh, you are relaxed, and that does wonders for your health, rather than being stressed about what you are eating and having to count things and be prescriptive. A relaxed relationship with food is incredibly important.

'I also really believe in the 90/10 principle. So 80 to 90% of the time, I aim to eat really well. The other 10%, I feel free to have whatever I like and just enjoy it, like I did when I had tiramisu for breakfast yesterday morning! It was leftovers from a barbecue last night. I had it with a cup of tea for breakfast,' she says, chuckling.

I'm sitting with Nadia in her backyard. It's small but beautifully manicured and full of fresh, green, leafy vegetables and herbs.

I ask Nadia if her cooking and recipes had changed much over time.

'Over the last seven years, my recipes have got faster and faster and simpler. That's been a reflection of me getting busier and busier and being a mum and needing to get dinner on the table by 5.30pm.

'I always thought, before being a mum, that my kids would eat whatever we were eating. Unfortunately, it didn't quite go according to plan. It was an idealistic way of thinking, but the reality is that we have met somewhere in the middle, I think. Sometimes my son gets what we have, but other times the dinners I cook will be with him in mind first.

'That was the situation last night. We had sausages and pasta with grated vegetables throughout because Bodhi looooooooves it. It's one of his favourite things. It had good-quality sausages with tomato, courgette, beetroot and carrot and grated cheese and spaghetti.

'I ended up eating Bodhi's cold leftovers. It's terrible – I don't like waste,
so I often end up eating his leftovers as well as my own dinner.'

I ask Nadia to share some favourite foodie things. At the top of her list is her daily smoothie ritual, she says.

'Most mornings, I have a green smoothie. It usually has some kale or spinach in it. Most leafy greens work, except I haven't had much success with watercress or rocket. I've tried those before and they weren't great.

'Then I add citrus, like orange or lemon, and put it in whole. Without the skin, though – I do take that off.

'I also really believe in making sure you enjoy your food. That is the most important part of your relationship with food.'

'Then I like to put frozen berries in the smoothie. That makes it nice and cold. It also gives it a nice flavour. Then I add turmeric and ginger [peeled and a small knob of each] and then add water and blitz it all up.'

Voilà! That's Nadia's secret healthy kick-start to her day. It's loaded with vitamin C and could well be responsible for her gorgeous, glowing skin. That and her amazing New Zealand and Chinese-Malaysian heritage, of course.

Next up, Nadia counts avocados as her second-favourite thing to consume.

'I would eat avocados most days throughout the summer, definitely. Throughout winter, I still have avocado, but it's frozen avocado. I buy them in bulk when they are cheap and then freeze them. Often, I put half an avocado in a smoothie to make it thick and creamy.

'Their colour and taste remain the same when frozen. So you've got to get them at the right stage, of course, and make sure they are not overripe or bruised. Freeze nice avocados – the firm and ripe ones. Freeze them whole – don't take the stem off or anything. They'll last about six months. Then, when you want to use them, just let them defrost. While the flesh will be all mushy inside, the taste and colour are the same in smoothies. It's only good for smoothies, mind. You can't use it for salads or anything else, because it turns to mush.'

I ask, 'Is it okay on toast?'

'Not really – the fat kind of separates,' she says. 'But they are perfect for smoothies.'

She adds that avocados are high in monounsaturated fats, which are good for your cholesterol and really high in folate (so good for pregnant women).

'They've got vitamin E, potassium … they've got a wide range of nutrients. They almost have everything in them. They have all three macronutrients: protein, fats and carbohydrates.'

Another favourite food item for Nadia is citrus.

'I have them all – tangelos, grapefruits, lemons … when I was pregnant, that was my craving. I ate 19 blood oranges in one go,' she says, laughing. 'How did no one catch on that I was pregnant? I don't normally do that. I just sat there, cutting them and eating them, one after another.'

She adds that these fruits boost vitamin C, which is good for collagen production and immunity. 'I have citrus in a smoothie or just by itself. I also add citrus to lots of dressings.'

Nadia eats meat and recommends we go for quality over quantity. Choose free-range and/or organic, and even wild meat, if possible, and eat smaller amounts.

'I love lamb. Another fave is probably wild rabbit. Our diet changes so much depending on where we go. We used to live in Gulf Harbour, north of Auckland, near a farm. Carlos used to bring back a lot of wild rabbit, which I would make into rabbit stews and pies, and then I would trade them back with our neighbour, who owned the farm, and she would often give us crayfish that she'd caught in return.

'We used to eat a lot more wild food, but then we moved into the city and our diets changed again.'

Nadia says her family has meat a couple of times a week now. 'We have it more because of Bodhi. I know he's getting enough iron, and he loves slow-cooked lamb.'

Nadia has found it really interesting how her diet has changed throughout her life. She says what you eat can come down to where you live, who else is in the household, your stage of life and, obviously, finances.

'It's very fluid. Just trust your instincts. At different stages of your life, you probably require different nutrients. Before pregnancy, I had super-high iron and zinc and my blood levels were fantastic. But after pregnancy, they were much lower. It's quite amazing how much pregnancy takes out of you – growing babies are like leeches! So that's another thing – your body does tell you what it needs sometimes.'

Next on Nadia's favourite food list are eggs, which boast protein and lots of good nutrients and vitamins.

'We have them every day. It's like our ritual every morning – poached eggs on toast. Occasionally, we have them scrambled.'

Lastly, Nadia says she can't live without the good oils.

'I don't hold back with oil. Carlos is like, "How do we go through so much olive oil in the house?" I've got olive, coconut and avocado oil, and I use all three often.

'I use olive oil the most. But if I'm baking, then I love to use coconut oil, as it gives it a lovely flavour. Olive oil is something I use for most savoury cooking. I use extra-virgin olive oil in salads. Avocado oil is something I use for higher-heat cooking because it has a high smoke point. I use coconut oil for cooking sometimes, if I think the flavour profile fits. It works really well as an alternative to butter, which I really love too, by the way.'

Nadia says we shouldn't be afraid of having good oils.

'Your cells need fat, your brain needs it, your organs ... it's good for cell function and your skin, and it's really important for when you are pregnant.'

Beauty foods – and why being broken can be beautiful

Popular Australian nutritionist **Lola Berry** is in my office – well, kind of. She's beaming up on my giant computer screen via Skype. She's sitting at her work desk too. She's in Bondi, Sydney. I'm in Auckland.

Lola is the bestselling author of a string of cookbooks and a regular spokesperson on nutrition and general wellbeing across TV, radio and print media. She has a TV presence in America too.

She runs the Happy Place smoothie and juice bar in Victoria, Australia, where you get a crystal with your smoothie order. She's a yogi too, and so I knew we'd hit it off. Before we get on to food, we chit-chat about crystals.

She holds a shiny brown stone up towards me, saying, 'It's a tiger's eye, which has the energy of passion.' It's among a handful of treasured gems in pride of place on her desk. She names about six gems, one by one, and raves about each special stone's attributes.

The girly-girl in me is mesmerised by all the sparkles, colours and shapes and their beautiful meanings. I'm transfixed by the grey/brown/greenish/blue/yellow mineral one.

'That's a labradorite stone,' she enthuses. 'This one is for making dreams come true. I put it under my pillow at night.'

'That's a labradorite stone. This one is for making dreams come true. I put it under my pillow at night.'

A self-confessed health nerd, Lola says her food approach is all about having foods that nourish. She also says food should be shared and savoured with loved ones. That's where the true joy in food comes from.

Lola is as passionate about real wholefoods as she is about her gems. On both topics, she sparkles. You can see immediately why she is a poster girl for eating good, nutrient-dense foods. Her big blue eyes are wide and alert, her skin glows, her beautiful blonde locks shine. She's got that quirky hippie style too, with her dress sense, and is wearing jewellery in the shape of stars and moons, dotted with gemstones.

On Instagram, Lola has mermaid-long hair, but I note she has short bangs the day we talk. 'I had my extensions chopped,' she tells me.

I learn Lola and I have a few more things in common other than yoga and a love for healthy food. She also does some running, and she shares that same don't-mess-with-me-and-my-dreams attitude.

I ask her about the challenges she faced in pursuing her food passions.

'Some people warned me off my dream to break into American TV,' she explains with a sigh. But this made her chase that dream harder. 'I had that dream for so long. So many people said, "Don't do it," but I was like, "SCREW YOU!"' she says, chuckling.

A self-confessed health nerd, Lola says her food approach is all about having foods that nourish. She also says food should be shared and savoured with loved ones. That's where the true joy in food comes from.

'I don't have huge hang-ups about certain foods,' she says. But, personally, she admits, 'I eat for vanity. I'm not going to lie! Look, I'd like to age gracefully.'

I reply, 'And who wouldn't?'

So that's why Lola eats wholefoods mostly and tries to resist too much sugar. She wants to have a bangin' bod into her old age.

Food to Make You Glow is one of my favourite books she has penned. This book is all about foods for happiness, energy, beauty, immunity, calmness, weight loss and detoxing.

I ask her for her top foods to bring anyone into balance and make them feel happier. First up, she says, 'you want a little bit of everything'. At the top of her list are good fats, though, like the ones from avocados (monounsaturated fats) and salmon (omega-3s).

'These are good for the brain and are good for keeping you happy,' she explains.

These two foods are in her favourite savoury meal. She loves to fry salmon in coconut oil in a pan until it is 'super crispy'. She then teams it with a side of smashed avocado and tops the meal with fresh coriander, chilli and a generous squeeze of lime.

She next raves about macadamia nuts as 'a hero food for beauty'. 'These are full of monounsaturated fats and protein – the latter is essential for cell growth, i.e. for nice nails and beautiful hair and skin. The oil from this nut can also be applied topically to combat ageing and aid skin healing. Macadamia-nut oil is rich in essential fatty acids, which gives it powerful anti-inflammatory properties and helps to moisturise the skin and aid scar healing.'

Lola raves too about the importance of good gut health. 'When your gut is well, so is your skin.' She says happiness is something that comes from the inside. So eating fermented foods will also help you to look radiant.

Next on her must-have food list for balance and happiness are blueberries. They are packed full of 'good sugars' (glucose) that help to fuel brain power. 'They are also a good source of the antioxidants anthocyanins, which give the fruit the blue colour and ultimately help with preventing cellular damage'. Decode: they're anti-ageing!

Then, there's raw cacao, says Lola. I love this excerpt from her book **Food to Make You Glow**: 'The main component of chocolate, cacao contains the amino acid called phenylalanine, which is needed to produce dopamine – a neurotransmitter that determines your alertness, learning, creativity, satisfaction, attention and concentration levels, as well as other brain processes that control movement and emotional responses.'

That paragraph explains why we all NEED chocolate in our lives. Amen.

Lola next has greens on her must-have list. 'You've got to have your greens, no matter what.' Everyone knows about the super benefits of greens like broccoli and silver beet, but Lola says her favourite is actually Brussels sprouts. Her favourite way to eat them is to cut them in half, fry them in a pan in olive oil and butter and then top them with pistachios and currents or cranberries. 'You can then choose to add bacon too, but I'm not a bacon girl.'

Lola says it's not just what goes inside our bodies that can make us happy. She's passionate about banishing negative self-talk. She has battled with this over the years, she says. I tell her I have too – and I think most women will agree it has held them back in life for periods.

Lola advises women to embrace self-belief. This philosophy got her through a pretty tough period, she tells me, when she released a diet plan 'which resulted in me being ripped to shreds'. It really divided people and resulted in some people in her life 'turning on me'.

'Everyone ran like cockroaches in a dark room when you turn the lights on,' she says honestly.

After that experience, she says she is so grateful for the true friends in her life who back her through thick and thin.

'And my self-belief was a big part of what got me through,' she says.

She believes strongly in turning negatives 'into positives'.

'You mean genuine resilience?' I ask Lola.

She says yes and then talks about a Japanese idea she loves.

'When something is broken, it is often mended with gold. You learn the biggest lessons when you fall, and so don't be afraid of falling,' she says.

I love this, so I later find the term Lola is talking about. It's kintsugi, a centuries-old Japanese method of repairing pottery with a special lacquer dusted with powdered gold, silver or platinum. In pottery that has been revived, you can see the glint and sparkle of the 'glue' and gold that hold the piece back together. The idea is to repair things with whatever you can to keep them in use. The Japanese see beauty in something being repaired and made stronger, changed, and believe there is even more beauty in imperfections.

I fall in love with this idea – because we are all damaged over the years in some way or another. We are all changed by harrowing experiences. We are all imperfect. There truly is beauty in imperfection, and the strong life lessons can be something we grow and strengthen from.

Lola next offers another idea that fuels her happiness on this planet, outside of food. She says she writes, or journals, regularly in a 'manifesto book' to fuel her wellbeing. It's where she jots thoughts and feelings.

I ask her where she got her gutsy, can-do attitude from. Who inspired her strong spirit? Her response: 'I'm inspired by awesome souls who live from their heart and who authentically live their passion with no apology.'

Her dad is like this. 'He always said, "Have goals, live your dreams, work hard."'

She also looked up to **Steve Irwin**, a nature expert, conservationist and larger-than-life TV personality. He passed away in 2006 after being pierced in the heart by a stingray.

'He believed his dream. He lived what was true for him,' she says.

And so she unapologetically follows her own unique pathway too.

Lastly, Lola urges people to tap into the healing powers of Mother Nature (biophilia), music, being around animals or doing yoga to fuel their health and happiness levels.

And, of course, adopt a gutsy and go-get-'em attitude like Lola, and you are likely to smile and shine bright in this life like a beautiful crystal.

Twenty nutrition hacks to help you look, feel and perform better than ever!

I've interviewed lots of nutritionists over the years, and it took me a while to decide which expert to approach for 20 nutrition tips. I chose **Cliff Harvey** because he is a researcher and also a relatable guy. Not only does he have the credentials to speak on food (ND, Dip.Fit, PhD candidate), he's able to cut though the geek-speak.

Cliff has many strings to his bow. Actually, the first time I interviewed him, I cheekily remarked, 'Is there anything you don't do?' He is a leading practitioner and researcher in lower-carbohydrate nutrition and metabolic efficiency. He is a naturopath, clinical nutritionist, strength coach, author and speaker.

'I love coffee. I drink it because it tastes amazing and gives me a kick in the butt.'

Cliff inspires through his writing, speaking and clinical practice and continues to lead the way with ongoing research. He is the founder of Holistic Performance Nutrition (providing nutrition education in carb-appropriate and real-food nutrition).

He has a great wild beard, and I love that he's a hoodie kinda dude, rather than part of the cardigan brigade that you might see often at universities. He's mild-mannered, except when you get him all fired up about different controversial food approaches – or dogs. Pitbulls, specifically. He hates that they are labelled a dangerous breed. He has a pitbull, Daisy, who he adores. I love how he stands up for things he is passionate about. I think this is missing a lot in the world.

We also share a love of coffee. He gives some cautions around coffee (see Hack 15 below) yet is upfront that he loves the brew. I threw Cliff into the media limelight a few years back with a newspaper article on coffee. He had read thousands of pieces of research on the good, bad and ugly sides of coffee, and so he talked about the science behind it. Coffee is not all bad and in some circumstances should be given a 'health halo' rather than a 'thou-shalt-not label'. He just cautions that if you drink it, you should ideally have your last cup of the day no later than 12–2pm.

Cliff makes me a coffee when I visit him at his home in Auckland. 'That's strong!' I say. But it's not fancy – just made from a plunger. I have mine white, while he has his black with a touch of cream. He averages three cups of coffee a day, he says.

'I love coffee. I drink it because it tastes amazing and gives me a kick in the butt. Personality-wise, I'm a sprinter, and I think that works well with my coffee habit. I work hard, do super-productive things and then chill big-time,' he says, grinning.

I'm with Cliff on this topic. I personally love it too and mindfully drink a cup (or two) daily. This amount can help me feel good, and I savour the cup, usually after a run or doing yoga in the morning. I know if I have more than two cups daily, though, it sends me off balance and turns me into a jittery, on-edge mess. I try not to have my second coffee after 2pm. After that, I'd order a decaffeinated brew if I was out at a social event with friends.

Anyway, you'll love Cliff's view on coffee, including the good, bad and ugly sides. But, ultimately, you decide if it's right for you or not.

Enjoy all his nutrition hacks (which he has personally penned) below. These can all help to uplift your life!

HACK 1: **Don't snack**

I know, I know … you've been told for decades that you should eat small, frequent meals and to snack and 'graze' throughout the day, but snacking is THE worst habit if you want to feel, look and perform better.

Humans are not built to graze. When we snack and graze, we tend to overeat, and it's seldom truly satisfying. How many times have you taken a BIG bag of almonds to work, only to notice that they are all gone by the end of the day?

Frequent snacking can also contribute to a perpetual increase in insulin levels. This hormone helps us to store fat, but, more importantly, even very small amounts can stop us freeing up fat from stores to use as fuel. So it hinders fat loss. Even if you're not gaining weight, having too frequent a release of even small amounts of insulin in response to snacking can stop you losing that stubborn fat. In fact, evidence suggests a strong link between snacking behaviours and both increased obesity and poorer-quality food choice. Snacks also tend to be lower in essential vitamins and minerals and healthy fibres and starches than complete, balanced meals.

A better option is to have similar-sized, well-balanced, complete meals throughout the day. This fits better with our natural pattern of 'fight or flight' (the stress response of sympathetic nervous system dominance), when we are most active, versus the 'rest and digest' (or 'relaxed state' of the parasympathetic nervous system) phase, in which we can digest food optimally. When we are 'sympathetic nervous system dominant' (i.e. when we are active and under pressure at work or play), blood supply is drawn away from the gut to supply the working muscles, while digestive enzymes and stomach-acid secretion are reduced and movement of food through the gut is slowed. So snacking, especially when we're 'on the run', reduces how well we can digest food and can result in cramping, pain and bloating, the common symptoms of irritable bowel, along with dysbiosis (bacterial imbalance in the gut).

HACK 2: Drink two large glasses of water first thing upon rising

Everyone knows how important drinking water is. Every cell in your body requires water to function correctly, and those functions inevitably include the processes that allow you to build and maintain muscle, lose body fat and think clearly. Without enough water, you will be unable to perform at your physical and mental best, and you may even feel hungrier! As little as a 2% loss in body weight from water can noticeably impair your physical and mental function. I don't need to tell you that drinking water is important … but a lot of people still have trouble remembering to drink water through the day. That's why having two large glasses of water first thing every morning is such an important hack for your daily nutrition. The body loses about 100ml of water each and every hour, and so by the time you wake up, you might have lost a litre or more of water. This is enough to affect your mental and physical performance, and until you replenish that water loss, you won't feel bright-eyed and bushy-tailed!

Having two large glasses of water creates a habit of hydration that starts your day off on the right foot and goes a long way towards making sure that you are optimally hydrated. We've also found in our practice that when people do this, they typically drink more water through the day and stay adequately hydrated without trying.

HACK 3: Eat when you're hungry!

This tip seems self-explanatory, and yet few people nowadays listen to their bodies and eat when they are actually hungry. Typically, we run between two extremes of eating 'by the clock' throughout the day (even when we don't need to) or eating to fill time, feel better (emotional eating) or as a distraction. We all do this from time to time, but if we are aware of eating meals and not snacks and mindful of eating only when we're hungry, we tend to slip into a very natural pattern of eating. This may, by the way, not be anywhere near the supposedly 'ideal' six meals per day. I, for example, regularly only eat two to three meals per day and never suffer from energy crashes or impaired performance as a result. It's like the old proverb says, 'Eat when hungry, sleep when tired.' Simple, really!

HACK 4: Eat until you're full

This tip goes together with the previous one. The question 'How much should I eat?' often arises, and the answer is simply, 'Eat until you're full!' And by 'full' I don't mean that tired old idea that you've probably heard time and time again of eating until you're 'moderately full'.

I mean, seriously … do you even know what it feels like to be moderately full? Because I sure as hell don't!

A more accurate way to think of being 'full' is in terms of satiety. Satiety is the state of being physically nourished and satisfied. I think we all know that feeling. It's the feeling we have when we say, 'I'm done,' and push the plate away from us. Many of us have been shamed into thinking that is a bad state to get to. But the human body has evolved to go out, find food and then, when we find it, eat abundantly! That's why it works so well to eat substantial, real-food meals until we're satisfied and then go some period without eating. It's also one of the reasons why fasting is not just normal for us but can also be so beneficial. If you're eating a diet that is based on natural, whole, unprocessed food, you are unlikely to overeat, even if you're eating until you're awesomely, satisfactorily … full.

HACK 5: Use apple cider vinegar in the morning

Apple cider vinegar is a time-honoured naturopathic remedy to promote digestion and improve the natural processes of detoxification in the liver. The old-timers suggest that the sour nature of these drinks help to kick-start your digestive processes and encourage the production of gastric enzymes. More recent evidence from both animal and human studies suggests that vinegar may help to reduce markers of cardiometabolic risk such as triglycerides (fats in the blood) and improve 'good' (HDL) cholesterol, along with aiding stability of blood glucose after meals and increasing insulin sensitivity in both diabetic and non-diabetic people. The active ingredient in vinegar, the short-chain fatty acid acetic acid, is also ketogenic and helps to encourage the creation of cool brain- and body-friendly ketone fuels, which are linked to improved satiety, reduced body fat and improved brain health.

HACK 6: **STOP and be mindful when eating**

In the modern world, we eat while distracted – working, watching television, playing around on social media – even though this is far from ideal for digestion and absorption of nutrients or for reducing stress. Most of these behaviours are inherently stressful, even though they don't appear to be. They are stimulating and can inhibit that natural 'rest and digest' phase (parasympathetic nervous system dominance) that is so crucial for optimising digestion and absorption of nutrients and reducing digestive upsets. This helps us to avoid the gas, cramping and bloating that can result from eating 'on the run'. When we're not mindful, we often eat too quickly. This, in turn, reduces feelings of fullness and satisfaction, leading to overeating. So slowing down and eating mindfully can reduce stress – and body weight. Chew food thoroughly and be mindful of the food you are eating. Be aware of the pleasure that good, natural foods provide, and allow the body to come to its natural point of fullness and satisfaction.

HACK 7: **Make too much dinner, so you have lunch for the following day**

Many people know what to do but struggle with how to integrate good eating into their lives, and lunch is often the most difficult meal to 'get right' consistently. We find ourselves at work or on the go and without a good option ready at hand. So we make the best choice available at a café or food hall, but all too often those choices are less than ideal.

One of the most effective strategies I and my clients use is to cook twice as much as we need for dinner and immediately put away lunch for the following day. This eliminates the need to prepare a healthy lunch in the morning and reduces the chance of having to find something whilst 'on the run' at a café, deli or food hall in which there may not be the healthiest options. When I was a competitive strength athlete, my day would involve writing in the morning, strength-coaching other athletes, working in the clinic and then training at night. There simply was NO extra time to worry about food prep, and so preparing too much at night to keep away for the following day's lunch (along with smoothies – more about that below) was a critical strategy for helping me to fuel myself for athletic success.

HACK 8: Use smoothies!

Protein is the base of any nutritious meal, and smoothies make an easy and quick meal option. I use them for morning or afternoon meals and after every training session to help encourage muscle repair. They are also a great way to 'front-load' nutrient-dense foods (that we typically don't eat enough of nowadays) into your diet. A smoothie provides the perfect 'hiding place' for extra veggies, berries and healthy fats. Veggies and berries are packed with vitamins, minerals, fibre and other essential nutrients. These little guys are like the spark plugs in your car – without them, you're not going anywhere!

Without essential and secondary micronutrients, the body cannot effectively utilise fuel for working muscles, organs and brain function, repairing tissue or building new components like the hormones and enzymes that direct all the myriad functions happening throughout the body. They also ensure we are in the best position to burn fat for fuel and store carbohydrates and protein where we want them to be stored (in muscle and other functional tissue). Data from the United States Department of Agriculture suggests that to get the same amounts of some nutrients in fruits, vegetables and berries, we may need to eat over one-and-a-half times the amount we would have needed 50 years ago. This is due to factors such as soil depletion and the prevalence of lower-nutrient, higher-yield crops. Suffice to say, to function at your best, you need to prioritise vegetables and berries, and there is no better way to sneak them into your diet than in smoothies.

Cliff's Perfect Smoothie

Start with 1 serve of a quality **protein powder**

THEN 3 x fist-sized servings of **leafy vegetables**

Add **berries** (to taste)

PLUS a few tablespoons of a **healthy fat source** (e.g. **olive, flax, coconut, macadamia** or **MCT oil**)

ADD **carbs** (**fruit, oats, cooked kumara** etc.) if you are active and carbohydrate-tolerant

BLEND with **ice** and **water** to desired consistency

HACK 9: Eat treats!

Life's too short to go without some of those foods that you love but that may not be ideal for your health, physique and performance IF you eat them all the time. The occasional treat won't upset your progress. In fact, having one or two treats a week can help you to mentally relax and feel like you are having some 'downtime'. Food is so very important for our mental, emotional and physical wellbeing, and when we allow ourselves to eat what I like to call 'foods for the soul', we honour that. It drives me nuts when I hear experts saying that 'food is just fuel'. NO, that's dead boring ... food is fun!

Above all, don't feel guilty about having the occasional treat. Remember that they are part of the plan, and if you do 'most things right, most of the time', you will get optimal results. Reread that: most things right, not all things right, all the time! Use this to reward yourself, but also make sure it's a positive, powerful, planned choice, not simply a resignation when you are feeling overwhelmed.

A great way to ensure that you are making empowered food choices (including treats) is to make treats fun and to make them an adventure! Don't have any old junk food just because you have allowed yourself a treat meal or because you are stressed out or exhausted and you 'gave up' on your nutrition plan. Instead, think of what you really desire. Go out somewhere and have something that you REALLY want to have. This makes the entire process an activity (an 'expedition') of powerful self-honouring and enjoyment. I always recommend leaving the house (because there shouldn't be 'treat' foods at home anyway – that's a sure-fire way to derail your progress) and being strong, proud and powerful in your conviction to go out and have a treat in the full view of other people.

So often I have clients tell me they feel guilty about the occasional treat and hide at home eating their favourite things. This only encourages weakened and disempowered associations with the foods we love. It is much better to treat ourselves with foods in a fun, playful and powerful way by going on a weekly or fortnightly expedition to have something wonderful.

HACK 10: Cut out fruit juice

For most people, eating fruit (in moderation) is great – but drinking it is not! Fruit juice can overload the body with too much fruit sugar, far too rapidly. You could not realistically eat the amount of fruit that you get from a large glass of fruit juice in such a short time, and most of us can't effectively deal with that large and consistent an influx of sugar if we do it too often. The best advice is that if you tolerate fruit, eat it but don't drink it!

HACK 11: Replace grains at meals with vegetables

Most of us should eat (a lot) more veggies and eat less pasta, bread and potatoes. We can kill two birds with one stone by eating lots (and LOTS!) of vegetables at our main meals to provide all those great nutrients –

without the extra carbohydrates. Put extra veggies on your plate where you would usually put carbohydrate-rich foods like bread and pasta! At each of your main meals (lunch and dinner), make sure you have at least three fist-sized servings of vegetables. That way, you'll get much closer to the now recommended 9+ servings per day of vegetables, fruit and berries.

HACK 12: **Base every meal on protein!**

Getting enough protein in your diet is essential for health and performance. Protein consists of strings of amino acids, which are the building blocks of all tissue and structures in the body. From them, we make neurotransmitters and hormones such as epinephrine and norepinephrine (our 'fight or flight' hormones) and serotonin, dopamine and melatonin, which are essential for a healthy mood balance, sleep and digestion, and the structure for every other cell, tissue and organ in the body! Eight of the amino acids that we derive from protein cannot be made in the body and so need to be included in sufficient amounts in the diet.

Protein also has a higher 'thermic effect of feeding' than either carbohydrates or fat. This means that you burn more calories as a result of eating protein foods compared to the same amount of either fat or carbohydrate.

Eating a higher-protein diet is associated with lower body-fat levels and increased fat-free mass (muscle). Eating sufficient protein will also increase satiety (feelings of fullness) and encourage greater stability in blood sugar levels – leading to better energy levels and a lessened desire to overeat.

To ensure adequate protein intake, start by ensuring that every meal contains a serving of a high-protein food. Good protein sources include grass-fed beef and lamb, poultry, free-range pork, eggs, fish and quality protein powders, or sprouted legumes, nuts and seeds (especially if you are vegetarian).

Despite some media reports, protein powders aren't dangerous to the body. In contrast, they are simply a convenient, easy option to provide that essential protein base for nutrient-dense smoothies, which can be easy-to-prepare, nutritious meals to fill the gaps in your day when you are unable to make a wholefood meal. They're certainly not better than wholefood sources of protein, but they can be a godsend for the convenience that most of us need from time to time to eat well consistently.

HACK 13: Take fish oil

Fish oil is quite simply the easiest way to supply quality omega-3 fats to our diet. In the modern Western diet, most people consume far too many omega-6 fats from the common vegetable oils found in processed and refined foods, factory-raised animals and cooking oils. These omega-6 fats in excessive amounts encourage inflammation and insulin resistance and are a possible causative factor for weight gain and obesity-related disorders. Omega-3 fats like fish oils help to redress this imbalance and encourage better overall health. Fish-oil supplementation is good for the heart and metabolic health, improves cholesterol and lipid profiles and reduces blood pressure. Benefits of fish-oil supplementation are also seen in depression and for joint swelling and pain in rheumatoid arthritis. Consumption of omega-3 fats from fish or fish-oil supplements reduces rates of all-cause mortality, cardiac and sudden death and possibly stroke.

But! These benefits are not necessarily seen with plant-derived oils that contain the 'base' omega-3 fat alpha-linolenic acid (like flax oil) because most people have very poor conversion rates of these plant-derived omega-3 fats into their usable metabolites.

HACK 14: Take a quality multi

Many of us don't get all the micronutrients we need to thrive from diet alone. This is especially true of vitamins A, B1, B6 and B12 and iron. A whopping 25% of us don't get enough zinc, while nearly 50% of us don't get enough selenium! So it makes sense that, along with eating a diet based on whole, nourishing foods, a quality multi can help to fill the gaps in your diet. Quality is key, though. Many multi formulas use poorer (cheaper) forms of vitamins (like synthetic B9 and B12) that either are not as effective or could even be harmful in the long term. Always choose a premium, high-quality multinutrient.

It's important for me to reiterate that food always comes first! But a quality multinutrient helps to fill in the gaps, and some compelling benefits have been seen in the research, including improved overall mortality, sleep and mental performance and reduced cancer and heart disease rates, weight gain, nausea, mood disturbance and stress.

HACK 15: Cut the lattes

Coffee and dairy are both fine for most people, most of the time. In fact, coffee intake is associated with reduced rates of diabetes, cardiovascular disease, liver disease, gallstone risk, cognitive decline, dementia and depression.

But some people are already stressed out, overworked and under-slept. If that sounds like you, the caffeine in coffee will not be helping you! And, perhaps more importantly, if weight loss is your goal and you're a real coffee fiend, the extra calories from milk in coffee can derail weight-loss efforts and can also lead to eating the odd extra 'treat' on your frequent coffee-shop expeditions! I have seen in clinical practice that for some people, the simple act of reducing coffee intake, and especially that of milk-based coffee drinks, can be a lynchpin for spurring weight loss.

So if you tolerate coffee well and don't overdo it, then continue to drink it, but if you think it might be holding you back, try having just black coffees or coffee with just a dash of milk (like a long macchiato), or simply take a break and see whether you are better off with or without coffee. (I love coffee, by the way, and you'll have to pry it from my cold, dead hands!)

HACK 16: Drink tea

Both green and black teas are packed with antioxidants. They are also potent thermogenics that can increase your utilisation of fat for fuel. Tea only has around one-third of the caffeine of coffee and so provides less of a stress effect than coffee if you are sensitive to caffeine's effects, and yet it still provides benefits for cognition, alertness and fat loss. It also gently relaxes you through the actions of L-theanine, an amino acid with proven benefits for mood, relaxation and cognition. Interestingly, many of the profound health effects of coffee are also seen to the same degree in tea drinkers.

HACK 17: Set limits on your alcohol intake!

Excessive drinking is harmful. Alcohol can reduce the body's ability to utilise stored fat for fuel, encourage the storage of both fat and carbohydrates as fat in the body and spur the breakdown of muscle. It increases inflammation, stresses our excretory systems and reduces our muscle-building efforts. Long-term overuse of alcohol is a known cause of cancer, liver disease and heart disease.

But a little alcohol in moderation is completely fine and may even be associated with modest benefits for health. An evaluation of the scientific evidence shows that one to two drinks per day is associated with a reduced risk of Alzheimer's disease, dementia and diabetes, reduced blood sugar, reduced risk for ischaemic heart disease (IHD), improved cardiac outcomes, improved cardiac markers, reduced risk for nasopharyngeal carcinoma and a 10% reduction in total mortality risk and isn't associated with kidney-function decline or weight gain.

However, many cancer types are increased at all levels of alcohol consumption, and oesophageal and liver cancers are increased even with moderate (approx. 2.5 drinks per day) alcohol use. The best advice is to limit alcohol intake to less than seven drinks per week for men and four for women.

HACK 18: Try using MCTs

Medium-chain triglycerides (MCTs) are one of my favourite supplements. In fact, I did my master's degree research on them! MCTs are a type of fat found in small amounts in dairy foods like butter and cheese and in palm oil and coconut oil. MCTs aren't digested and absorbed in the same way as normal dietary fats and instead are taken up directly into the liver from the gastrointestinal tract, where they are converted to cool, brain- and body-friendly fuels known as 'ketone bodies'. MCTs promote fat loss, especially in and around the belly. MCTs can also help us to stick to a healthy diet more easily by reducing voluntary food intake, increasing the desired time between meals and improving our portion control. Even relatively low intakes of MCT (as little as 15g or 1 tbsp per day) as part of the diet enhance how many calories we burn day-to-day.

HACK 19: Save your treats for after dinner

This tip seems like heresy ... BUT if you are following the tips outlined here (eating meals based on wholefood etc.), it's likely that you are 'crowding in' the good stuff and eating an appropriate amount. So if you do want a treat, the best time might be after dinner when you have already eaten, over the day, several good, healthy, satiating meals. This means that you are less likely to overeat treats later in the day than if you are trying to moderate them through the day. I use this strategy and find that if I eat well through the day and make sure I am getting in LOADS of vegetables, quality protein and healthy fats, it is difficult to overeat at night!

HACK 20: Restrict your feeding windows

Fasting has become a big thing. I started looking at the research around fasting way back in the late 1990s and was surprised to find that it wasn't detrimental to health and performance and, in fact, had a lot of health benefits. I say surprised because, at the time, everyone was still obsessed with having to eat many small meals throughout the day. One of the most compelling reasons to have fewer meals is often forgotten, though. When we limit our feeding windows, we simply eat less! What I mean is that if you have fewer hours to eat, you'll eat less. This is a consistent finding in our clinical practice, and so, for adherence and to keep getting consistent results for body-weight maintenance or for mental and physical performance, finding the number of hours or mealtimes that allow you to eat to satisfaction without overeating is a real blessing! I find that having a high-protein, vegetable-packed meal with plenty of healthy fats for either breakfast or lunch (depending on when I first get hungry) and the same for dinner allows me to, as mentioned earlier, also have some extra 'free foods' after dinner, and I'm not able to eat enough in those few feedings to put on extra weight!

Parting words from Cliff

Fitness expert **Jack LaLanne** (often referred to as the 'Godfather of Fitness') once said, 'If man made it, don't eat it.' And you know what? He was right!

Highly processed foods are most commonly the ones that promote inflammation, encourage fat gain and sabotage our energy levels, and so, to improve health and performance, the priority is not how much but what you are eating. Foods that are natural, whole and unprocessed are typically more nutrient-dense than processed and refined foods. This means that they contain greater levels of the essential vitamins and minerals and many more of the secondary nutrients like antioxidants. These secondary nutrients are not 'essential' (in that you don't need to eat them), but they are extremely health-promoting. Natural, unprocessed foods also have, in general, lower levels of carbohydrates and less potential to contain damaging inflammatory fats. Research indicates that a 'real-foods' diet (like the paleo lifestyle) may reduce obesity and many cardiac risk factors (blood pressure, average insulin, average glucose, total cholesterol, LDL cholesterol and triglycerides) while improving HDL cholesterol (commonly called 'good cholesterol') as well as body composition (your muscle-to-fat ratio).

If you do ever 'fall off the wagon', simply get straight back on track. Remember that we are in this skin a long time. One slip-up does not make for a complete failure! In fact, if you get straight back on track and take the learning from the deviation, you will continue to move steadily towards your goals.

Beware – those 'healthy' snacks may in fact be energy bombs

Do you know what's in that drink or seemingly healthy snack you're about to devour? Check out the label carefully. It could be a kilojoule-loaded 'energy bomb'.

So says **Dr Clare Wall**, associate professor of nutrition and dietetics at the University of Auckland.

She says some people think they are choosing a quick and healthy snack or drink, but it's worthwhile checking the ingredients carefully. Your snack may contain mega amounts of kilojoules (kJ), may be low in nutrients and won't necessarily make you feel full.

She says the Ministry of Health recommends a daily energy intake of 8700kJ for an average adult, but this will vary on individual needs and lifestyle. For instance, some muesli bars 'are like small cakes in disguise'.

'People think they're being healthy eating this, when sometimes they're having the equivalent of a cake, as they're high in sugar and fat,' Clare says.

A medium latte (about 360ml) with full-cream milk can contain more than 800kJ, and if you add cream, that's 300kJ more. Having three or four of these coffees daily can seriously increase your energy intake. Worse still, these caffeine fixes do not add much to the quality of your diet.

And don't get her started on those chilled Frappuccinos at some takeaway joints. There are at least 1000kJ in most of these, and some may have as many as 1900kJ.

As for alcohol, Clare says a 200ml glass of wine contains more than 800kJ and a beer has approximately 650kJ. These are 'empty kilojoules' because they have no nutrients, she adds. 'A bottle of wine has the same energy as a family-size block of chocolate.'

> 'Do you know what's in that drink or seemingly healthy snack you're about to devour? Check out the label carefully. It could be a kilojoule-loaded "energy bomb"'

After some snack ideas?

I've included some smoothie ideas in this book – some are super healthy, while others are more calorie-dense. There are even some cakes, because I believe in quitting the guilt around having the occasional treats.

Here are some of my other go-to snacks:

- Nut butter in Medjool dates – for a sweet treat. Add a drizzle of dark chocolate on top and this is heaven.
- Nut butter on its own from a spoon. Or I put a spoonful in celery and chomp it.
- Handful of nuts. I keep lots of different varieties in the freezer: walnuts, almonds, pecans, Brazil nuts, hazelnuts, macadamia etc.
- Yoghurt and berries like raspberries, blueberries or blackberries.
- Avocado with a squeeze of lemon or lime juice, salt, pepper and a sprinkle of chilli flakes on paleo crackers.
- Canned salmon or tuna. There are loads of varieties. I like the variety that are mixed in with beans and capsicum.
- Dinner leftovers, e.g. heated veg and kumara or some chicken. I often add salad leaves from the garden (after I've washed them under a tap, obviously).
- Small cubes of cheese.
- Piece of fruit that's in season.
- Bliss balls made of nuts, coconut oil, cacao, pumpkin seeds – whatever nuts and seeds I have in the cupboard at the time.
- A few squares of dark chocolate. I sometimes combine this with nuts too!

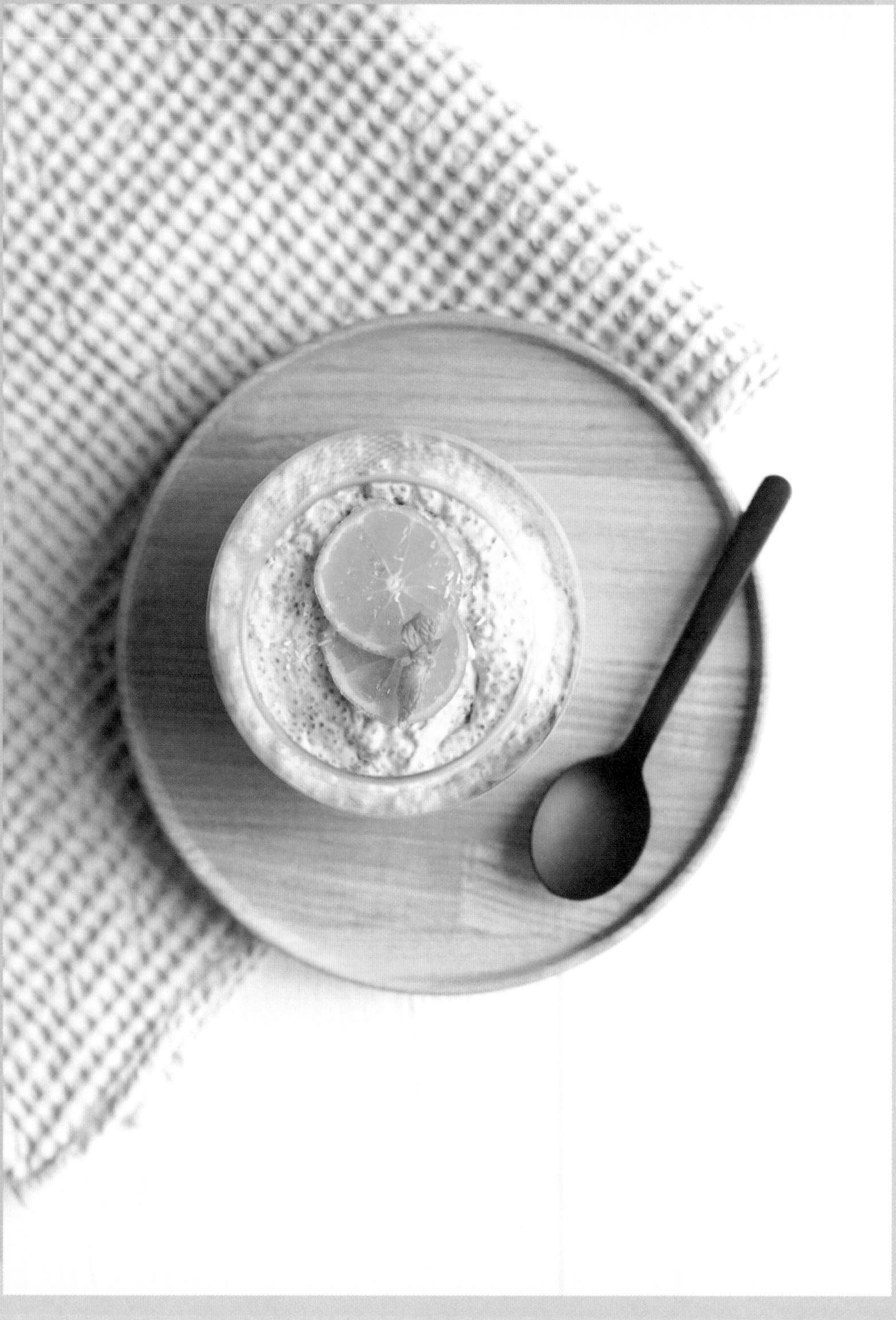

Sweet thangs, you make my heart sing₊

Everything in life can be enjoyed in balance. Here are some sweet treats, cakes and snacks. If you eat healthy most of the time, then the odd sweet treat should be savoured and enjoyed. This is the philosophy I live by – and how I coach my clients too. After all, life is too short to eat salad all the time, alone.

Hazelnut Bliss Balls

½ cup **hazelnut pulp**
(left over from the recipe on
page 68 or use ½ cup hazelnuts)

½ **orange** (juice and grated zest)

1 cup **fine coconut**

1 tbsp **coconut oil**

½ tsp **cinnamon**

1 tbsp dark **cacao powder**

1 tsp **vanilla essence**

pinch **salt** (kelp salt preferably)

Optional: chunks of your favourite
(store-bought) dark chocolate for the
centre of each bliss ball.

Optional: I like to sift cacao powder
over the balls after they are made for
an added taste of cacao and that
fancy-pants styling factor.

Place all the bliss ball ingredients
(except the chunks of chocolate) into a
bowl and mix well. Then roll balls out of
the mixture. For added wow factor, push
a chunk of chocolate into the centre
of each bliss ball while shaping them
in your hands. You can choose how
big you make the bliss balls. I generally
make them quite large so they can go in
my kids' lunchboxes. This is good energy
food! I sometimes put these bliss balls
on a platter when guests come around
along with wedges of chocolate, a
bunch of grapes, strawberries and
other dessert-style treats.

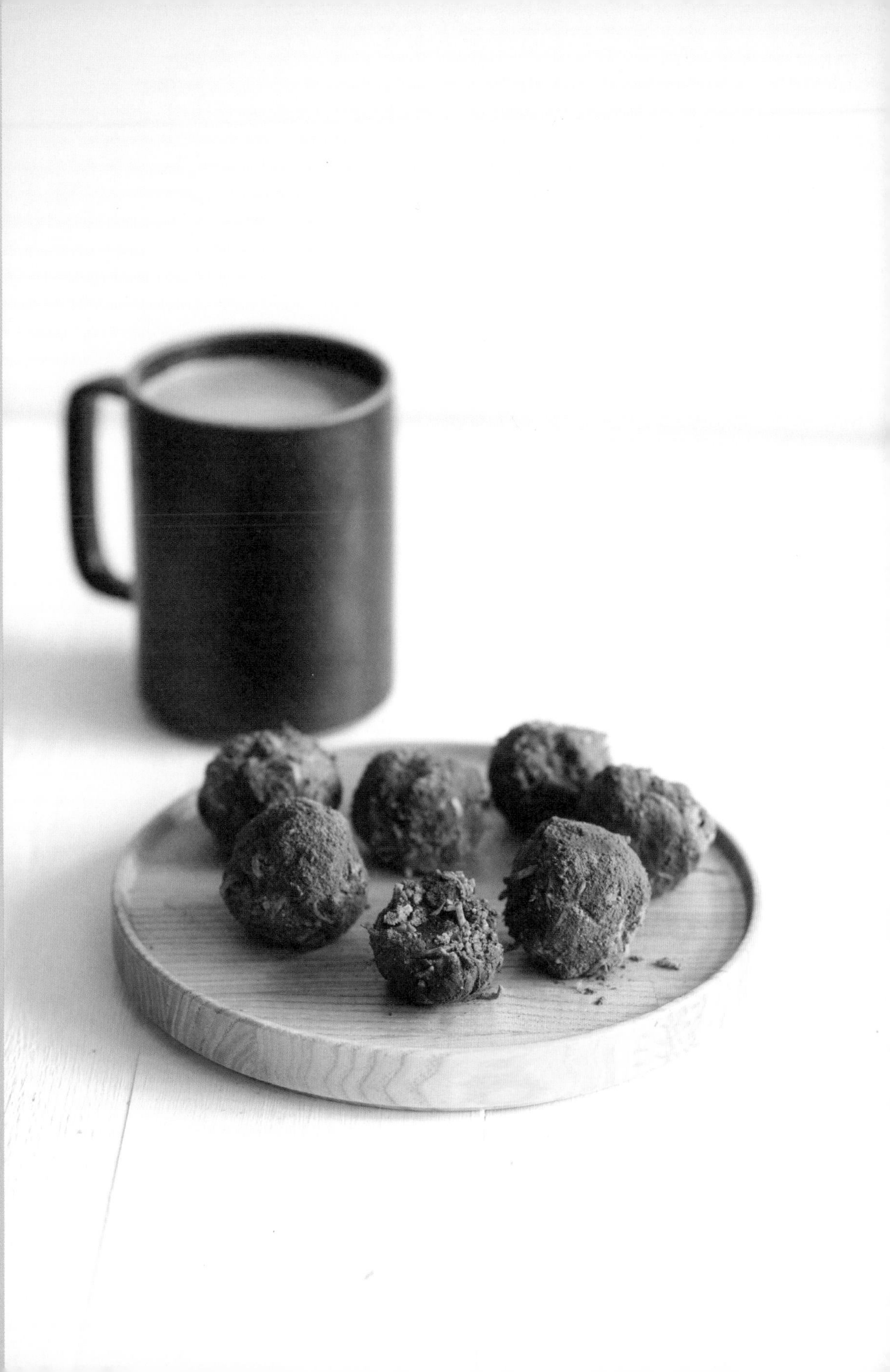

Choc Cherry Bliss Balls

When you gift something handmade, it means it is made with love. Make this for a friend who loves healthy snacks. Thinking of others in a small way like this can be uplifting. The snacks are also easy to make. My kids love these bliss balls in their lunchboxes.

Gift the jar of ingredients, or make the bliss balls up – your choice.

WHAT YOU NEED IF YOU ARE GIFTING THIS RECIPE:

A large glass jar with lid + large ribbon

1 cup raw **almonds**

1 cup shredded **coconut**

½ cup **Medjool dates**

⅔ cup **cacao powder**

¼ cup **dried cherries** (or cranberries)

⅓ cup small **dark chocolate bits**

pinch **salt** (I use kelp salt)

1 large **orange**

TO MAKE THE GIFT:

Measure out the dry ingredients and then gently layer all of these (one at a time) into a clean jar. Put the lid on top and add a ribbon. Gift this (and one large orange also) to someone you love.

TO MAKE THE BLISS BALLS:

Place all the ingredients (except the orange juice and zest) into a blender and blitz. Next, use a grater to get the zest off the orange and then cut the orange in half and squeeze all the juice. Place the zest and juice into the main mixture. Blend all the ingredients together. If it's not wet enough to bind, then add a little water (this happens if you use a small orange sometimes).

Using your hands, roll large bliss balls from the mixture, place into a container and store this in the fridge or freezer. When serving, sieve some extra cacao powder over the bliss balls. This gives them a light 'dusting' and they look prettier.

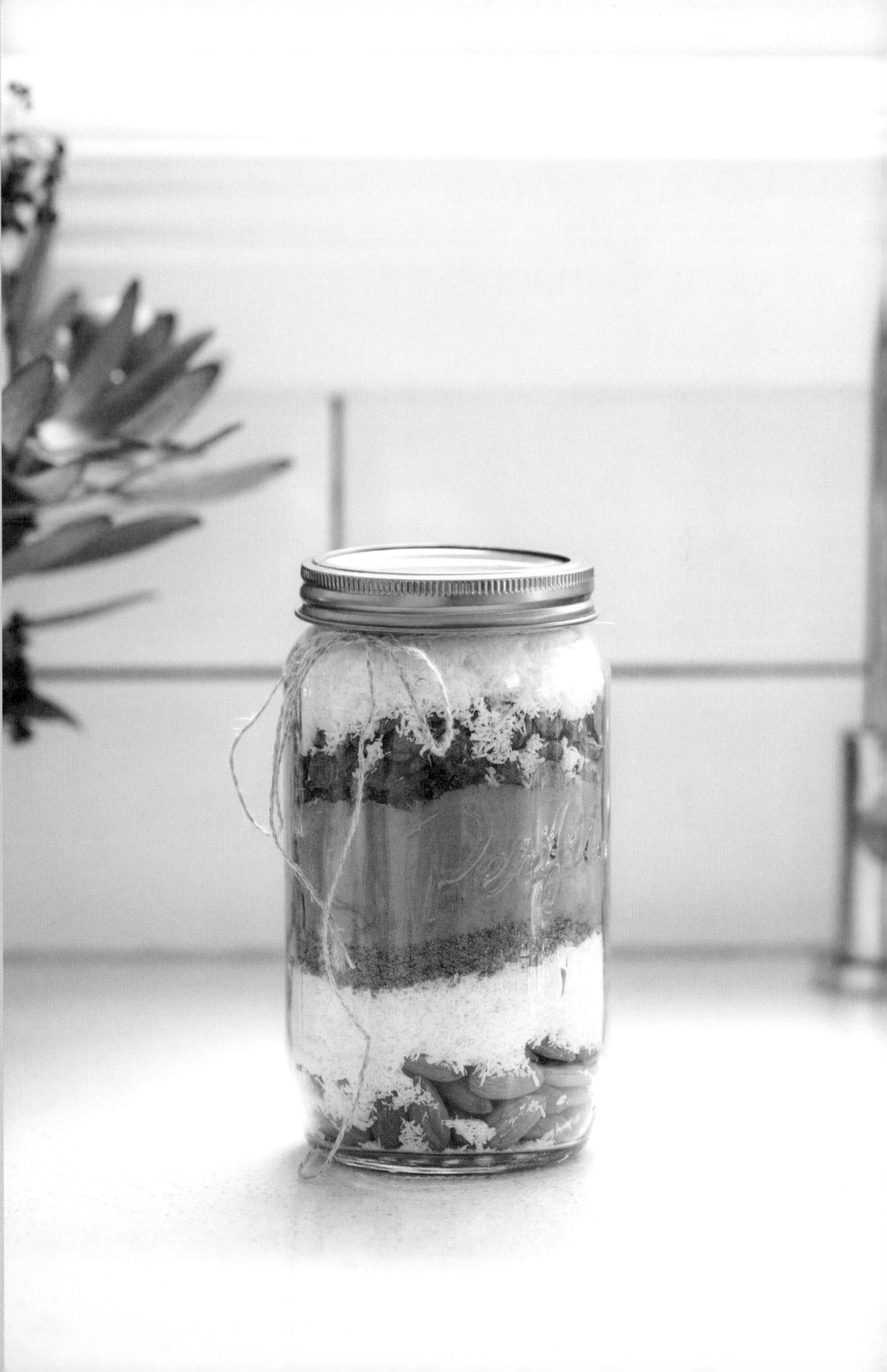

Gluten-free Choc Beetroot Cake with Choc Ganache

'Live life in balance.' That means you can have your cake and eat it too. I eat cake and chocolate and drink the occasional glass of wine. Life is for enjoying and occasional treats are to be savoured. Just have these things as treats sometimes, not all the time. I hate the idea of feeling guilty about having treats. We all need to let go sometimes. You know, enjoy the moment, and be social with others. Then get back to sticking to your regular way of living to fuel your body well at the next meal.

250g **butter**, softened

1½ cups **coconut sugar**

3 large **eggs**

1¾ cup **gluten-free flour** (1 cup rice flour, ¾ cup potato flour and 2 tsp xanthan gum)

2 tsp **baking soda**

2 tsp **baking powder**

½ cup **cacao powder**

2 tsp **vanilla essence**

½ tsp **salt**

1¼ cups **sour milk** (just use normal milk and add 1 tbsp of vinegar)

1 large **beetroot** (peeled and then finely grated, which makes up about 1 cup grated beet)

Preheat your oven to 180°C and line a cake tin with baking paper. Spray with oil or use a little butter.

Place the softened butter and sugar into a bowl and beat until whipped together. Then add the eggs one by one, beating in between each addition. Sift the dry ingredients into this bowl. Then add the remaining ingredients and mix until the mixture is smooth. Pour the mixture into the lined baking tin and bake for roughly 45 minutes (depends on how wide/deep your tin is – and so keep an eye on your cake in the oven!). Cool on a wire rack and then, when cool, sift some cacao powder over the top or add chocolate ganache.

TO MAKE THE GANACHE:

Put a can of coconut cream in the fridge for a few hours – or I usually leave one in the fridge overnight. Open the tin, scoop off the clear liquid and save this in a cup in the fridge to use in your next smoothie. Put the thick coconut cream in a bowl with ½ cup cacao powder, ½ cup natural sweetener (I use maple syrup usually but you can use what you like. My husband uses xylitol sugar). Next add ½ tsp vanilla bean powder. Mix and then spread on top of the cooled cake. Keep the cake in the fridge if you put ganache on it. Otherwise, the cake on its own can keep in a container on your bench for a few days if it's not warm weather.

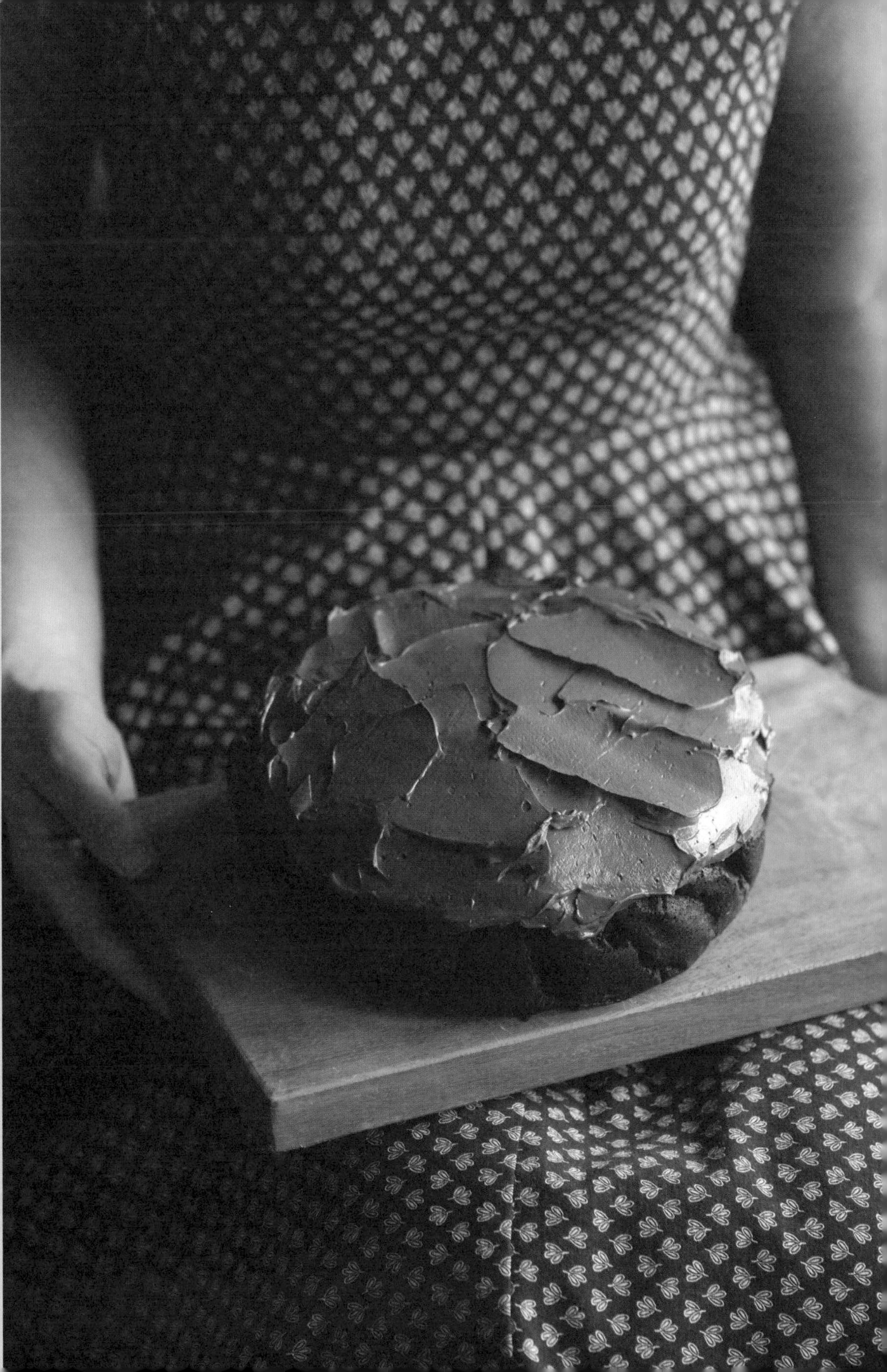

Gluten-free Carrot + Walnut Cake

1¾ cups **flour** (use any type you like. For a gluten-free cake, try 1½ cups rice flour, ½ cup chickpea flour, ¼ cup potato flour and 2 tsp xanthan gum – the latter is thickening agent)

2 tsp **baking soda**

2 tsp **cinnamon**

1 cup **coconut sugar**

pinch of **salt**

4 **eggs**

½ cup **rice malt syrup** (or maple syrup)

1 cup **oil** (I use coconut oil)

1 tsp **vanilla bean paste**

3 medium **carrots**, peeled and grated

1 cup **sour milk** (just mix 1 tbsp of lemon juice to 1 cup of milk)

½ cup **walnuts**, chopped

Turn oven to 180°C. Put baking paper in a baking tin and spray this with cooking oil.

In a bowl, sift the flour, baking soda, cinnamon, sugar and salt. Put this to the side. In another bowl, whisk the eggs, syrup, oil, vanilla paste, carrots and sour milk. Next, combine both bowls of ingredients together and then mix the chopped walnuts in gently with a spoon. Place the mixture in the tin and bake for 55 minutes (or a bit longer if you use a deeper, smaller baking tin). Just keep an eye on it!

Cool on a wire rack. Have as it is, or I sometimes put cashew-cream icing on top.

To make the icing, I put 1 cup of raw cashews in a bowl of filtered water for about two to three hours to soften. I then rinse them, put the cashews in a blender with just a little fresh filtered water and blitz them until smooth (add a little maple syrup to the cashew cream while blending it together if you'd like to sweeten this a little). I put the cashew cream in the fridge to thicken up and then later spread it over the cake once cooled.

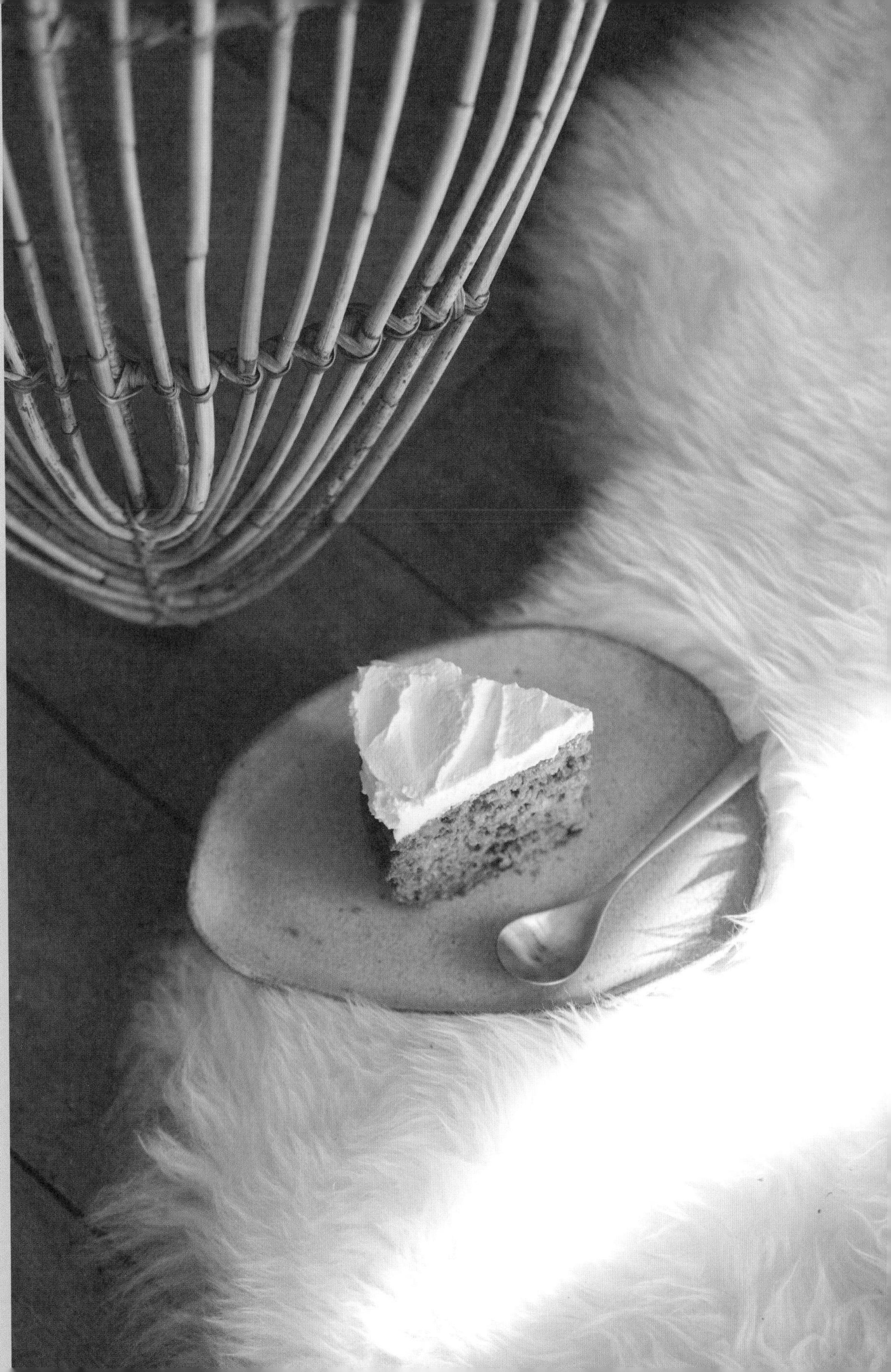

Lemon 'Licious Poppyseed Cake

When life gives you lemons, don't make lemonade – make this cake. It's gluten-free and mouth-wateringly good.

2 **lemons**

2 cups **ground raw almonds**

2 cups **coconut sugar** (or use white sugar if you want the cake to look more of a pretty yellow colour rather than a browner colour – your choice)

2 tsp **baking powder**

2 tbsp **poppyseeds** (optional)

5 **eggs**

OPTIONAL TOPPING:

1 **lemon**

2 **oranges**

maple syrup

Preheat the oven to 160°C. Put baking paper in a round tin and spray with oil.

Place the lemons in water in a pan on the stove and pop a lid on the top. Boil for 30 minutes, until they are soft. Drain and put to the side to cool. In a bowl, place the almonds, sugar, baking powder and poppyseeds (if you want the latter ingredient). Now leave this to the side.

Remove the pips from the cooled lemons and then put the lemons in a blender and blitz until a smooth consistency. Put the cooled smooth lemon mixture in with the dry ingredients and then mix in the eggs. Pour the mixture into the cake tin and bake for 75 minutes (depending on the shape/depth of your tin – so remember to keep an eye on it in the oven).

I eat this cake as is or add some yoghurt or whipped cream on the side. An optional topping that looks pretty neat is this idea: thinly slice an orange and lemon and put them on a lined oven tray. Drizzle maple syrup on top of these to glaze. Bake at 160°C for about half an hour to dry them out. Once done, I put them on the cake and then drizzle maple syrup on top.

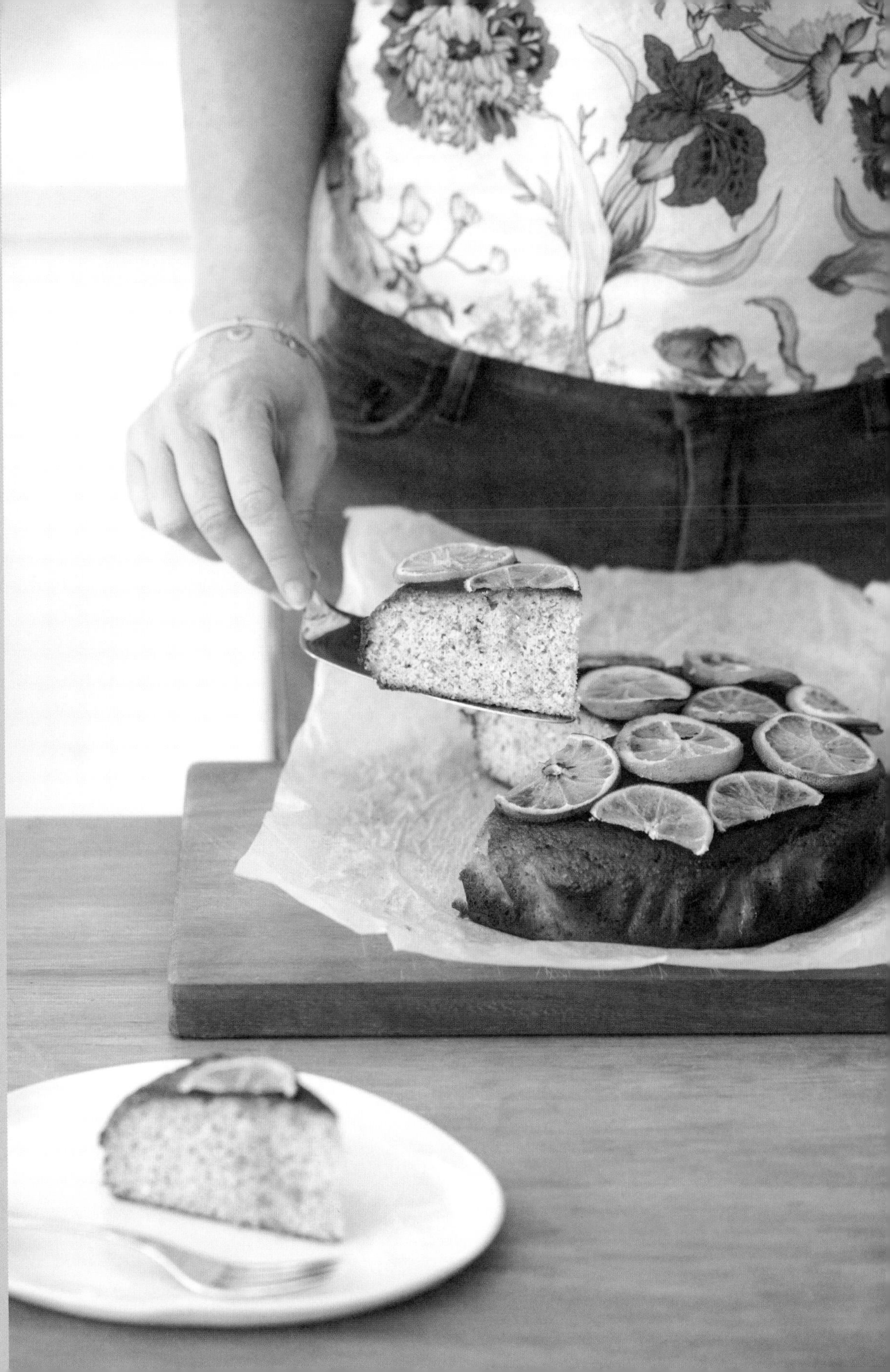

Raspberry + Apple Crumble

Warm desserts in winter are a heart-lifter. There's something just so comforting about a traditional crumble. This one has a lot of crumble on top of the fruit, which stops fights over there not being enough topping in my household! I bet this doesn't just happen in my house, right? Everyone loves the crumble, I'm sure.

6 apples

1 cinnamon stick

squeeze lime juice

2 cups raspberries (I use frozen ones generally)

1 cup whole oats

1 tsp cinnamon

1 cup coconut flour

½ desiccated coconut

½ cup coconut sugar

¼ cup ground hazelnuts

100g butter

Turn the oven on to 180°C. Slice the apples and then place them in a pot with water and the cinnamon stick. Boil these for 10 minutes roughly and then take them off the stove. Leave this to the side while you make the crumble.

To make the crumble, place all the dry ingredients into a bowl, chop the butter into small pieces and use your fingers to rub the butter through the mixture. Now leave this to the side.

Go back to the cooled apples and cinnamon. Blitz this in a blender after adding the lime juice (or feel free to leave the apple in the sliced form if you prefer, along with the cinnamon stick).

Place the cinnamon apples into a baking dish and then add the frozen raspberries, scattering them on top. Next place the crumble on top and place this in the oven for about 20 minutes, until it browns slightly on top. Serve this with yoghurt or whipped cream. My kids love it with French vanilla ice cream. Enjoy!

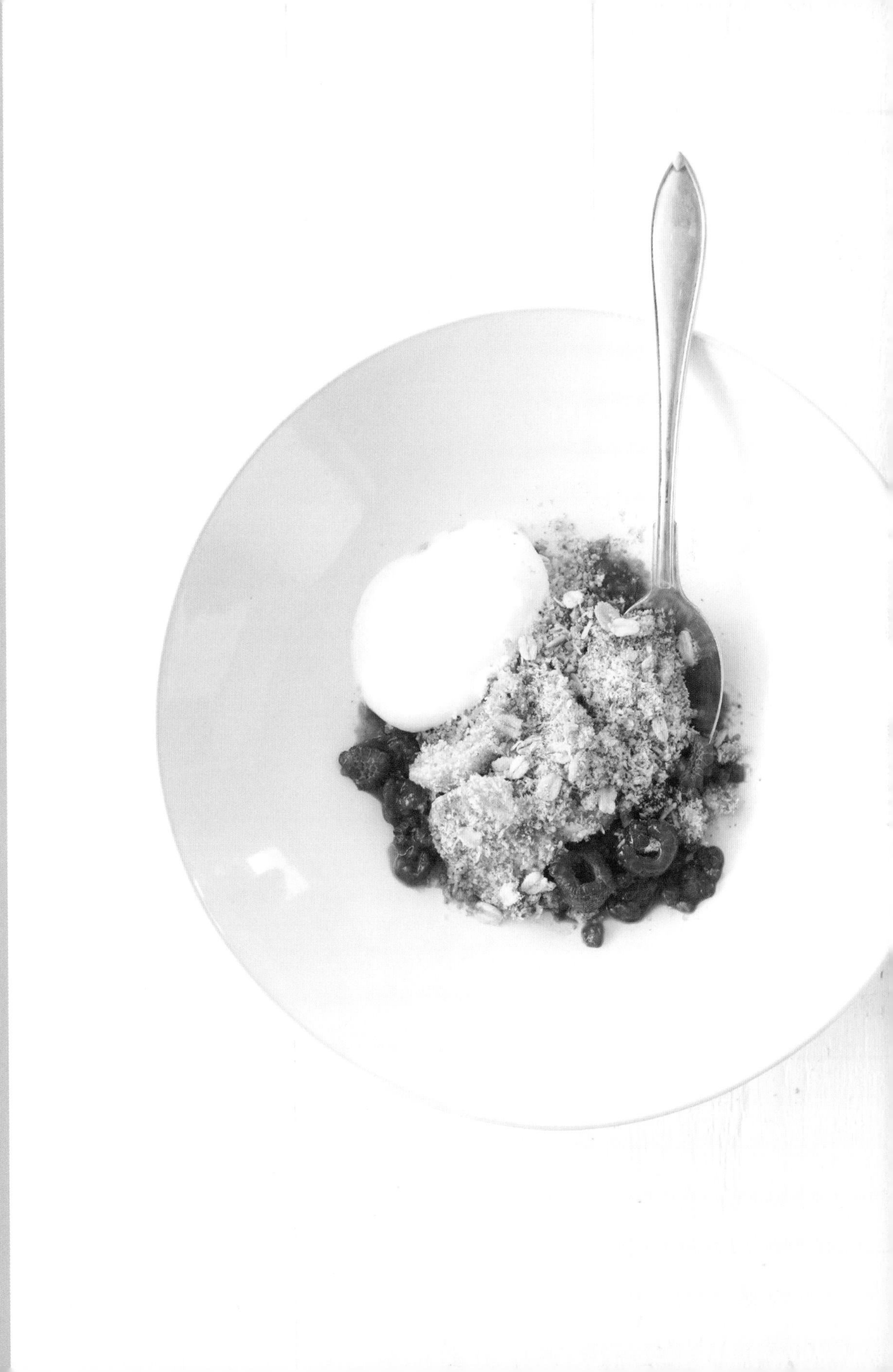

Gluten-free Gingerbread Men (and Women)

These gluten-free gems are delicious and crunchy. One useful 'ingredient' is that I use my kids to help me make these. But this is not a requirement. It just makes things more fun, and messy.

3 tbsp **golden syrup**

½ cup **sugar**

1 tsp **mixed spice**

1 tsp **cinnamon**

1½ tsp **ground ginger**

1 tbsp **water**

50g **butter**

½ tsp **baking soda**

200g sifted **gluten-free flour**
(I use 150g brown rice flour, 50g potato flour and 2 tsp xanthan gum – the latter is a binding ingredient)

1 tsp **baking powder**

Turn oven to 180°C and grease a tray with butter or a light spray of oil.

Place golden syrup in a pan, along with sugar, mixed spice, cinnamon, ground ginger and water.

Heat on a low heat until sugar dissolves and then turn off the element and allow the butter to melt in this mixture.

Take the pan off the element and let it cool for five minutes. Then add baking soda and mix.

In another bowl, put sifted gluten-free flour and baking powder. Then add the heated ingredients from the pan and mix until a workable dough. Keep adding more flour until you get a dough you can roll out (using a rolling pin). I use cutters for the gingerbread men and then a spatula to lift the shapes up from the bench and on to the tray (so they stay in one piece).

Bake these on the greased tray for about 10 minutes. As soon as they are cooked, use a spatula underneath each biscuit to lift them off the tray and put them on a wire rack for a few minutes to cool. Then eat one before the kids have the rest.

Tip: I love making these for the kids at Halloween. I just use bat cut-outs and then sprinkle red edible glitter on top of them for that fun factor! Or I coat them in melted dark chocolate and they go down a treat too.

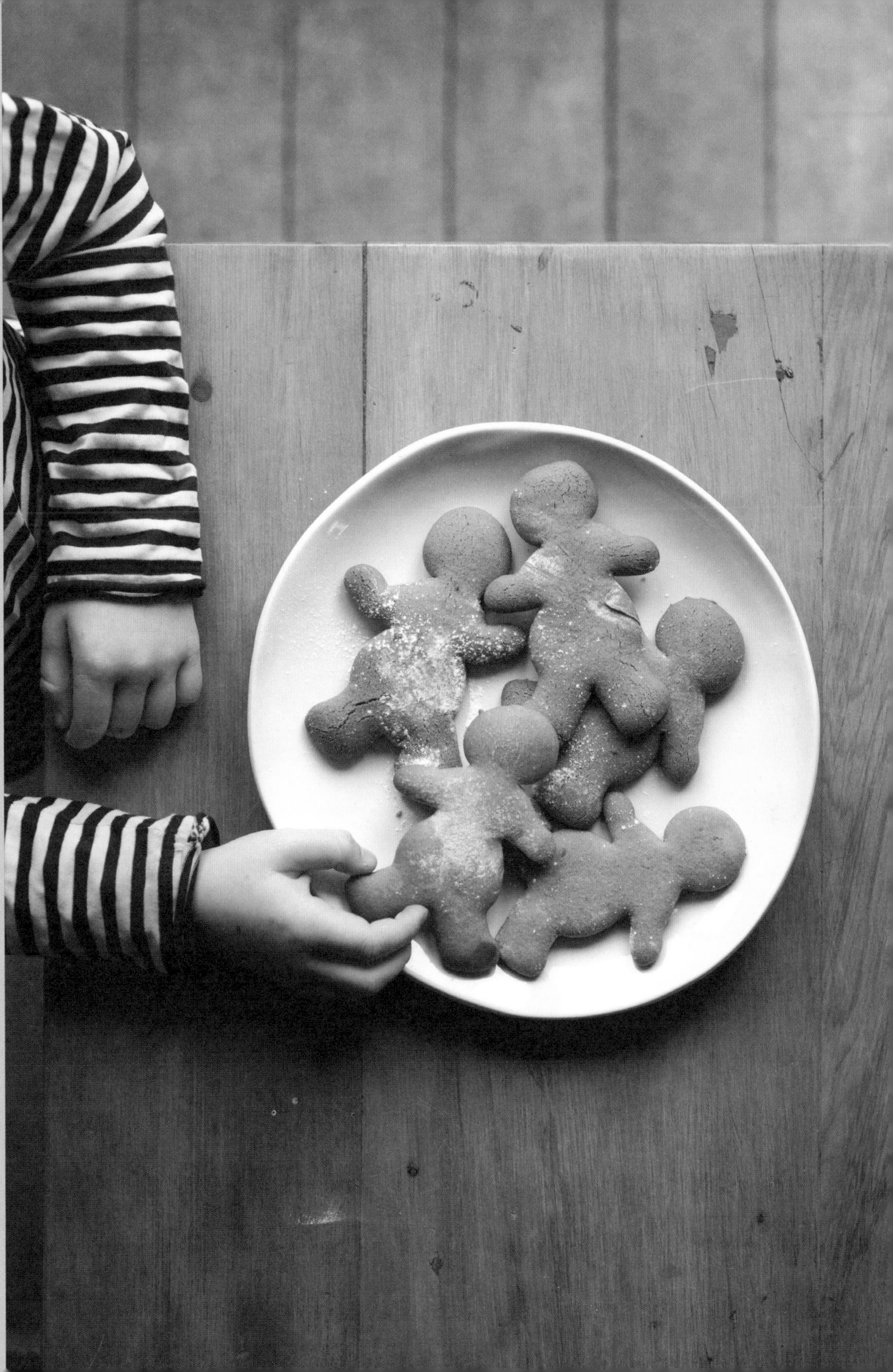

Mango Tango Chia Pudding

I love making desserts when friends come around for dinner. There's always dessert at my place; I believe in balance of all good things in life!

If it's winter, I'll bake. But during summer, an easy dessert I love to make is chia puddings. This mango chia dessert is creamy and delicious, and shows off the mango fruit. I was inspired after a visit to Bowen, in the Whitsundays, in Queensland. Here the fruit grows in abundance. This recipe is like that feeling of sunshine on your face on a blissful, relaxed summery Sunday. There's joy with every spoonful. In Bowen, there's a giant mango which cost about $90,000 to build. This giant mango makes the place memorable and there's a shop nearby where you can buy local frozen whipped mangoes in a pot, which are a terrific thirst-quencher.

Every time I make this dessert it transports me to the Whitsundays. It's often not just the taste of a meal but also the memories attached to food that really make the overall experience bliss.

1 fresh **mango**

1 cup **coconut yoghurt**

½ tsp **cinnamon**

¼ cup **white chia seeds**

Roughly cut up the mango (removing the skin and pip) and put this into a blender. Add the coconut yoghurt and cinnamon and blend until smooth. Then add in the chia seeds and stir in gently with a spoon. Place this into glasses and leave in the fridge for 30 minutes (or ideally overnight) to let the chia plump up. Then top with whatever you like. The topping here is a couple of slices of fresh mandarin (because they were in season at the time) plus a hint of mint.

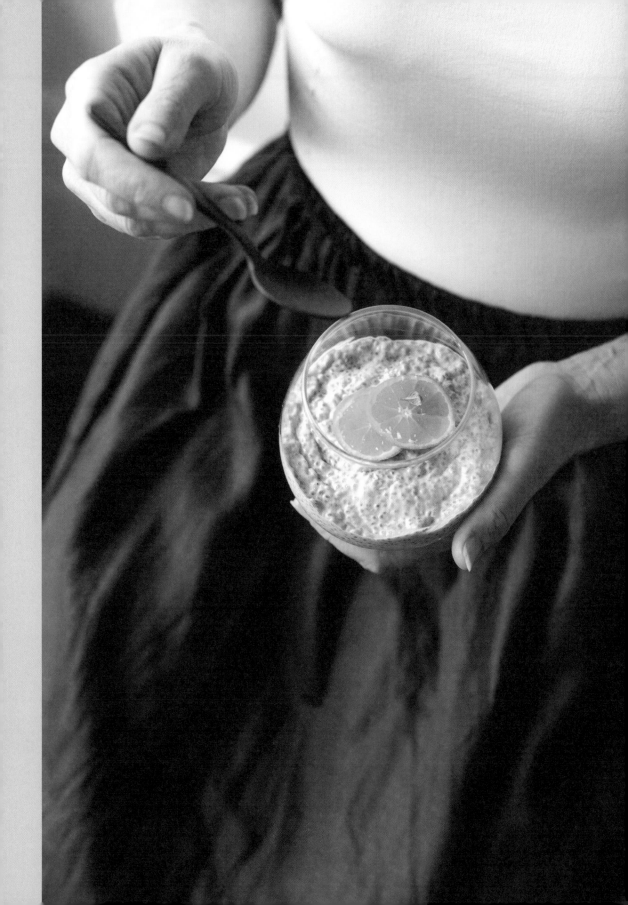

Homemade Chocolate

This is on repeat at my house because it's so yum.

300g **cacao butter**

½ cup **cacao powder**

pinch **kelp salt**

½ cup **maple syrup**

Place a pan on the stove with a little water and put this on a medium heat. Then place a glass bowl in the pan. Put the cacao butter into this bowl to gently melt. Once melted, place this to the side. In another bowl, put the rest of the ingredients. Then add these ingredients to the cacao butter and stir until a smooth texture. Next line a tin with baking paper and pour the chocolate mixture into this. Place this in the freezer for a few minutes so it can start to harden. Then bring it out of the freezer and top with whatever you like. You could just use shredded coconut, for instance. On this one I put hazelnuts, pistachios, coconut chips and crumbled freeze-dried mandarin. Leave it to set fully in the freezer and then eat later as you wish.

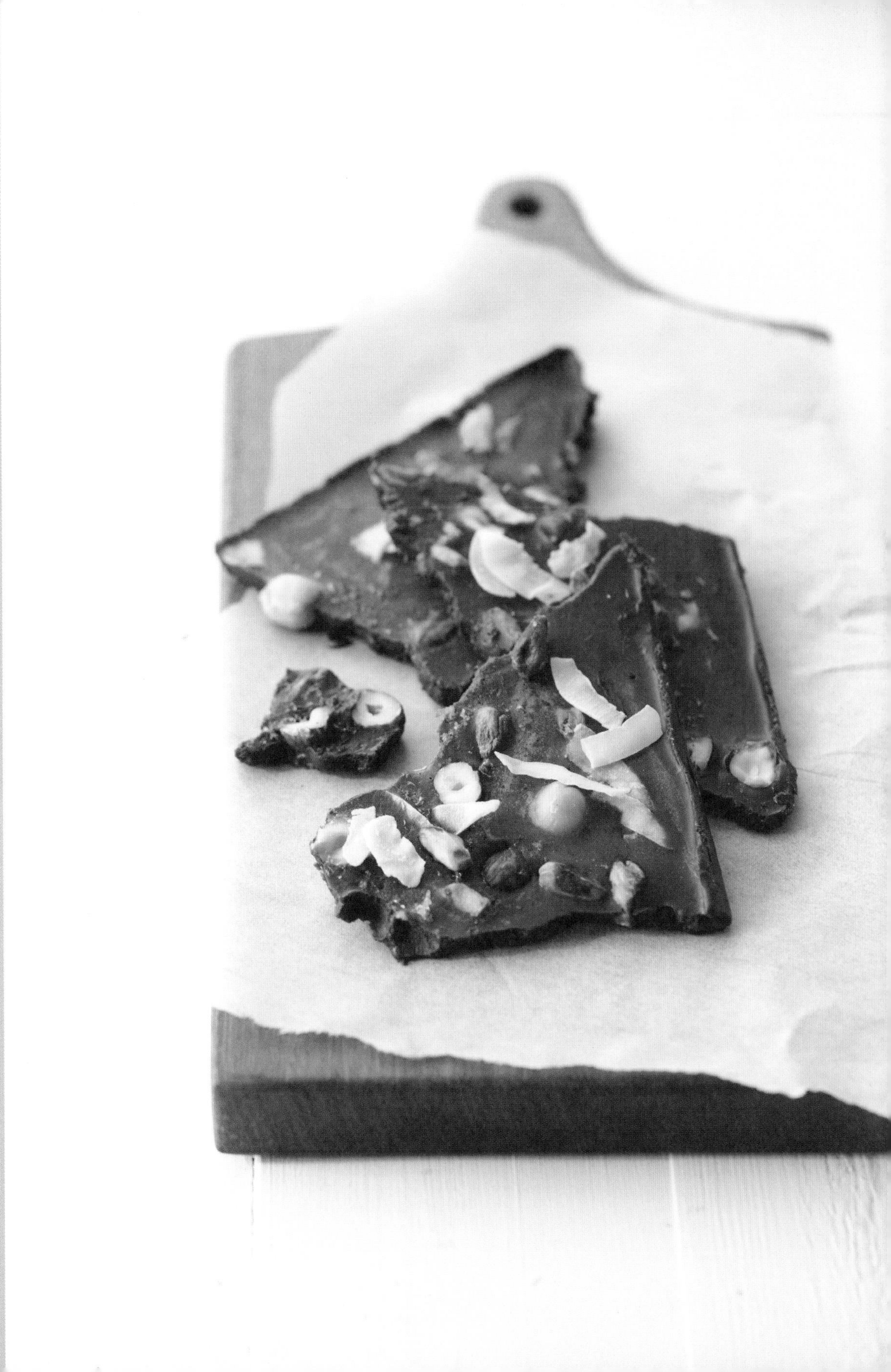

The gimme-gimme-more way of life₊

Money shouldn't be your only life metric. Money can help with opportunities and give you more options. It can help with happiness and help boost satisfaction levels up to a certain point. But more and more money will not necessarily buy more and more happiness.

Life ultimately is about experiences and authentic connections with people you care about and love, not stuff.

Instead of finding more happiness, I'd recommend finding your flow. I did a presentation on flow – or, essentially, around Hollywood happiness versus authentic happiness – in 2017 for the active-watch company Fitbit. The topic of the talk was 'Finding Your Life Flow'.

I spoke about things which boost real happiness and the way you feel. Some of these things include getting sufficient sleep, eating nutrient-rich foods, drinking enough water, self-care rituals, mindful living with not too much stress, having a positive mindset and feeling successful. Then I talked about connecting well with others and also, as the ultimate, finding your flow.

Psychologist **Mihaly Csikszentmihalyi** writes about flow being 'the secret to a life worth living'. What he means is that you can find authentic happiness and pleasure and lasting satisfaction through doing activities that put you into a state of flow.

The requirements for finding flow generally include a reasonably high skill set. You need to have practised something lots, but you should also still be challenged by it. Musicians can find flow through playing an instrument, while surgeons can go into flow too – a state of 'doing'. You know that expression 'getting lost in the moment'? It really means something.

I personally find flow through running. It took me years to learn how to run well and get better at it. I had to work at this skill over quite a bit of time. But now I can run with ease. I feel freedom while running. It's joyful and like moving meditation for me. Running takes me to my happy place, so to speak. I can feel lost in the moment while in motion.

When I did that speech for Fitbit, I asked the audience to think about something they liked doing and then advised them to spend time doing this regularly to raise their life enjoyment. But remember, what helps me to go into a state of flow is not necessarily what another person might enjoy. We are all different, and so the message is to find something that resonates with you and helps you to feel happy.

At this talk, I told the audience how long it took me to find flow through music as an example. I recall learning how to play the alto saxophone when I was 11 years old. In the beginning, I tortured my parents with loud, squeaky honking sounds and felt frustrated at not being able to play a song well. But, slowly, over many years, I mastered the keys, tone and timings better and my enjoyment levels started to soar. My parents' enjoyment levels at listening to me also changed dramatically. Once, they suffered through my honks with the instrument. Now, they would tell me how much they loved listening, and I'd often hear them humming the songs I played long after I finished practising.

I then got to a level where I could play in an orchestra. I wasn't a brilliant musician, but I could learn to play songs well if I worked on them. I could read music with ease, and playing music was satisfying and uplifted my soul. It helps me find flow now, too, all these years later. It's even more uplifting to hear my son Zach play this instrument. That's about being a proud parent, really, rather than finding flow, but it still makes me happy!

In life, you need activities or interests outside of work stresses. You need something for yourself that's fun and helps you to feel good. This is the magic of flow. It's like a reset button. Too much work and you will feel out of balance. Too much play and you won't feel challenged enough. In the yoga world, we call it finding effort and ease (or rather sthira and sukha).

Decluttering

This is one thing I'm working on myself. I do have too much stuff. All those handbags in my closet really need a rethink. And my wardrobe could do with a sort-through. I'm certainly not perfect. But I do try to buy things that last and that I have in mind to keep longer-term, rather than buying lots of cheap throwaway items. I believe that every dollar we spend can have an impact.

I speak with **Rachel Hoffman**, author of **Unf*ck Your Habitat: You're Better Than Your Mess**, to get some tips around how to declutter. She's the expert here, not me!

We talk via Skype. She is in Rhode Island, a US state in New England, while I am in Auckland.

Rachel appears for our chat and confesses immediately that she is in her PJs. It is late at night in her part of the world. I tell her I love her for this! I love anyone who doesn't take life so seriously. I feel immediately at ease and like I am chatting to someone who lives life in a realistic fashion, rather than by perfectionism.

I tell her that after reading her book, I realised there were so many areas of my life that I needed to declutter.

Rachel is so excited to hear this. 'Oh, good, oh, good. But did you get them done, though? That is the question,' she probes.

'Reframing your thinking from being all-or-nothing to every-little-bit-counts can be transformative.'

'Er, no. It's on my to-do list,' I admit, chuckling. I immediately confess that my emails need a serious clear-out. I don't confess to my handbags or clothes, however, this early on in our chat!

I tell her my takeaway from her book is to declutter a little bit at a time and that this eventually adds up to a lot of mess-clearing.

'Reframing your thinking from being all-or-nothing to every-little-bit-counts can be transformative,' she says.

Here are her thoughts on that whole gimme-gimme-more way of life which I named this chapter after.

She says: 'I think when we accumulate so much stuff over the course of just living our lives, what happens is we get completely overwhelmed with the amount of stuff we have. It's as if you feel like the more you have, the better you are doing or the more successful you are. You associate things with happiness or success.

'I'm not a proponent of extreme minimalism or getting rid of everything until you are down to one chair and two dishes! There's definitely an amount of stuff that we need to exist today. I just want people to have a better relationship with their stuff.

'So, rather than accumulating all these things and feeling stressed out in having to deal with them, we should have a balance and ask ourselves,

"What are the things that I need and what are the things that I love?" The rest can go. Ask yourself, "How can I interact with all of this stuff that allows me to enjoy my home?"

I ask Rachel if her approach is like feng shui, which includes clutter-clearing. She says it is entirely different. Her approach is to have systems for decluttering that are practical, rather than philosophical.

'My goal is to get into how people actually live their lives and to devise strategies that work within everything else that is going on. We need systems that take into account that you might work full-time, that you are a student or that you are a shift worker. It's important to find a way to adjust and adapt to the reality of your situation,' she explains.

For example, you may have a mental health issue and be struggling to declutter. Feeling mentally unwell can be closely linked with a cluttered environment, she says.

'Depression, anxiety, ADHD, any of those things that affect your everyday life can then get reflected in your living space. Some people may not get out of bed for a couple of days. Having an anxiety attack can make cleanliness hard. Then the mess can become overwhelming and they don't know what to do with it.'

Rachel came to write her book as a result of starting a blog on decluttering about eight years ago. Back then, she had a different tone, because it was mostly her friends reading her words.

> "What are the things that I need and what are the things that I love?" The rest can go.

'I would tell them to do stuff and then report back when you've done it. What I found is it was holding people accountable and they would come back and tell me about it. It grew from there.

'It started out kind of mean, jokingly drill-sergeant-like, and then I found that over time the approach got much more compassionate. I found people with disabilities or mental-health issues, or children of hoarders, needed kinder guidance,' she says.

So she stopped being 'judgemental' around mess. However, she does still try to hold people accountable.

I ask Rachel if her house is immaculate now.

'My house is entirely average. It's pretty messy right now, because I have a bunch of things to do and I've got kind of caught up,' she says. 'So it needs a little work.'

Rachel tells me she lives with three chihuahuas. 'So it is not all entirely my fault,' she says, chuckling.

I love Rachel's response. She's relatable and real, and, again, she comes back to guiding people through living a life in balance, not perfectionism, when it comes to tidiness. After all, who has a tidy house all the time?

Rachel then tells me she refers to herself as a 'reformed messy person'.

'I've been there, and so I can understand a lot of what is holding people back,' she explains. 'People who are not naturally neat and tidy do not know how to get through this.

'Having an anxiety attack can make cleanliness hard. Then the mess can become overwhelming and they don't know what to do with it.'

'Number one is to get off social media and go wash your dishes. Now! Then, don't put things down. Put them away instead.'

'I understand some of the obstacles because I have them, and I understand some of the excuses and some of the troubles. Overall, the experiences I've had allow me to reach people on this topic.'

I ask Rachel to share some of her top tips on decluttering.

'Number one is to get off social media and go wash your dishes. Now! Then, don't put things down. Put them away instead. This means you will not have to deal with it later and you are not building your mess. A couple of seconds' tidying in the moment can save you a lot of time down the road. It's about changing small habits. It's about doing little things for small amounts of time.

'I wish I could tell people to stop doing your whole house one weekend or one day. Tackle a little bit at a time instead. Don't save it all up to do it all at once and then get frustrated or overwhelmed. The only way people know how to clean is top to bottom, and I encourage people to reframe their thinking.'

Rachel says people often tell her the mess is 'too overwhelming' or 'too bad'.

'This is because they are looking at it as one big problem to solve, rather than doing 20 minutes at a time. And doing 20 minutes at a time can make a big difference.'

I ask Rachel if her email inbox is in need of a clean-out – like mine.

'Actually, it's okay! I delete what I have to delete, unsubscribe when I have to,' she says.

She wants people to let go of this idea that everything has to be perfect.

'We need to be more forgiving of ourselves. We tend to judge ourselves very harshly when things are getting a little messy at home. But be kind on yourself. Remember you can do a little bit at a time, you don't have to do it all at once. It will get done in the end.'

Rachel says she ultimately wants people to enjoy the space they live in and be comfortable in it. This is not about feeling bad when you are not in a magazine-worthy and super-tidy home.

Rachel says she ultimately wants people to enjoy the space they live in and be comfortable in it.

10 hacks for sustainable living

'Buy Less; Become More.'

These words are in bright pink letters on the cover of Australian author **Sarah Wilson**'s latest recipe book, **Simplicious Flow**. This book is about nutritious eating with zero waste.

I could have put Sarah in the nutrition part of my book. I absolutely love her recipes and she's a superstar at creating nutrient-dense food that people love. She's viewed as one of the top 200 most influential authors in the world for good reason. She has penned a string of cookbooks and also one book on anxiety called **First, We Make the Beast Beautiful: A New Story About Anxiety**. Sarah lives with anxiety and shares, openly and passionately, an approach to life that helps her now thrive, in the hope it will help others too.

So, back to why I asked Sarah to be in this chapter. Her new cookbook has not only amazing food but also a passionate striving for more sustainability. She's passionate about us all collectively caring for the planet more. She hopes to inspire others to live life more consciously and thoughtfully. You could also call her approach mindful living. Actually, I don't care what you call it. Just do what she preaches.

She doesn't just care about eating good food that fuels her body well. She also gives a stuff about not stuffing up the planet with needless waste along the way.

She's passionate about us all collectively caring for the planet more. She hopes to inspire others to live life more consciously and thoughtfully.

I asked Sarah to share some hacks on living a sustainable life because this is a heart-led thing for her and she has some cool tips to share on how to do it.

I'll confess, meeting Sarah was a huge highlight for me as a health journalist. I first met her to interview her for a magazine column, and I'm embarrassed to say I got a bit tongue-tied and might have even gushed at the start. I was anxious as hell because she is a bit of a hero of mine. But I also knew she'd be okay about my anxiety and gawkiness because she has anxiety too.

Actually, the meeting went okay. I gushed once and then got over it pretty quickly. Thankfully.

I guess my meeting Sarah was kind of the equivalent of a sports-mad bloke meeting his sporting superhero. Sarah inspires me to do more for the planet and thus 'to be more'. Yeah, she's got glowing skin and is beautiful. But what I really dig are her forward-thinking 'smarts'.

I was cheeky enough to ask her to be part of this book, and I was blown away when she said yes. She's not only a famous author, she also does not have a bad bone in her body, obviously. (She also likes old bones – read the hack that includes them. It did get me thinking I'm a bit more conservative than Sarah when it comes to zero food waste. But I like that she's stretching my way of thinking.)

Here are a series of hacks that Sarah does for sustainable living and which we should all be doing to save money and save the planet. These are in no particular order.

1. Use your head: use your feet

'I walk. Walking is the multitasker's dream thing to do. I cover this in my book **First, We Make the Beast Beautiful**. There's so much science attached to this in terms of helping to manage anxiety. The part of the brain that modulates the walking motion is the same part of the brain that controls flight or fight, and it's the oldest part of the human brain. It is a mono-tasker. It's like your grandfather; it can only do one thing at once. While you are walking, you can't be anxious.

'That's one study. There are other studies to show that walking goes at the same pace as discerning thought, too. That in itself can modulate anxiety. It also helps you think. Philosopher Friedrich Nietzsche said that no good idea had not come about through walking. Charles Darwin walked, Virginia Woolf walked …

'Don't own a car, because then it forces you to walk and ride. You get creative. I love working out, "Oh, all right, I'll walk to there and get the ferry there, walk there, and then get the train from there …" Just work it out. You've even got a phone now that works it all out for you.

'The cost of a car is incredible, and there are the environmental factors. I'm part of a car-share scheme. There are cars parked all over Sydney that you can use. So if I've got to go and pick up some stuff or drive quite a distance, I hire one.'

2. Be wheelie cool

'When I travel, I ride a bike. In London, Paris, Slovenia or New York, wherever I am, I sign on to the bike-share scheme. That's how I get around. I'll ride all across New York on a bike. It means you get to see the city, get to meet people. You are part of the local system. 'Sustainability can be about engagement, too. Once you are engaged, it goes into flow. Part of my mantra with this is, "Start somewhere." Like my book – there are 52 challenges. Just start somewhere and you will start to get a kick out of flow. You get a taste of it and you want to try something else. Being engaged and riding a bike is wonderful for that.'

3. Be a butter scavenger

'This one horrifies my friends! You know when they bring out the little thing of butter at cafés? I collect that.'

I tell Sarah I'm amazed she has the courage to do this with her anxiety.

'Some things are bigger than my anxiety, and one of those things is my outrage around food waste. Look, to be honest, a part of it is that I feel a sense of responsibility. It's kind of what I do, and I'm trying to influence people [not to waste food].'

Sarah adds that she does the same with bones from other restaurant tables. She can tell I'm squeamish over that recommendation and almost takes delight in it.

'They're good for boiling!' she raves. 'You are going to boil them at a high temperature and simmer them for two hours. There's not going to be anything resembling a germ left, right? Use your common sense. That's the thing.'

I ask her if this is really just going back to how our grandparents lived.

'Being frugal is cool. It's actually a rare moment to be a renegade against this consumer culture. It's a way of standing up to it.'

4. Limit liquids

'Don't indulge in liquids. I only drink three things: red wine, coffee and tap water. Choose a few things that you really enjoy drinking. Be aware that anything liquid tends to come with a tonne of sugar, which is very hard to digest and hard to metabolise because it travels so quickly to the liver. It's extremely deceptive – a large glass of juice could include six teaspoons of sugar, which is beyond the daily limit, and you drink it in about a five-minute hit. And your liver will store that instantly, like it would any toxin, and store it as visceral fat.

'Then there's the sustainability point of view. Drinks are usually in single-use containers. Then there are the straws, the plastic lids and cups ...'

I ask Sarah if cardboard straws are okay.

'If they recycle them, but I doubt they do. But at least they don't kill turtles.'

5. Ditch takeaways

'Don't do takeaways. Or, if you do, take your own container and ask for "food only" – that is, you don't want the serviettes, chopsticks, containers and so on. This is something the Americans do. And then walk to pick it up. That's flow – it's an opportunity to walk with your boyfriend or your husband, too. And you also worked up an appetite along the way.'

6. Cursing takeaway coffee cups

'It's a huge part of our culture to get a takeaway cup even if you are sitting in a café, which just baffles me. People say to me, "Do you use a keep cup?" I always allow five or 10 minutes to just sit and drink my coffee out of crockery. I think the whole takeaway culture is dreadfully unsustainable. I mean, 70% of coffee cups are non-recyclable or not biodegradable. Everyone thinks that you can recycle them, but, no, they tend to have plastic on the outside to keep the heat in. Coffee cups, plastic bottles and straws are the biggest contributors to ocean pollution. So cut them out, eat in, use your mouth. I don't even use keep cups. It's just another thing to buy.

'Everyone is craving five minutes to collect their thoughts. Do so while you are having a coffee. I drink a black coffee every day. Or if you do like takeaway coffee, then make your own takeaway coffee cup. Make your own with a glass jar with rubber bands around the outside to grip. I can stick mine in the dishwasher, and it's all fine.'

7. Buy in bulk

'Buy at bulk food stores, plus take your own jars and containers. Herbs and spices here are a tenth of the price, and you can often get bargains like broken nuts and things like that.'

8. Eat everything on thy fruit

'Don't peel things. I don't peel pumpkin. I eat orange peel because I like it. Don't peel kiwifruit. If you are using strawberries in smoothies, then why would you take the hull off them? Why would you take the green stuff off those strawberries when you are only going to add kale? Things like beetroot leaves – whack them in. Eat the whole food.'

9. Buy organic chicken and eggs

'Always buy chicken and eggs organic. It's one of those foods where it really does make a difference. In my book, I've got how to make 14 organic meals from one organic chicken. When you use an organic chicken, you can then feel confident about boiling the bejesus out of the bones to get the stock and so on.'

10. Freezer smarts

'Lean how to use your freezer. It runs more economically when it is full, because solids freeze at a higher temperature than air, so the freezer doesn't have to work so hard. I freeze leftovers, nuts and bananas when they are in season.'

How to reset to find your happiness+

Take time for yourself. Don't feel guilty. Make sure you have time to reset and have that balance.

Do something you love. It helps your brain to function at a higher level, inspires creativity and helps you to reset your happiness levels.

Everyone needs me time. It nurtures us and helps us to shake feeling overwhelmed. However, what one person enjoys might be another's nightmare. For example, I love running, but a lot of my friends consider this some kind of self-inflicted torture. They'd only choose to run if they were being chased by a tiger. I get that!

Some people like crafting, knitting, mindful drawing, gardening, baking, listening to bands or playing a sport. Whatever you dig, do it often.

Never let being 'too old' be an excuse with learning. My husband, for instance, started learning to play the piano in his late 30s. You just have to embrace the idea that you will not be very good at this new skill for a while and that it will take some time to get better. But with practice, your ability and enjoyment levels can soar.

Strength in stillness

We live on a stressful and sped-up planet. Everything is getting faster and more efficient.

But going faster isn't always better. It can lead to burnout. So it's important to prioritise time to feel calmer and have more clarity. There is power in pausing and doing meditation. We can then reset and strengthen.

When I teach yoga and meditation, I share with students that meditation is like music. You know those pauses in a song? They can be as powerful as the lyrics. Those pause moments help us to appreciate the loud, powerful notes and beauty of the piece. If all the notes were loud, the piece wouldn't have the same impact. Those pauses can also be like a piece of art. The softer, finer strokes in a painting are as beautiful as the darker, more intense shades.

Meditation slows us down so we can speed up. It can help us cast aside the mind clutter.

Meditation can improve your focus, sleep, resilience, memory, cognitive functioning and cardiovascular health. Some experts prescribe 20 minutes twice daily. I prescribe a couple of minutes daily for normal meditation.

Meditation can allow us to be more present and centred during stressful experiences. It's powerful for reducing stress. We have more 'restful alertness' during meditation, and it makes us smarter, happier and more relaxed.

Meditation slows us down so we can speed up. It can help us cast aside the mind clutter.

I teach mindfulness, which is another style of meditation, at health retreats at the Polynesian Spa in Rotorua.

Lots of clients ask, 'How do I start?' I teach them to start with two minutes daily, which is easy for any busy individual. There's true power in meditating even for two minutes. You can build on this time if you wish.

Find a space where you feel comfortable – it could be outside or inside. If it's outside, you might like to observe the clouds and their colour and movement in the sky. Next, notice the swaying of the tree branches, listen to birdsong and notice the warmth of the sun on your skin. While doing this, breathe slow and take deep belly breaths. These moments of stillness can help you feel more present. They're an antidote to stress.

I now know how to use this technique and use it often. I even feel like my running is moving meditation now. It's so uplifting.

It's normal for your mind to wander when you first start meditation, by the way. Meditation expert Bob Roth calls it the 'gotta-gotta-gotta mind'. He wrote that we often have a hyperactive mind that's thinking, 'I gotta do this. I gotta do that. I gotta call him. I gotta call her. I gotta make a list. Then I gotta slow down. I gotta get going. I gotta get to sleep. I gotta get up.'

Sounds familiar? I felt this way when I started too. I was the worst fidget. Everything was a distraction: non-stop thoughts, sounds … I felt self-conscious.

I teach them to start with two minutes daily, which is easy for any busy individual. There's true power in meditating even for two minutes. You can build on this time if you wish.

'Meditation is a tool I now use often to feel grounded.'

But I have learned how to enjoy these pause moments. They give me a powerful reset. I'm not always in this state – I'm a mum and run a health business. But meditation is a tool I now use often to feel grounded. Teaching it has also become one of my biggest gifts to share. I love empowering others to find strength through stillness too.

The power of sleep for performance

If anyone can help you reconsider how many zzzzzzz's you are getting, it's **Dr Adam Storey.** He makes the science around sleep relatable and presents the facts in an astonishing way, likening a lack of sleep to being intoxicated.

Adam is the former Sports Science Manager and Assistant Strength and Conditioning Coach for the Blues Super Rugby team in New Zealand. This is an elite team that performs at the highest level of professional rugby.

He is also a research fellow at Auckland University of Technology's Sports Performance Research Institute, where he supervises PhD and master's students whose research relates to strength and conditioning and exercise physiology.

He loves the science around sleep.

I met Adam in 2017 when we were both speakers at the launch of the Fitbit Ionic watch. As well as telling the time, this watch tracks things like sleep, calories, steps and heart rate.

'It's not necessarily about how hard you train. It is more about how well you recover.'

Dr Adam Storey

I spoke at the launch about how exercise can help people find flow (and happiness), while Adam spoke about the benefits of adopting a blissful sleep ritual. He explained some of the benefits of a good night's sleep. These include:

- Increased energy
- Sharper concentration
- Better decision-making
- Improved memory
- Increased ability to manage stress
- Improved muscle regeneration
- Better immune system

The final point – having good immunity – is important for professional rugby players due to their demanding travel and competition schedules, says Adam.

'Their ability to catch a bug while in airports or on planes is right up there,' he explains.

Adam says sleep deprivation is the 'enemy of top performance' – for his players and for anyone. 'It's not necessarily about how hard you train. It is more about how well you recover.'

Adults, in general, need eight hours' sleep a night. But his athletes ideally need 10+ hours' sleep during hard training periods, so they have adequate time to recover. 'Sleep like a baby, train like a beast' is Adam's motto.

He says a good sleep fuels top performance. Previous evidence has also shown that getting less than eight hours' sleep can increase the likelihood for injury by a whopping 170%.

HOW TO RESET TO FIND YOUR HAPPINESS+

Sleep deprivation can also lead to faster exhaustion, greater perceived effort, decreased power output, slower reaction time and worsened short-term memory performance.

Not getting enough sleep, in real terms, can result in players turning up to training 'grumpy' (which disrupts team dynamics) and can mean that they struggle to remember new drills from the day before.

When Adam likened lack of sleep to drinking alcohol, I started looking at sleep in a different light. These figures, which equate functionality after a night's sleep with functionality after drinking beer, blew me away:

6 hours = 2–3 beers

4 hours = 5–6 beers

2 hours = 7–8 beers

0 hours = 10–11 beers

I love Adam's view of alcohol here and the relatable way it can impact on your lifestyle. I tend to be a lightweight nowadays – I have a glass or two of wine at celebrations – but I remember how I felt on those bender nights in my teens and 20s. I remember my brain shrouded in a foggy haze. So it's easy to see why getting a good night's sleep, as Adam says, 'is a no-brainer' (and is so good for the brain).

I catch up for a coffee with Adam at the university where he works to ask what other health tips he gives to his elite players. I think anyone can learn from what elites do to function at an optimal level – even if we don't all perform like beasts on a rugby field!

On the topic of coffee, Adam recommends to his players that they don't drink this brew too late in the day.

Adam, by the way, has a double-shot coffee while we chat. I have a decaffeinated brew. I've personally learned that two cups a day is the maximum I can drink to function at my best. After that, I can get jittery.

I ask him for his other top tips for a good night's sleep.

'Use your bedroom for sleep and sex. Resist taking things like screens, iPads and mobile phones into the bedroom. Or at least resist looking at screens an hour before bedtime. The blue light from screens is potent and can impact melatonin levels, i.e. keep us awake. In addition, the electromagnetic waves that are emitted from devices can disrupt our various sleep stages [light, deep, REM, awake patterns].'

Adam also says it is smart to 'wind down' after each day. So it's wise not to check in on social media, as this doesn't aid chilling out.

If we have 'chill-out time' to wind down, then this helps us to combat 'self-chatter' and will 'let the mind settle', he explains.

'All too often, our cell phones are the first thing we pick up during the day and last thing we put down. We are so invested with what other people are doing in the world. Be selfish about yourself and stay off your phone before going to bed.'

He adds that the ideal temperature for sleeping (if you have a home heating and cooling system) is around 18–18.5 degrees. He also backs using mindfulness to tap into feeling calmer and happier.

'Use your bedroom for sleep and sex. Resist taking things like screens, iPads and mobile phones into the bedroom.'

Dr Adam Storey

HOW TO RESET TO FIND YOUR HAPPINESS

He reveals a cool insider secret next. The players have a shot of tart cherry juice (about 50ml) after big late-night games.

'This helps them to wind down,' he says.

It is thought that these little berries pack a health punch because the antioxidants support joint mobility and help protect the body from free-radical damage. The berries are also full of vitamin A and beta-carotene.

Adam sends me a link to some research that the University of Texas Health Science Center in San Antonio has done around cherries. It claims the juice enhances immune-system function, has a potent anti-inflammatory effect and may increase melatonin levels to help people sleep. Melatonin essentially helps with the biological rhythm of every cell within your body.

If you are wanting to replicate this juice idea at home, prepare for a small hole in your wallet. It's about $50 for the cherry juice concentrate (946ml) that the players use – that's about $2.60 per shot. I'd bet it's worth every cent for them, though. They're always looking for a competitive advantage.

Back to more bedtime advice. Adam says 10pm–2am is the 'golden window' for the best sleep, so tuck up before 10pm if you can.

So tapping into a good night's sleep is smart – whether you are a rugby player or anyone. We all want to function at our best.

'Sleep is definitely one of the best recovery methods, and it's free, so there is no excuse not to prioritise it,' adds Adam.

Yoga for finding calm

Yoga is a great vehicle for feeling calmer. It gets your muscles moving but also your mind. The movements and incorporating your breath are ultimately a good distraction from work deadlines!

Yoga has many elements to it. Movement is just one limb; there are others too, and essentially yoga is a way to live a kind and caring life.

When I trained to be a yoga teacher, I learned to calm my nervous system in a matter of moments through the power of doing diaphragmatic breathing. I love teaching this to my yoga students now. A friend who is a physiotherapist uses this technique too to reset and feel calm between helping patients.

How do you do it? Take time to stop, be still and take 10 long, slow breaths whenever your heart races – or you feel stressed. You should feel your belly rising and taking in the oxygen, rather than chest-breathing. If I'm at my desk, I do this while sitting during breaks. But it is wonderful also to stand at home and stretch my arms up to the sky (on the inhale of breath) and then bring my arms down by my sides (on the exhale). This can be invigorating and feels like it resets my body and mind.

Rachel's two favourite restorative yoga poses

- **Legs-up-the-wall.** This is exactly how it sounds! Lie on your back with your bum close to the wall. Then extend both legs up the wall and rest them vertically or, if you have tight hamstrings, on a slight lean. Don't go too close; you should feel no stretch down the backs of your legs at all. It should be completely restful. You can even use a bolster (or rolled-up towel) under your hips to elevate them slightly if you wish. Close your eyes and put your hands by your sides with palms facing up. Add slow, long, deep belly breaths and this will be so restful. This pose is not only great for relaxation and feeling super calm, it also helps reduce swelling in your legs and feet, relieves tired leg muscles and helps your mind to reset.

- **Child's pose.** Come on to your knees. Have your big toes together and spread your knees apart. Then sit back on your heels, bow down with your forehead on your stacked hands (if you can) and do slow, long inhalations and exhalations. Place your arms by your sides if you prefer. This pose is so calming for the mind. It's also lovely for your back and the perfect rest pose in between harder yoga poses.

Pet a pet, and why workplace wellness matters

Pets can influence that feel-good factor. As a home-based freelancer, I have my British Blue cat, Hermione, as my constant companion and my best distraction from writing deadlines. When I pick Hermione up for silky-soft snuggles, I get an immediate pick-me-up and smile. Stroking her fur and hearing her purr is soothing.

There are also benefits from stroking pets. The combination of the caring gesture and the calm, rhythmic patting has been shown to release a string of feel-good chemicals in the brain.

I often laugh out loud, too, as Hermione jumps on to my work chair to swipe at my hair. Or she pounces on my desk wanting to play. She's mischievous and joyful. She forces me to take time for play.

Jarrod Haar, Professor of Human Resource Management at the Auckland University of Technology, calls Hermione and other pets 'mood influencers'.

'A growing body of research suggests pets are powerful health champions.'

A growing body of research suggests pets are powerful health champions. That's why some boutique companies are allowing pets into the workplace. A growing number of employers now have pet-friendly policies, he says.

'The pause we take when we stroke a pet or engage for a few seconds helps employees disconnect from their work, so even after 10 seconds, they are better able to refocus on the task at hand. Relaxed and happy workers tend to perform better, too.'

Jarrod says research tells us that being able to focus on work and get a task completed (perhaps after that cat pause) allows workers to feel satisfied in their work-related tasks, which leads them to be happier. In turn, research shows us that happiness may really be the key to success – including better income and job performance as well as relationships, community involvement and mental and physical health.

Wellness programmes in workplaces are on the rise in some places, for good reason. Jarrod says wellness initiatives can influence better productivity, better workplace retention and less absenteeism and result in a healthier 'bottom line'. These wellbeing programmes can help employees achieve better wellness and happiness – and become better performers.

Wellness initiatives can influence better productivity, better workplace retention and less absenteeism and result in a healthier 'bottom line'.

He says this is linked to the 'contagion effect'.

'Essentially, if you work in a healthy and happy team, you "catch" people's moods,' he says. So co-workers and leaders who are in a good mood are contagious.

Jarrod says benefits to staff in general 'help a company to have a competitive advantage. The benefits signal to employees that the company cares.' Workplace wellbeing can also help with the 'social exchange theory'. This means that when we treat people well, they want to 'give back', i.e. work well, be less absent and decide not to leave.

'Employees who feel their company cares about their wellbeing are less likely to consider leaving. They might feel they owe the company for their care and goodwill. They also might recognise that other employers do not offer as much or care as passionately. These all lead employees to stay, perform better and be organisational champions!' he explains.

'Employees who feel their company cares about their wellbeing are less likely to consider leaving. They might feel they owe the company for their care and goodwill.'

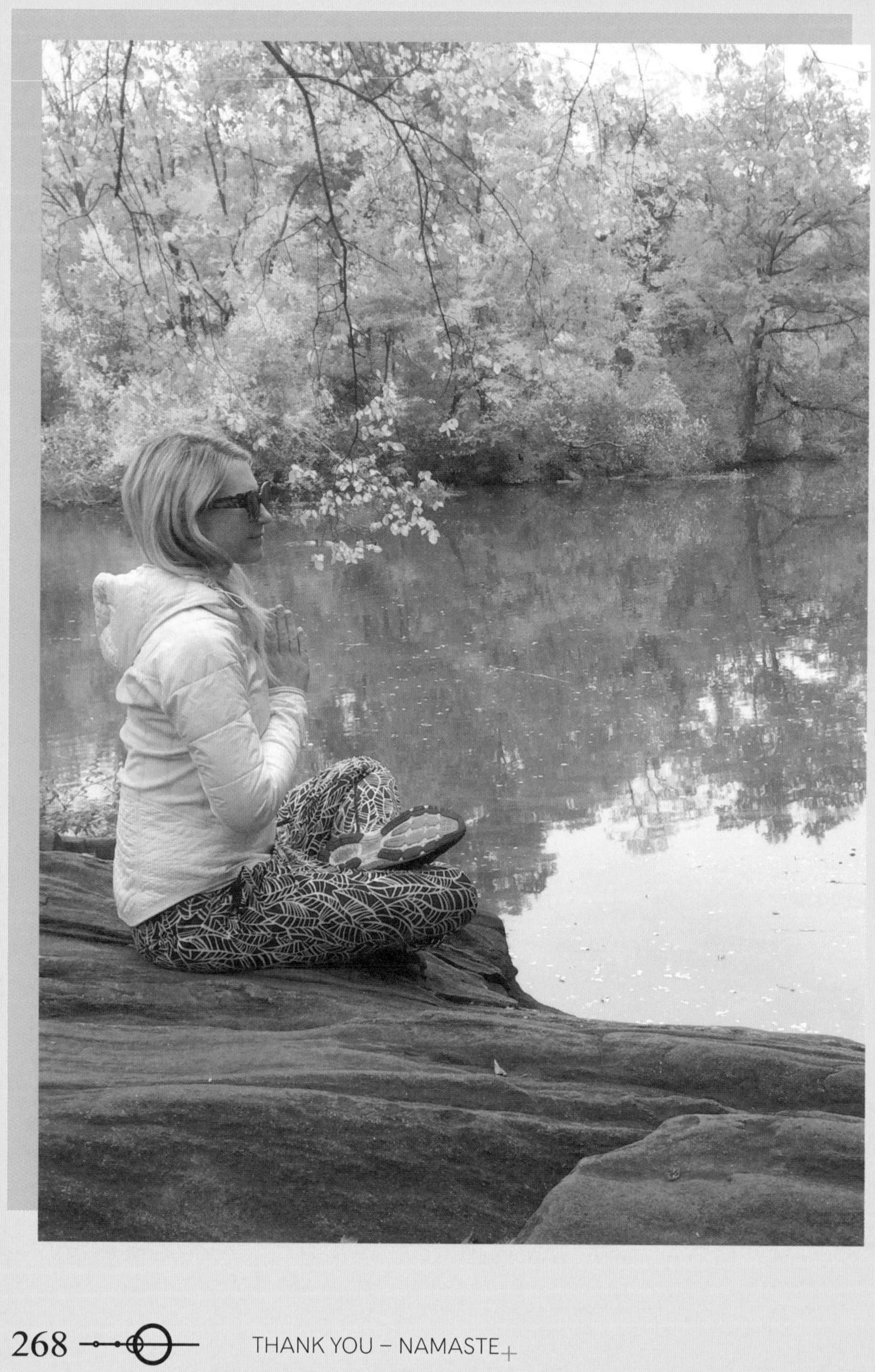

Thank you – Namaste₊

At the end of teaching yoga, I bow to my students, with hands in prayer position, and say, 'Namaste.' The translation is, 'I bow to you.' It's an acknowledgement of the soul in one to the soul in another.

It's a ritual.

It's an acknowledgement and a thank you. It's really a thank you from the heart.

Thank you from the bottom of my heart to all the contributors in this book. You are all inspirational beyond words. It's an honour to have crossed paths with you all. Thank you for sharing your wellness wisdom with me – and the world.

Thanks to Beatnik for saying yes to this project and for your support. I skipped down my hallway that day.

Thank you to **Good magazine**'s talented, kind and caring editor, Carolyn Enting – also a true friend. Thank you to other editors and journalists too who have nurtured me through the years and let my writing passion grow and evolve. There are too many to name – but you know who you are.

Thank you to Aimee for your stunning photography and passion behind this project.

Thank you to my husband, Damien, for being hands-on to help raise the kids while I worked. Thank you too for being a rock and encouraging me to follow my dreams.

Thanks to my kids, Zach, Lachie and Finn – my everything. My greatest wish is for you all to be healthy and happy. Do life your way and however you dream.

Thank you to everyone in my life who has cheered me on. It takes a community to make each one of us really great. I'm lucky to be surrounded by incredible hearts and minds. I learned some magic from you all. And when you gather enough bits of magic and learnings, you can become a slightly better human. That's my aim, anyway. I'm still a work in progress, though. Everyone is, right?

Thanks to two teachers I had in high school who told me I was 'smart enough' to have a career. You helped me at a young age to believe in myself to a whole new level and helped to propel me forwards in life. I think I doubted myself a lot up until then. I think of this often and the power that a few kind words can make.

Thanks to my Grandma Anne, who in recent years has become blind. She taught me to see life through a glass-half-full lens, always. She taught me true kindness and the importance of a smile and joy-filled laughter. She taught me how to live mindfully before I even knew the term. She is the definition of kindness.

Thanks to my parents Nick and Chris, sister Bex, brother Jamie and wider family, who love me and are there for me always.

Thanks too to my kids for being my chief taste-testers with the recipes.

Thanks to all my friends – you are like my family too. You all inspire me – not just in sports, at a CrossFit box, on the yoga mat or on a running track. You are part of 'home' for me.

Lastly, thank you to anyone who reads this book and feels inspired to change something – even if it's the smallest thing – to be healthier or happier. I hope you find something in this book that uplifts you and helps you to smile more.

Connect with Rachel

www.inspiredhealth.co.nz
Facebook: @InspiredHealthNZ
Instagram: @RachelGrunwell